RELIGION AND CULTURE IN THE MIDDLE AGES

Medieval Blood

Series Editors
Denis Renevey (University of Lausanne)
Diane Watt (University of Wales, Aberystwyth)

Editorial Board
Miri Rubin (Queen Mary, University of London)
Jean-Claude Schmitt (École des Hautes
Études en Sciences Sociales, Paris)
Fiona Somerset (Duke University)
Christiania Whitehead (University of Warwick)

RELIGION AND CULTURE IN THE MIDDLE AGES

Medieval Blood

BETTINA BILDHAUER

UNIVERSITY OF WALES PRESS
CARDIFF
2006

British Library Cataloguing-in-Publication Data
A catalogue record for this book is available from the British Library.

ISBN 0-7083-1940-8

Printed in Great Britain by Cromwell Press, Trowbridge, Wiltshire

CONTENTS

FIGURES

Series Editors' Preface

Religion and Culture in the Middle Ages aims to explore the interface between medieval religion and culture, with as broad an understanding of those terms as possible. It puts to the forefront studies which engage with works that significantly contributed to the shaping of medieval culture. However, it also gives attention to studies dealing with works that reflect and highlight aspects of medieval culture that have been neglected in the past by scholars of the medieval disciplines. For example, devotional works and the practice they infer illuminate our understanding of the medieval subject and its culture in remarkable ways, while studies of the material space designed and inhabited by medieval subjects yield new evidence on the period and the people who shaped it and lived in it. In the larger field of religion and culture, we also want to explore further the roles played by women as authors, readers and owners of books, thereby defining them more precisely as actors in the cultural field. The series as a whole investigates the European Middle Ages, from c.500 to c.1500. Our aim is to explore medieval religion and culture with the tools belonging to such disciplines as, among others, art history, philosophy, theology, history, musicology, the history of medicine, and literature. In particular, we would like to promote interdisciplinary studies, as we believe strongly that our modern understanding of the term applies fascinatingly well to a cultural period marked by a less tight confinement and categorization of its disciplines than the modern period. However, our only criterion is academic excellence, with the belief that the use of a large diversity of critical tools and theoretical approaches enables a deeper understanding of medieval culture. We want the series to reflect this diversity, as we believe that, as a collection of outstanding contributions, it offers a more subtle representation of a period that is marked by paradoxes and contradictions and which necessarily reflects diversity and difference, however difficult it may sometimes have proved for medieval culture to accept these notions.

Acknowledgements

It is a pleasure to acknowledge the generous support I have received from so many people and institutions in writing this book. Though it bears little resemblance to my doctoral thesis, it is based on much of the same research, and heartfelt thanks are therefore first due to Mark Chinca, my Ph.D. supervisor, for his respectful and meticulous guidance; and to my examiners, Miri Rubin and Christopher Young, who have encouraged and advised me beyond their official role in so many ways. I am also very grateful for the financial support of my doctoral studies to the Arts and Humanities Research Council, the Master and Fellows of Pembroke College, Cambridge, and the Tiarks Fund of the Department of German at the University of Cambridge. To the Master and Fellows of Emmanuel College, Cambridge, I am deeply indebted for providing me with an extraordinarily unpressured and stimulating post-doctoral research environment.

Many other teachers, colleagues and friends have also generously commented on various versions and sections of the work, including Dirk Driessen, Karina Kellermann, Liz Herbert McAvoy, Peggy McCracken, Bob Mills, Greg Moore and Ian Steed. Anke Bernau, Barbara Bodenhorn, Maria Diemling, Lauren Kassell, Harry Jackson, Nigel Palmer, Maggie Schleissner, Soumhya Venkatesan, Tessa Webber and Colin Wilcockson have provided helpful further guidance. I am particularly indebted to Dennis Green for his tireless backing. Thank you all very much. In Cologne, Joachim Bumke and Dietz Bering sparked my interest in the Middle Ages, and Ursula Peters was the first person to support my idea to write on blood, for which I am grateful.

This volume could not have been written without those friends who have shared their workspaces and ideas with me over the years and never tired of discussing blood, bodies and theories in reading groups, dining halls, computer rooms, kitchens, pubs and trains – you know who you are, and I thank you.

Introduction:
Making Bodies through Blood

> What then is the body? Provided that no one asks me, I know. If I want to explain it to an enquirer, I do not know . . . I confess to you, Lord, that I still don't know what the body is, and I further confess to you, Lord, that as I say this I know myself to be conditioned by it.
>
> (After Augustine of Hippo, *Confessions*)

What is a body?

K nights bathing in blood, mystics sucking blood from Christ's wounds, priests drinking the blood of Christ, women killing babies with their menstrual blood, physicians using bloodletting as a universal cure – medieval people were fascinated by blood. This book aims to understand this fascination. I argue that this interest is the corollary to medieval definitions of the body: blood served to confirm a view of the body as a bounded entity that was useful and necessary in medieval culture, but not self-evident. Blood secured this body in four crucial ways: through functioning as revelatory proof of the body's existence; through being regulated by taboos and thereby affirming the body's contours; through excluding some bodies from such integrity and thereby marking gender and ethnicity; and through the widening of this conception of the enclosed body to include social bodies, so that collective and individual bodies could reaffirm one another.

What, then, is the body? This, like Augustine's query about time, is a deceptively easy question.[1] The *Oxford English Dictionary* defines the body as 'the material frame of man [*sic*]', which singles out materiality and humanness as main features, with the word 'frame' suggesting a bound entity, carrying and unifying the human being. But this idea of a body as a material, bounded entity is far from self-evident in contemporary everyday understanding, let alone in scientific and philosophical research or in history, in ways worth considering before plunging into the topic of medieval blood. As regards spatial boundedness, 'commonsensical' experience suggests that, while the body may be in most situations the area enclosed by skin, this is by no means an absolute external boundary. Humans cannot live without taking in food and air and expelling waste. Far from providing a smooth envelope, skins constantly receive and emit fluids through pores and cells, so that it is impossible to determine which atom, say, is still part of the epidermis and the intestinal lining and which is not, and which pork molecule has turned into a human molecule. Even the 'inside' of a body is full of skins, opening up many surfaces. As Shannon Sullivan has suggested, drawing on John Dewey, we live 'as much in processes across and through skins as in processes "within" skins'.[2]

Moreover, the internal coherence of this bodily space is also open to question. The idea that the body is the area over which we have conscious control is challenged by the fact that there are many body parts and functions which humans can never consciously control, and many over which we can gain or lose power depending on age and health. Despite our perception of the body as an internally coherent organic system, each cell is to an extent an independent organism that can reproduce without a larger body around it, sometimes work against it and be incorporated into another body. Thanks to transplant technology, even whole organs can be exchanged between bodies. Cross-species transplants and genetic manipulation can theoretically create bodies that contain elements of more than one species and are thus potentially not entirely human anymore. Donna Haraway's seminal 'Cyborg manifesto' has pointed out that many bodies are not even fully organic, with tooth fillings, prostheses and implants or the linking of organic bodies and machines in cyberspace, realizing Gilles Deleuze and Félix Guattari's visions of bodies as part of larger 'desiring machines'.[3] Worries about the continuity of personal identity when 'I' live with someone else's heart or brain are expressed both by people with transplants and in countless science fiction fantasies.

While organ transplants and implants can cause concern, the question of numerical identity becomes even more acute when several 'whole' organisms share the same bodily space. The body of any pregnant woman 'contains' that of one or more other prospective human beings, as feminist philosophers like Christine Battersby have highlighted.[4] Siamese twins and the concept of 'multiple personalities' are challenges to the 'one body, one person' correlation that attract much media and cultural attention. The microbiological observation that we all share the apparently so clearly enclosed space of our body with a multitude of other organisms, bacteria, parasites and fungi, has also filtered down into popular knowledge. Tied up with the issue of spatial definition of the body is that of temporal continuity. Since every cell of the body is regularly replaced, 'I' have no single cell in common with my teenage self – am 'I' still the same person?[5] Moreover, it is not clear when the body comes into existence – at birth, at some stage in the womb, at conception, or when the relevant egg and sperm cells are first produced, say? Similarly, when does the body end – when the heartbeat stops, when the brain ceases to function, when the soul departs the body, when the body is decomposed?

Finally, the distinction between a material body and an immaterial mind, soul, spirit or consciousness has remained philosophically and scientifically problematic, and is undermined even by religious beliefs in the resurrection of the body. Most philosophers and scientists locate consciousness in the brain, and thus see body and mind as inextricably linked. Quantum theory argues that matter and non-matter are not clearly distinct anyway, but are part of the same continuum of energy. Despite the usefulness of the model of the body as a separate, enclosed unit, then, this view is not at all obvious, and instead needs a lot of cultural work to be upheld.

Medieval bodies

Just as avant-garde research, art and thought question the fiction of the self-evident body as we know it, so the historical observation that the body has not always been conceptualized in that way highlights its contingency. The splits in the continuum of existence – between a body and a soul, a subject and an other, an embodied subject and everything outside it, human and other bodies – were made at some point in the history of humankind. The Middle Ages are often used to postulate the existence of an alternative understanding of the body. There are two contrasting, but frequently combined views of 'the medieval body'. One is that this body was actually even more fixed and circumscribed than our own, that the unity of embodied subjects was guaranteed by unquestioned religious and social beliefs. David Hillman and Carla Mazzio summarize this well:

> The medieval Christian understanding of the relation between corporeal fragmentation and wholeness tends to adhere to the Pauline view that 'as the body is one and hath many members, and all the members of that one body, being many, are one body: so also is Christ'; thus Erasmus could use almost exactly these words at the beginning of the sixteenth century in his discussion of the nature of bodily multiplicity. By the end of the century, however, such a profession of confidence in the ultimate unity of religious and social systems modelled on bodily organization was no longer viable.[6]

According to this view, medieval thinkers (here including Erasmus) envisaged the body as an unproblematic model of wholeness, assuring the coherence of social bodies formed in its image. The individual, with complex issues and a need to negotiate his role in the world, including his body, was only born in the Renaissance.

The second commonly held opinion is that medieval people imagined bodies as precisely the kind of fluid and open body that much contemporary theory proposes as ideal. In *Rabelais and his World*, Mikhail Bakhtin finds in medieval literature and carnival an image of the body as grotesque, open, fluid, monstrous, fecund and abundant, and contrasts this with the sterile, enclosed body typical of modernity:

> Contrary to modern canons, the grotesque body is not separated from the rest of the world. It is not a closed, completed unit; it is unfinished, outgrows itself, transgresses its own limits. The stress is laid on those parts of the body that are open to the outside world, that is, the parts through which the world enters the body or emerges from it, or through which the body itself goes out to meet the world . . . The body discloses its essence as a principle of growth which exceeds its own limits only in copulation, pregnancy, childbirth, the throes of death, eating, drinking, or defecation. This is the ever unfinished, ever creating body, the link in the chain of genetic development, or more correctly speaking, two links shown at the point where they enter into each other . . . The unfinished and open body (dying, bringing forth and being born) is not separated from the world by clearly defined boundaries; it is blended with the world, with animals, with objects.[7]

The body as imagined in modern and classical literature and culture, on the other hand, is as enclosed in its skin as contemporary 'common sense' understands it:

The Renaissance saw the body in quite a different light than the Middle Ages, in a different aspect of its life, and a different relation to the exterior nonbodily world. As conceived by these canons, the body was first of all a strictly completed, finished product. Furthermore, it was isolated, alone, fenced off from all other bodies. All signs of its unfinished character, of its growth and proliferation were eliminated; its protuberances and offshoots were removed, its convexities (signs of new sprouts and buds) smoothed out, its apertures closed . . . The inner processes of absorbing and ejecting were not revealed. The individual body was presented apart from its relation to the ancestral body of the people.[8]

That the Middle Ages thus celebrated a more fluid body, a body since disciplined and sealed through the 'civilizing process' of increasing restraint of emissions and manners, has become a commonplace among cultural historians of the body as diverse as Norbert Elias, Michel Foucault, Klaus Theweleit or Thomas Laqueur.[9] But whether 'the medieval body' is described as a natural guarantor of unity or as naturally unrestrained, it appears in both cases to be unequivocal and taken for granted, rather than complicated by modern cultural freight.

A similar binary of wholeness vs volatility characterizes many descriptions of the role of blood in the Middle Ages.[10] Caroline Walker Bynum, for example, has recently drawn on the imagination of the body as either intact or fluid to postulate a similar division of the functions of blood:

Body – in some basic physiological sense container and identity, constituted by edges and boundaries, intricately connected to growth and decay, to taking in through eating and therefore to food – tends to be a symbol of community and of self. Blood is, both physiologically and symbolically, more complex and labile because finally contradictory. Blood is life and death. It is *sanguis* and *cruor*, for Latin shares with other Indo-European languages a distinction between inside blood (in some sense, life) and outside blood or bloodshed.[11]

If the body is seen either as enclosed and filled with blood, or as vulnerable and bleeding, then blood can also only be interpreted either as life (when it fills the intact body) or as death (when it has left the body). Modern scholars often present this binary of blood as life-giving and death-inducing as a 'natural' and primeval distinction based on the 'fundamental human experience' that blood flows out when people die and must therefore be the 'life-fluid'.[12] Such reasoning ignores not only that humans much more frequently experience non-lethal blood-loss and non-bloody deaths, but also that this is a retrospective attribution of our own categories into an unknown past. As well as backwards in time, the death–life dichotomy often deployed in descriptions of the role of blood can easily be expanded sideways to include violation and wholeness, pollution and cleansing, sin and redemption. But I suggest that such pairs always already rely on and enforce the concept of the bounded body, where blood is either 'inside' or 'outside'. Instead of seeing the body 'in some basic physiological sense' as a container consti-tuted by boundaries, I argue that this view is culturally constructed; instead of seeing blood as fundamentally 'more complex', I contend that the seeming complexity of blood depends on the seeming stability of body, and vice versa. Blood was only separated into matter 'inside' and 'outside' the body because its movement was crucial in making this distinction, and body appeared as an enclosed container because one location of blood is perceived to be outside and another inside.

Medieval concepts of the body, I shall show, were as complex and difficult as modern ones.[13] Medieval authors struggled to forge integrity and boundedness from the plethora of bodily phenomena, too. Where exactly the body spatially ended, for example, caused considerable concern even to medieval theologians, philosophers and scientists.[14] Did food become body, did it cease to be body when emitted? Did cut hair and nails belong to the body? Did spilled blood? The fact that ancient and medieval physiological theory holistically imagined the body as a microcosm, in direct communication with the planets and the weather, made a sophisticated delineation necessary. Body parts were in the Middle Ages also understood as acting independently of the body as a coherent whole, as was the case with relics of saints' bodies, the myriad eucharistic pieces of Christ's body and drops of his blood, or the grotesque mobile body parts of medieval fabliaux, like the penis that has its eyes transformed into women's breasts, or the one that wanders into a nunnery, much to the excitement of the assembled nuns.[15] As today, actual and fictional bodies could also contain other bodies in part or as a whole, even across the species divides, for instance, when Nero in 'Moriz von Craûn' is 'pregnant' with a toad in his stomach, when monsters were believed to be composed of parts of different species, or in the much-debated issue of cannibalism.[16] The relation between body and soul was also intensively discussed, with an emphasis on their unity; the soul was usually believed to share all physical characteristics of the person, and the body to be resurrected. Matter was believed to be just one ingredient of the body, for whose generation form was also necessary.

I argue, then, that the dominant medieval view of the body, as today, was that of a closed container, and that the awareness that this model could not always be upheld caused more anxiety than enthusiasm. As today, alternative models of a more open body existed, for example, in mysticism or in ideas of collective bodies and, as Jeffrey Jerome Cohen has recently found, even in depictions of the body of the knight forming a conglomerate with his horse, bridle, armour and weapons.[17] Both affirmation and challenges to the dominant view of the body were played out, crucially, through blood. By exploring such medieval constructions of the body, I hope to be able to 'make strange' our own assumptions, by contrast and comparison with the equally contingent medieval ideas. I shall do so with the help of three recent philosophical, anthropological and psychological theories on the constructions of bodies that will also prove useful for understanding the medieval body.

Modern theories

The most significant and illuminating current theory on bodies, especially on how bodies come about as distinct, material entities, has been proposed by Judith Butler. In the context of her problematization of the notion of woman and of heteronormativity in *Gender Trouble*, she spends a considerable amount of thought on how gender comes to be embodied and how gendered bodies come into being; and she returns to this topic in more detail in *Bodies that Matter*. One of her main challenges is to the belief that the body is a pre-given, pre-discursive entity, matter inscribed by culture:

> This 'body' often appears to be a passive medium that is signified by an inscription from a cultural source figured as 'external' to that body. Any theory of the culturally constructed body, however, ought to question 'the body' as a construct of suspect generality when it is figured as passive prior to discourse.[18]

By arguing that the body, like all other concepts, is discursively constructed, Butler does not go as far as Michel Foucault and other radical constructivists in suggesting that bodies are brought about by words. She does, however, contend that the *concept* of a body, our idea of what counts as a body, where a body ends and what it is, is brought about by language. Models with which we think, like 'the body', never do full justice to reality, to actual bodies. Like many contemporary philosophers, Butler assumes that there is always a remainder that cannot be expressed in our conceptual schemes, a part of the continuum that does not fit into any 'either–or' logic, and that is thus abjected into an area outside discourse, like the 'real' in a Lacanian and Žižekian sense. This is not an abstract, merely epistemological process, for real people enact this idea of how bodies should be. Butler sees the body as always in process, created through repeated performances. In her understanding, one of the key ways in which normative ideas about bodies become reality and are 'lived' is by the exclusion of those bodies that do not fit our conceptual schemes, not only from view, but also from existence:

> Given this understanding of construction as constitutive constraint, is it still possible to raise the critical question of how such constraints not only produce the domain of intelligible bodies, but produce as well a domain of unthinkable, abject, unlivable bodies? This latter domain is not the opposite of the former, for oppositions are, after all, part of intelligibility; the latter is the excluded and illegible domain that haunts the former domain as a spectre of its own impossibility, the very limit to intelligibility, its constitutive outside. How, then, might one alter the very terms that constitute the 'necessary' domain of bodies through rendering unthinkable and unlivable another domain of bodies, those that do not matter in the same way.[19]

Bodies thus become, for example, male or female by disallowing any intermediate 'performances', by branding cross-dressers, 'butch' women and 'femme' men as freaks and exceptions to be kept in the closet.[20]

Unlike Butler I am not concerned with how actual, lived bodies are shaped by discourse, but more with the discursive models of how such bodies can and should be imagined, with the body as a sign within a text. I thus stay in the realm of discourse in this sense, although I am interested in what is marginalized and excluded by discourse. It would have been impossible in any case for medieval people to step out of discourse, out of the conceptual categories that their cultures and languages offered. On the most basic level, the idea of what a body is and how it functions proposed in the medical and physiological texts that I investigate will have had effects on real bodies, surgical procedures, diseases and deaths. Actual people too will have fashioned themselves according to the ideal bodies of men, women and courtiers in fictional literature. More generally, there was no other way to be embodied than the one suggested by discourse, no way to think of a subject other than in relation to the idea of the body, be it in contrast, modification or acceptance of the dominant model. My interest is precisely in how these bodies were imagined, in what people *believed* a body was, which was inextricably linked to what it actually might have been. When, in the following, I speak of bodies being constructed, like Butler, I am not implying that they are 'made up' and do not really exist, but simply that they are fashioned in a certain way so that they become accessible to our understanding, in the sense of 'conceptualized' or 'conceived'.

Where Butler explores how normative bodies were enforced by some embodied subjects counting as normal and others not, I look into the abjection not just of other bodies, but also of an outside of one's individual body. This is why, while I agree with Butler that bodies cannot be imagined without gender, I do not ascribe it the leading role. I do discuss ways in which the normative, male, Christian, able body is upheld with the help of the (devalued) bodies of women, Jews and monsters, but I think that bodies are defined in contrast not only to these other bodies, but also to an outside that is not other embodied people, but air, blood, matter or the world.

Butler briefly discusses two theorists who have thought a lot about the body along those lines, Mary Douglas and Julia Kristeva. Mary Douglas's *Purity and Danger* deals with the body in the context of her interest in taboos and fears of pollution, which, according to her, safeguard social distinctions by declaring anything that does not fit into the existing categories either taboo, sacred or polluting. The boundaries of the body, she argues, are beset with a string of taboos and rules in most societies because they are seen to symbolize the inner or outer boundaries of a society:

> The body is a model which can stand for any bounded system. Its boundaries can represent any boundaries which are threatened or precarious. The body is a complex structure. The functions of its different parts and their relation afford a source of symbols for other complex structures. We cannot possibly interpret rituals concerning excreta, breast milk, saliva and the rest unless we are prepared to see in the body a symbol of society, and to see the powers and dangers credited to social structure reproduced in small on the human body.[21]

So the body is a symbol of society, and *therefore* substances such as bodily fluids that leave its boundaries are seen as violating the integrity of the social group, and are hence policed by taboos. As an example, she cites the ancient Israelites' concern with keeping the external ethnic boundaries of their community intact, which made them regulate each individual's contact with bodily fluids. Only because they were a 'hard-pressed minority', a body politic with threatened boundaries, maintains Douglas, was the integrity of the individual body of such concern to them that any excretion, including blood, was seen as polluting.[22] The reason why boundaries and emissions in particular are paid so much attention in rituals and taboos, for Douglas, is a sense of danger that any exchange with an imagined outside can bring to an imagined inside:

> Any structure of ideas is vulnerable at its margins. We should expect the orifices of the body to symbolise its specially vulnerable points. Matter issuing from them is marginal stuff of the most obvious kind. Spittle, blood, milk, urine, faeces or tears by simply issuing forth have traversed the boundary of the body. So also have bodily parings, skin, nail, hair clippings and sweat. The mistake is to treat bodily margins in isolation from all other margins. There is no reason to assume any primacy for the individual's attitude to his [sic] own bodily and emotional experience, any more than for his [sic] cultural and social experience.[23]

In a creative misreading, Butler interprets Douglas to mean here not that the skin symbolizes the outer boundary of a society, but that it stands between the body and society, that it delineates the distinction between what counts as body and what counts as its outside, the social. Commenting on Douglas, Butler writes:

> Her analysis suggests that what constitutes the limit of the body is never merely material, but that the surface, the skin, is systematically signified by taboos and anticipated transgressions; indeed, the boundaries of the body become, within her analysis, the limits of the social *per se*. A poststructuralist appropriation of her view might well understand the boundaries of the body as the limits of the social *hegemonic*.[24]

Butler unfortunately does not take further such an appropriation of Douglas's analysis for thinking about the relationship between body and its exterior, except by offering a brief explanation of why gay and lesbian exchanges of fluids are seen as polluting, as evidenced by the homophobic hysteria about AIDS as a 'gay disease'. She here returns to the Douglasian view of the individual body as mirroring the social body when she claims that the fear of AIDS is not due to any practical, medical considerations, or a wish to delineate the body, but because of a concern for the social body that is represented by the individual bodies. Douglas's argument could be further appropriated along the promising lines initially suggested by Butler, and reversed as a tool for thinking about individual bodies. Douglas clearly does not believe that rituals and taboos surrounding bodily fluids serve to enforce the bodily boundaries themselves; this would be pointless, as the body, to her, is always already self-evidently bounded. Instead, such rituals only make sense to her if they symbolically point to and deal with something else, something beyond, the social 'body'. But might the taboos concerning bodily emissions not simply aim at those emissions directly, rather than symbolically at social groups? If 'the mistake is to treat bodily margins in isolation from all other margins', as Douglas states, then perhaps this also works in the other direction. No more than there is 'reason to assume any primacy for the individual's attitude to his [sic] own bodily and emotional experience', as Douglas has it, is there reason to assume the primacy of her 'cultural and social experience'. In this sense, Douglas's analysis of pollution and purity in relation to the boundaries of *social* bodies can thus be deployed to understand the concern with the integrity and limits of *individual* bodies, too.

Julia Kristeva, discussing Mary Douglas's work in *Powers of Horror*, argues precisely for the significance of bodily boundaries not only for society, but also for the subject. She believes that social and subjective bodies correspond to one another, without either the subjective or the social taking precedence.[25] Kristeva then sees it as her task to explain pollution fears and disgust surrounding bodily fluids not only in terms of the function that the body might have as symbolizing society, but also in terms of the function it might have for the individual subject. For her, the boundaries of the body are constituted through abjection, through the expulsion of something internal that is then discharged from the body:

A wound with blood and pus, or the sickly, acrid smell of sweat, of decay, does not *signify* death. In the presence of signified death – a flat encephalograph, for instance – I would understand, react, or accept. No, as in true theatre, without makeup or masks, refuse and corpses *show me* what I permanently thrust aside in order to live. These body fluids, this defilement, this shit are what life withstands, hardly and with difficulty, on the part of death. There, I am at the border of my condition as a living being. My body extricates itself, as being alive, from that border. Such wastes drop so that I might live, until, from loss to loss, nothing remains in me and my entire body falls beyond the limit – *cadere*, cadaver.[26]

Kristeva then enquires further into which functions the view specifically of bodily fluids as polluting might have, wondering why excretions like blood in particular are abjected.[27] Her Lacanian answer is that prohibitions and pollution fears concerning excretions aim at abjecting the maternal body. Kristeva assumes a model of human development, both in terms of the individual and the species, in which basically the baby initially perceives itself as one with the mother in the pre-verbal, 'semiotic' stage. The separation process is especially associated with learning to control one's bodily emissions (as well as with learning language, thus entering the 'symbolic order'). The separation from the mother leaves the subject with a constant sense of lack and a desire to return to the semiotic stage and be one with her again. But at the same time, such a return would be the end of its existence as an individual; it thus feels threatened and horrified by the idea. So repulsion keeps the desire to return at bay. Polluting bodily fluids are in Kristeva's view either excremental or menstrual, because both are associated with the initial unity with the mother:

> Those *two* defilements [excremental and menstrual] stem from the *maternal* and/or the feminine, of which the maternal is the real support. That goes without saying where menstrual blood signifies sexual difference. But what about excrement? It will be remembered that the anal penis is also the phallus with which infantile imagination provides the feminine sex and that, on the other hand, maternal authority is experienced first and above all, after the first essentially oral frustrations, as sphincteral training.[28]

As with Lacanian accounts of a subject's development in general, there are three main problems with this view: a nostalgia for a lost fullness, a conflation of phylogenesis and ontogenesis, and a merging of women and physicality. From a feminist perspective, Kristeva's equation of women with mothers, and of mothers with bodily fluids (which 'goes without saying' in the above quote) is dubious, as it perpetuates these patriarchal constructions. Butler further rightly criticizes Kristeva's notion of an initial union with a maternal body, to which any return is psychotic and must therefore be barred by taboos. It is never clear whether this story of human development refers to each individual or the species, and both are used to justify one another, but ultimately, neither view really holds. However clear links between mother and menstruation may be for adult writers, why would a baby associate menstrual blood, with which it probably rarely comes into contact, more with its mother than, say, skin contact? Rather than such a linear account of individual development stemming from an initial loss, a model that sees identity as always in progress, always in a continuing process of being constructed, seems more useful.

If we choose not to follow Kristeva down the line of the abjection of the maternal body, this permits the development of her argument in a different direction. Her concept of abjection can work without assuming that the abjected is a pre-discursive unity with the mother. Instead, we can interpret abjection in a Butlerian spirit as a more future-oriented process, which produces an embodied subject and distinguishes it from an outside through the repeated and regulated expulsion of bodily matter. Such an understanding of abjection as an ongoing process of identity construction will prove useful in the reading of blood as an ever-present threat to physical integrity.

Medieval blood

In order to understand the role of blood in medieval thought and conceptions of the body, I focus on a range of texts in which the fascination with blood is particularly strong, written in the thirteenth to fifteenth centuries in German. In late medieval German-speaking areas, the devotion to the blood of Christ and the saints as well as the 'blood-libel legend' accusing Jews of blood-thirst was particularly widespread; and blood was of concern across discourses like medicine, philosophy, Christian devotion and theology, courtly fiction and law.[29] By combining a broad interdisciplinary interest in anything blood-related with detailed readings of remarkable texts, I hope to be able to elucidate medieval conceptions of the body in fresh ways. This should also make accessible to an English-speaking public some classic and some almost forgotten German texts whose concepts of blood and bodies have for the most part never been investigated, and which in many cases have hardly been studied at all.

However, my observations about the significance of blood for constructing bodies are relevant not just to this geographical and temporal spread, but, in varying intensity, would seem to apply to the European Middle Ages in general, as I will show with reference to examples in other languages. Medieval literate culture was not only interdisciplinary, with courtly, scientific and religious texts strongly influencing each other and being read and written by the same group of people, but also 'international', with science, theology, devotion and the ethos of knighthood being developed across geographical and linguistic boundaries. While Uli Linke's *Blood and Nation*, for example, identifies a particularly German fixation on blood in the National Socialist cult of blood and in post-war Germany, she diagnoses in the Middle Ages an interest in blood across Europe. The most extensive study of medieval blood to date, Peggy McCracken's examination of French romances *The Curse of Eve, the Wound of the Hero*, shows that men's (unlike women's) blood was overwhelmingly a valued sign of heroism, sacrifice and valour, which contrasts with my observations of men's blood in German fiction as much more ambiguous.[30] However, this has less to do with medieval geographical distinctions than with the differences between McCracken's approach and mine. While McCracken exposes gendered patterns, I focus more on the occasions on which these patterns break down. Moreover, the concern with bodily boundaries and with their negotiation through blood started long before the Middle Ages and has not ended since. In fact, the interest in blood increased as the Middle Ages waned, in sixteenth- and seventeenth-century discourses of witchcraft, anti-Judaism and nobility. Given the scarcity of research specifically on blood, it is difficult to make more detailed claims about spatial or temporal concentrations of different uses of blood at this stage.

My central thesis is that blood affirms the body as one of the major tenets of medieval thought and identity. 'The body' is not a given, enclosed, unified entity, always already different from the mind and from its surroundings. The concept of such an enclosed body is instead produced by various strategies, of which several use blood. The first chapter, 'The Secret of Blood', argues that blood is ascribed a huge value in establishing the truth. First and foremost, it reveals the integrity of the body in a circular conclusion in cases ranging from Christ's body on the cross and in the eucharist to murder and the generation of embryos. 'Blood Taboos', my second chapter, discusses how situations in which the body bleeds are marked as transgressive and accordingly punished, thus paradoxically confirming the idea of the body as *normally* integral. Prohibitions of bloodshed and of other contact with blood thus work to uphold the model of a bounded body. However, the idea of an invulnerable, completely enclosed body is also exposed as an unattainable fantasy in medieval fiction. Taboos surrounding conception, pregnancy, birth, infancy and the process of dying safeguard the *temporal* limits of the body as well. 'Bodies that Form', the third chapter, investigates how some bodies are not granted integral status and instead defined as bleeding: the bodies of women, Jews and monsters. These not fully embodied subjects are also imagined as endangering the integrity of bounded Christian men's bodies in three keys patterns: by polluting men with blood-flow, by sucking them out and by mimicking and rivalling their enclosure. The fourth chapter, 'Bloodlines', turns to social bodies, which are imagined not just as analogous to, but in various ways composed of individual bodies and blood. Bodies were one of the 'concepts to think with' most central to medieval thought with its penchant for analogy and concrete models. Families as well as the communal body of the Church were constituted through a shared blood. Boundary transgressions were in the same way important and marked as transgressive as those of individual bodies.

1

The Secret of Blood

The man [Alex Ferguson, long-standing manager of Manchester United,
who play in red] is United. Cut him and he will bleed red.

(Alan Brazil, quoted in *Private Eye*, 28 May 2004)

Truth games

In the Swiss town of Brugg, a thief steals a monstrance, finds three
hosts inside and throws them into a brook. When a shepherd later
passes by with his flock, the animals kneel down on the embankment and
refuse to leave. The shepherd notices the hosts in the water, each adorned
with 'three pure blood drops'.[1] He calls the priests, and they ceremoni-
ously bring the hosts 'with the living blood of God' to Zurich, Brugg
and Basle.[2] This story, told in a few simple words by an anonymous
Swiss writer in a fifteenth-century collection of short narratives, proves
for the narrator that the eucharistic bread is truly the body of Christ:

> Hiebi so weis ich wol,
> das daran nieman zwiflen sol,
> das sich der allmächtig gott
> selber berge in das helig brot,
> das die priester niessent allgemein
> das fleisch und das bluote rein
> und ouch alle cristenheit,
> die ir gelouben daran leit.
> wer gottes lib hierinne nit gewesen,
> ein sölich zeichen wer hie nit geschechen.[3]

This shows me clearly, so that nobody should doubt it, that the omnipotent God hides himself in the holy bread; that all priests partake in the pure flesh and blood, as do all Christians who put their faith in it. If God's body had not been contained therein, such a sign would not have occurred.

In the opinion of the narrator, the blood appearing on the host (together with the worshipping animals which lead to its discovery) reveals beyond doubt the hidden presence of God's body. Such a proof by blood is a frequent occurrence in the eucharistic miracle cults and tales flourishing in the late Middle Ages, and not just there. As I shall explore in this chapter, blood functions as proof in a variety of medieval discourses like medical diagnostics, theological and mystical writing and drawing as well as courtly fiction, confirming not only the presence of God's body in the host, but also the incarnation, the superiority of men's knowledge, the authenticity of specific texts, the idea that guilt requires punishment, and, most fundamentally, the conception of the body as a bounded entity.

Many miracle tales, like the one about Brugg, explicitly claim to show the truth of the doctrine of transubstantiation (the belief, which the Fourth Lateran Council in 1215 established as doctrine, that the eucharistic host and wine are in fact transformed into the body and blood of Christ) or of the idea of concomitance (the belief current from the twelfth century that both body and blood are contained in each bread and wine). This is the case, for example, in the miracle tales collected between 1219 and 1223 by the Cistercian monk Caesarius of Heisterbach in his influential *Dialogus miraculorum*. The legends are here embedded in a dialogue, in which a monk uses them to convince an inquisitive novice of the truth of a range of Christian beliefs. The narrator assures us that, while this conversation between monk and novice is fictional, all the reported events were witnessed and related to him by 'religious men' and 'not fashioned from imagination'.[4] One of the twelve 'books' of the *Dialogus* is reserved for eucharistic miracles. This book is introduced by a special mystifying caveat stating that this particular subject is to be approached with 'fear and trembling', since faith is required here, not reason.[5] This warning is repeated by the monk, who proceeds nevertheless to carefully summarize the Church's new teachings on transubstantiation.[6] The novice then demands to hear of miracles that would prove that the body and blood are indeed present under the species of bread and wine, and that those who believe in this are rewarded, while the unworthy communicants are punished. The monk duly furnishes him with the desired illustrations, painstakingly giving a place and sometimes a time and witness for these events. Most of the miracles consist of the body and blood of Christ appearing visually in the sacrament, either to benefit the pious or to punish or convince the doubters. To provide evidence for the transubstantiation of the wine, for example, there are seven stories in which either the wine in the chalice turns into blood not just in substance, but also in appearance, or in which spilled eucharistic wine leaves blood stains. These legends convince the novice that the wine does turn into Christ's blood:

> Sic mihi satisfecit oratio tua, ut iam non dico credam, sed quod amplius est, sciam post consecrationem sub specie vini verum esse sanguinem Christi. Cum enim Apostolus dicat, *fidem esse substantiam rerum sperandarum, argumentum non apparentium*, quae visu tam manifeste ut dictum est percipiuntur, iam non creduntur, sed sciuntur. Quod sub tam multiplici testimonio visum est, me vidisse reputo.[7]

> What you have said has so thoroughly satisfied me that I do not say I shall believe, but more than that, I know, that the wine becomes the true blood of Christ after the consecration. For when the apostle said that *faith is the substance of things hoped for, the proof of things not seen* [Heb 11: 1], things which are seen so plainly as you have told me, can no longer be said to be believed but known. And what has been seen under such ample testimony, I count myself to have seen.

So the method for establishing the truth is here reference not to the teachings of the Bible and the Church, but to tales of miraculous events. More specifically, according to the novice, the crucial factor in making these stories work as proof is that the previously hidden blood is now 'seen'. Faith would believe in the transubstantiation of the wine, the 'things not seen', but the visual appearance of hidden blood here, as in the story from Brugg, furnishes the incontrovertible evidence that Christ's body and blood are present in the eucharist: a detection of blood reveals the truth.

Michel Foucault was one of the first thinkers to draw attention to the central importance of blood in medieval spirituality and mentality. In *History of Sexuality*, I, he describes the 'threshold of our modernity' as a change from a 'society of blood' to a 'society "with a sexuality"'.[8] Foucault, however, denies that, unlike the modern concern with sexuality, the medieval interest in blood had anything to do with its status as proof. According to Foucault, 'we' moderns are obsessed with sexuality because it links two key areas that must be controlled in modern societies, the body and population growth. In the same way, he claims, power in the Middle Ages crystallized around blood because important fields of power like kinship, nobility, war, execution and death over-lapped here. But to Foucault, the difference between the Middle Ages and modernity is not simply a change of focus from blood to sexuality, but also from reality to knowledge, from ontology to epistemology. Unlike sexuality today, Foucault writes, medieval blood was not complicatedly constructed as an object of knowledge. In the Middle Ages, 'power spoke *through* blood . . . blood was *a reality with a symbolic function*', whereas later, 'power spoke *of* sexuality and *to* sexuality', he maintains, and claims that: 'the new procedures of power that were devised during the classical age and employed in the nineteenth century were what caused our societies to go from *a symbolics of blood* to *an analytics of sexuality*'.[9] While medieval blood was simply a symbol or a reality, then, modern sexuality has become an object of analysis, of what Foucault later calls 'truth games' or 'regimes of truth':

> Each society has its régime of truth, its 'general politics' of truth: that is, the types of discourse which it accepts and makes function as true; the mechanisms and instances which enable one to distinguish true and false statements, the means by which each is sanctioned; the techniques and procedures accorded value in the acquisition of truth; the status of those who are charged with saying what counts as true.[10]

Foucault's main example of such a truth game in *History of Sexuality*, I, is precisely the confession of secret sexual behaviours and desires, as in psychoanalysis and the Catholic sacrament of confession. These sexual confessions are meant to give insights into the true personality of the confessing subject, and are thus one of the fundamental truth games through which we experience ourselves, and which Foucault describes as 'the games of truth in the relationship of self with self and the forming of oneself as subject . . . the games of truth and error through which being is historically constituted as experience; that is, as something that can and must be thought'.[11] The air of secrecy surrounding sexuality adds to its perceived truth value, makes even speaking about it excitingly trans-gressive, and turns sexuality into an object of knowledge that has to be unveiled before it can reveal further truths about the embodied subject. Foucault denies that this modern 'analytics of sexuality' has any parallel in the Middle Ages, where blood is just a 'reality' or 'symbol', and thus less conditioned by a discursive and epistemological technique.

This distinction between modern sexuality as an object of knowledge and medieval blood as a reality has rightly been criticized for being at odds with Foucault's own sophisticated ideas on historiography, stated and evidenced elsewhere throughout his works.[12] Specifically, it relies on a simplistic view of medieval sexuality, of medieval constructions of knowledge and of periodization. A more fundamental inconsistency, however, is that Foucault here implicitly excludes blood from the discourses that according to his theories shape everything accessible to human understanding. He attributes unmediated authenticity to blood, and thereby uncritically buys into precisely the truth game that turns bodies and in particular blood into 'natural proof'.[13] Blood in his view is somehow outside discourse, pre-discursive and absolute.

A similar truth game with reference to the body in general (rather than blood in particular) as immediate, incontrovertible proof is used in the essentialist argument for the gender divide. The erudite analyses of this truth game by feminists like Judith Butler can help us understand how the deployment of blood as proof fits into a wider framework of biology corroborating social and cultural categories. As Butler demonstrates, in Western thought, physical sex is artificially distinguished from social gender, only in order to use the former to 'prove' the inevitability of the latter.[14] To simplify, essentialism presents 'biological functions of a woman's body' as radically different from social roles, in order to be able to show tautologically that women's social roles are dependent on their 'biological' make-up, and conclude that these roles are necessarily given. Greater authenticity is ascribed not only to biological sex but to physical facts in general, which are often artificially distinguished from social ones so that they then can be employed as 'natural' proof for the social facts. Sciences like biology are among our most respected mechanisms for establishing truths about humans and nature; but even independent of any scientific verification, 'biological facts' are credited with a high truth value in medieval and modern Western societies. Facts like brain size or shape of genitalia have been deployed as incontrovertible proof for everything from the alleged inferiority of women or Africans to the perceived unnaturalness of homosexuality. Blood is another one of these physical facts that is used to substantiate cultural assumptions.

Of all biological facts, as we shall see, those about blood held a particularly high status as proof in the Middle Ages.[15] As is the case today in expressions like 'it is in my blood' or 'blood is thicker than water', blood is given an almost instant authenticating value. A mention of blood is often intended to make an immediate truth claim and to silence any opposition. The appeal to blood as revealing an innermost, inalienable fact is a truth game that works across different discourses – biology, confession, literature, Christianity, and law. The logic goes that if it is blood-related, it must be true. In eucharistic miracle tales and elsewhere in medieval writing, references to blood were often used to make a truth claim forceful enough to count as absolute, incontrovertible proof.

As we shall see, the most fundamental truth confirmed by blood in the Middle Ages is the existence of the integral body. In the eucharistic miracles, it is Christ's invisible integral body, unharmed by non-believers' attacks, that is evidenced by blood. What counted as Christ's body was often proven through blood, as when a desecrated host begins to bleed. But it is usually now overlooked that the bodies of other Christian figures and indeed of ordinary humans were as much in need of confirmation as that of Christ. Again and again, blood furnished such authentication not only of Christ's, but also of any human body. The argument runs that it bleeds, therefore it must be a body. In fact, one of the main reasons for the medieval fascination with blood, and for its ability to function as proof for a large number of claims, was the value ascribed to it in verifying the existence of an integral body. The stakes were high, because blood confirmed what was 'body' and could therefore count as a biological fact in the first place. Moreover, the idea of an integral body was used to essentialize and back up further distinctions, such as that between fully embodied subjects and imperfect bodies like those of women and Jews.

Many of the 'proofs' supplied by blood rest on circular conclusions and questionable premises. In the eucharistic miracle tales, for example, blood is said to appear in the sacrament, thereby allegedly proving the doctrine of transubstantiation, but this assumes that the audience believes the truth of these events in the first place. But why would someone who did not already trust that the host was Christ's body be swayed by such legends, why would such a person give them more credence than the Bible and the Church's teachings? It merely furnishes more stunning proof for the already converted. Here and elsewhere, triple layers of secrecy surrounding blood hide the circular nature of the argument. Blood is usually conveniently hidden inside the body and cannot be further scrutinized. If it does become visible, as in the eucharistic miracle tales, this is in itself a shocking revelation that has a ring of authenticity about it.[16] Not only is blood usually hidden, but so is what it reveals: here Christ's body. As we shall see in this and the following chapter, as well as uncovering the existence of a specific unseen body, blood often lays open the unspoken *concept* of the body. The texts discussing blood frequently add a third layer of textual secrecy, such as Caesarius' caveat to approach the miracles of the eucharist with particular trepidation: the stories stress that they themselves contain secret knowledge, which they reveal to be about the normally hidden blood, whose uncovering in turn reveals intimate secrets.

Blood and the humoural body

One of the key discourses classifying blood as secret knowledge, only to unveil it, was medicine. The *Bartholomäus*, for instance, the most widely used German medical handbook in the thirteenth century, begins with a mystifying build-up, promising to impart hidden truths that all turn out to be about blood. Despite being a pragmatic compilation of recipes from different Latin sources, the *Bartholomäus* initially describes itself as based on a Latin translation of writings by the famous 'Greek' authorities Hippocrates, Galen and Constantinus Africanus, 'proven to be true' by the experience and experiments of 'Master Bartholomäus'.[17] It thus claims to convey the most authentic information available in the truth game of medieval medicine: that which stems from Greek written sources, academically mediated and confirmed by experience. The text proceeds to arouse the reader's curiosity further by promising that, if he or she 'wants to know' these proven truths, the book will disclose them, giving an example of how it is going to decipher knowledge for its readers by citing and then translating a Latin incipit.[18] After this self-aggrandizing and deliberately obscurantist opening, the promised knowledge is finally specified:

> Swer nû wil wizen, von wiu ein igelich siehtuom chom den der mensch habe, der sol daz merchen bî der varwe, die daz harn hât, daz von dem menschen chunt. Swenne daz harn ist rôt unde dicke, daz bediutet daz daz bluot rehte chraft unde guoten gewalt hât in dem lîbe. Swenne daz harn ist dunne unde rôt, daz bediutet daz der mensch ist colericus: der hât des pluotes ze vil unde der fiuhte ze luzil von dem wazer, der muoz durch nôt gâhmuotes sîn, wan im diu galle schiere enbrinnet sô starche, daz ir diu fiuhte nicht widerstên mach. Sô daz der harn ist wîz unde dicke, sô ist der mensch flecmaticus; der hât des pluotveimes ze vil gevangen, der ist

lanchraeche unde swîget gerne. Ist der harn dunne unde wîz, so ist der
mensch melancolicus; der hât des pluotes sô vil, daz iz ist erswarcet; der
wirt schiere grâ.[19]

Whoever wants to know the cause of any disease that the human being
might have shall detect this by the colour of that person's urine. If the urine
is red and thick, this means that the blood has the right strength and
healthy power in the body. If the urine is thin and red, this means that the
human being is choleric: he has too much blood and too little watery
moisture; he is inevitably irascible, because his gall is quick to be incensed
so strongly that moisture cannot defy it. If the urine is white and thick, the
human being is phlegmatic; he has caught too much blood foam; he is
patient and likes to be silent. If the urine is thin and white, the human
being is melancholic; he has so much blood that it has turned black; he will
quickly become grey.

If the recipient 'now wants to know' the cause of all human sickness, he
or she must analyse a patient's urine, and will find that the answer to be
uncovered in each case is blood: an excess of blood, an excess of blood
foam or so much blood that it has turned black. Whenever a cause of a
specific disease is mentioned in the following recipes, it is also blood.[20]
Health, on the other hand, depends on the 'right strength' of blood. So
the text builds itself up as a bearer of secrets and then reveals that this
arcane medical knowledge is, at root, knowledge of blood. Blood is itself
hidden not just as an object of knowledge in the text, but also inside the
body, where it can be uncovered by urine analysis. The *Bartholomäus*
hence presents blood as a secret, which, if uncovered, reveals further
hidden mysteries of the body.

As a medical handbook, the *Bartholomäus* is interested in finding out
the truth about blood not for its own sake, but for what it in turn
reveals about the inside of the body: the balances and imbalances of
fluids in the body which will determine health and sickness. The great
importance given to uncovering the state of the blood here thus also
confirms the *idea* of the body as essentially an enclosed container of
fluids. This conception of the body, and the significance attributed to
blood in asserting its validity, is typical of medieval medicine and of the
ancient Greek physiology upon which it was based. In medical thought
and practice, the key to understanding the body was to understand the
state of the blood. Blood was hidden in the body, but inferences could
be made through urine diagnosis, through an analysis of the colour
and consistency of samples from bloodletting and through examining

the external appearance of a patient and taking his pulse.[21] Once this knowledge of blood was unveiled, it revealed in turn the condition of the whole psychosomatic unit. Medical writing and practice thereby constructed the embodied subject as a homogeneous, coherent system of blood and bloody derivatives, bounded by the skin. Put simply, human bodies were seen as containers of blood, phlegm, black bile and yellow (or red) bile. These four 'humours' determined the balance of the essential qualities of temperature and moisture (hot or cold, and moist or dry), which in turn was responsible for the 'complexion', that is, the temperament and personality of the person – sanguine, phlegmatic, melancholic or choleric. The sanguine type was usually given the most positive attributes – among them strength and friendliness. The diagnostic list quoted above from the *Bartholomäus* goes so far as to pathologize the other three types, although according to orthodox humoural theory some imbalances of humours were natural variations rather than disorders. Blood was seen as the most important humour, since it contained and transported the three others. Food was processed in various stages of digestion into blood, with the residue expelled, and the purified blood nourishing the individual parts of the body, where it was used up. All other bodily fluids such as semen, menstrual blood and the humours were at some point separated from blood and digested further, and were thus considered variant forms of blood.[22] Diseases were defined as an unnatural dominance of one humour in the body. Despite the theoretical importance of all four humours, the *Bartholomäus*, like other medieval German texts, tends to neglect all but blood, not even naming the other three, which it describes instead as 'blood turned black', 'blood foam' and 'excess blood'.

So the text convolutedly presents itself as uncovering a method, urine analysis, which allows one to access hidden knowledge about an individual's blood; and blood in turn reveals the state of the body, and on another level shows that the body is basically a container of blood: if all the physician needs to know about the body to cure it is the state of the blood, then the body is, medically speaking, a container of blood. If the body is medically a container of blood, then all the doctor needs to know is the state of the blood. By virtue of being hidden, blood makes this circular conclusion seem convincing.

Similarly, therapeutic methods implicitly confirmed this view of the body. The medieval panacea was bloodletting, recommended for any disease in order to regulate the balance of the humours. For instance, Ortolf von Baierland's *Arzneibuch*, which replaced the *Bartholomäus* as the most popular German medical handbook in the fourteenth century, describes bloodletting as the first task of the physician.[23] Ortolf was probably a practising physician at Würzburg, who summarized and augmented the standard Latin university textbooks up to about 1250 in a book that was more systematic than the *Bartholomäus*, with an introduction to physiological theory and health regimen, sections on urine, on the pulse and on diseases from head to toe, and on wounds.[24] For each of the illnesses, Ortolf gives the symptoms and potential physiological causes and suggests treatments and medications. He begins again by establishing the trustworthiness of the narrator, who confidently introduces himself by name, as a medical practitioner and 'master' of his field, using Latin books and Hippocrates as sources, and then gives the following general recommendation:

Ef eynen menschen eyn sucht wyl besteyn eder eyn grot suchte, vnde dat he sere krang wert, so saltu merken, ef et von ouerricheme blode sy eder von anderme gesuchte. Jst ez von blode, so is der harn rot vnde de aderen an dem arme vnde an deme houede slan eme sere; so sal men eme to hant laten to der aderen, er de nature vnde dy craft eme entghe.[25]

If a disease or an illness overcomes a person, and he becomes seriously ill, then you have to note whether this is caused by surplus blood or by any other disease. If it is caused by blood, the urine is red and the veins on his arms and head are pulsating vigorously; in this case, you should let his blood at once, before his essence and strength leave him.

So again, the truth revealed by the urine and the veins visible and tangible under the skin is the amount of blood in the body, and that in turn is the most likely reason for any disturbance in the homogeneous system of fluids. Therapy will thus have to attempt to restore the balance of humours in the body. The underlying view of the body is again that of a container of a finite amount of fluids.[26] Aside from bloodletting, therapeutic measures included regulating the intake of food (which was turned into bodily fluids), encouraging digestion, and staunching bleedings and excessive excretions in order to keep the body's liquids in balance. By putting such an emphasis on the adjustment of fluids within a closed system, where a flow through the skin meant a 'loss', a removal from the system, medical practice affirmed the concept of the body as a normally enclosed container. Moreover, every time a real patient was apparently healed through this

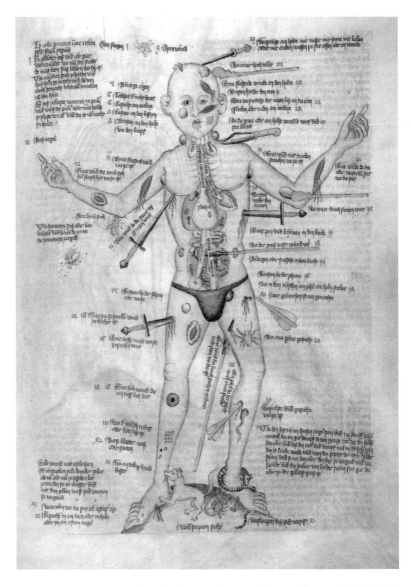

1 Woundman (*c*.1420, Thuringia). London, Wellcome Library, MS 49, fol. 35r. By permission.

regulation of humours, this would have furnished further convincing proof of the theory.

A different way in which blood as an object of knowledge proved the concept of the bounded body is visible in the aptly named 'woundman'. This figure often accompanies the treatise on wounds from Ortolf's *Arzneibuch*, which was in fourteenth- and fifteenth-century manuscripts transmitted separately as a self-contained text in Latin and German. The woundman in the fifteenth-century Wellcome Apocalypse manuscript, the first illustrated translation back into German, for example, is being struck, bitten, cut and pierced from all sides; by swords, arrows, clubs, spears, a knife, a nail, a twig, snakes, a bee, a spider, a dog and a scorpion (Fig. 1).[27] Strikingly bright, opaque red blood flows from the numerous wounds in all parts of the man's body. As the captions and images specify, there are deep wounds, running wounds, swollen wounds, wounds still containing parts of the weapons, putrid wounds, wounds to the veins, to the neck, to the head and so on. Blood emerges from many of these injuries and spreads onto the skin and the surrounding space. This is an image of a porous, permeated and leaking body, and blood shows up this vulnerability and seepage. But at the same time, this is a medical diagram helping to treat such injuries and bleedings. The figure serves as a visual index to the accompanying treatise on wounds; the inscriptions around it describe the depicted injuries and give reference numbers to the relevant therapeutic instructions. Next to the gushing wound in the figure's left arm, for instance, the caption reads '32 A wound where veins are severed, wherever they are' (*32 Eine wunde do di adir vorsnytten sint wo die sint*); and under number 32 in the treatise, a recipe for a medicated plaster to treat such wounds is listed. So the woundman, an image of a body under threat, in conjunction with the text becomes an image of a body about to be treated and hopefully healed.

So while we see blood streaming out of a human body here, we are assured that the body will nevertheless be fully integral, since all such horrifying bleedings can be stopped with the help of the medical knowledge transmitted in the text. In other words, the multiple bleedings are contained conceptually in the function of the image as a medical diagram. They are also visually contained: the text neatly frames the bleeding body at the centre; the blank spaces have been filled with additional recipes. Bright red is not only used to indicate blood, but also for the orderly index numbers. Other medical diagrams put blood even more to the service of visual containment and order; for example, the popular 'bloodletting man', an image similar to the woundman indicating where and when to let blood as a cure for which affliction, regularly uses red lines, sometimes dramatically identified as blood through drops and beads, to connect the bloodletting points on the body to signs of the zodiac.[28] Moreover, the unperturbed expression of the woundman and the fact that his stomach has been opened up not by another weapon, but to allow the artist to depict injuries of the inner organs, remind us of the fact that this is a didactic display rather than a portrait of a sick person. What at first glance might seem a frightening depiction of the fragility of the bleeding body thus functions as a confident assertion that its integrity will not be destroyed, and visible blood again plays a central role in showing this.

Blood and Christ's human body

Since the groundbreaking work of scholars like Caroline Walker Bynum, Miri Rubin, Sarah Beckwith and Stephen Greenblatt, Christ's eucharistic body has been rightly recognized as a central and much-contested focus of late medieval and early modern theology and devotion; the debates surrounding transubstantiation, concomitance, or the withholding of the chalice from the laity are well researched.[29] Somewhat less attention has been paid to the fact that Christ's body was also under debate in other forms, as a human body on the cross and as the collective body of the Church. Even the central Christian belief that God became flesh, that Christ had a body in the first place, was still contested, and in need of miraculous and theological confirmation. Again, blood was often used to supply such evidence. In many stories similar to that of the bleeding host of Brugg, it is not a wafer, but an image of the crucified Christ that is attacked and begins to bleed. Caesarius' monk in the *Dialogus miraculorum* tells his novice how, during a battle in St Goar in 1201, an artillerist shoots a bolt into the arm of a crucifix, so that blood flows:

> Mox mirum in modum antiqua renovantur miracula, et ad instar venae humanae, sanguis de loco vulneris coepit stillare.[30]

> At once in a wonderful way the miracles of old are renewed and blood begins to drip from the place of the wound, as if from human veins.

THE SECRET OF BLOOD

That the 'miracles of old' visually substantiated here are not only previous stories of bleeding crucifixes, but also Christ's original incarnation, is perhaps implied by the fact that even a Jew attests to the truth of this story, a man whose religion precisely denies that Christ was God's son made flesh. That such tales indeed primarily aim to demonstrate that Christ gained a human body is even clearer in a similar miracle in the *Dialogus miraculorum*, according to which in Weissenburg during the same conflict, a combatant tries to steal a linen tunic covering a crucifix high up in a church, and while attempting to pull the tunic down with his lance, pierces the figure on the cross repeatedly, so that it begins to bleed, the monk tells us:

> Dominus vero ut sibi factum ostenderet, quicquid eius imagini inuiriae vel contemptus irrogatur, egit sua potentia ut de singulis punctionibus sanguis ubertim emaneret. Semel enim adhuc mortalis confixus atque lanceatus est in terris, et tamen quotidie sendens ad dexteram Patris se configi per Prophetam conqueritur dicens: *Et me configitis gens tota die.*[31]

> The Lord to show that any damage or insult inflicted upon His image was done to Himself, by His power made the blood gush freely from each of the wounds. For only once whilst a man He was pierced with a lance on earth, and yet each day sitting at the right hand of the Father he complains in the words of the prophet, that He is pierced, saying: *And ye people pierce me all day.*

According to the monk, damage done to the image is damage done to Christ, just as an attack on a host is an attack on Christ's own body and provokes the same bleeding. But he interprets this differently: while the wafer's bleeding shows that Christ is present in each host, to claim that the crucifix's bleeding demonstrated that Christ's body was present in each crucifix would be a heterodox belief. Instead, the monk relates this appearance of blood to that of Christ's past bleeding on the cross and his continued suffering for us, which suggests that it is the incarnation itself that is confirmed here rather than any animation of statues.

Christ's wounding with the lance 'whilst a man' of course refers to the passage in the Gospel of St John where a Roman soldier, in the Middle Ages identified as Longinus, pierces the crucified Christ: 'but one of the soldiers with a spear opened his side, and immediately there came out blood and water'.[32] Not just in popular piety, but also in learned biblical exegesis, this passage, and in particular the visible blood, was taken as proof that Christ did have a human body. Thomas

Aquinas (d. 1274), for example, writes of this flow of blood and water in his commentary on the Gospel:

> Quod quidem factum est ut Christus ostenderet id quod erat, scilicet verus homo. In homine enim est duplex compositio: una scilicet ex elementis, alia ex humoribus. Unum elementorum est aqua; inter humores autem praecipuus est sanguis.[33]

> This proves that Christ showed what he was; if you like, a true human. For humans are of a double composition: on the one hand, if you like, of the elements, on the other of the humours. One of the elements is water, and amongst the humours, the principal one is also blood.

Water and blood prove that Christ had a human body, according to Aquinas, because these were the two key elements of the body in humoural theory. In Greek and medieval natural philosophy, water – like fire, air and earth – is one of the four elements out of which all physical beings are composed, and its presence therefore shows that God had a body. The bleeding, moreover, demonstrates that Christ had blood during his lifetime, and therefore evidenced the second essential quality of every human that Aquinas mentions: the presence of humours. Other theologians argued that Christ's blood showed his human nature because it had come from Mary, his human mother (see chapter 3). Aquinas describes the fact that blood confirmed Christ's humanity again as a revelation of truth. Several texts went so far as to call blood 'of the truth of human nature', such as the treatise about the mass ascribed to Innocent III (d. 1216):

> Si enim capillus de capite vestro non perit, quanto magis sanguis ille non periit qui fuit de veritate naturae.[34]

> For if a hair on your head shall not perish (Luke 21: 18), how much more will blood not perish which was of the truth of [human] nature?

Veritas humanae naturae is a technical term much used in the debates on the resurrection of Christ and of all Christians' bodies for all that is essential rather than accidental to the body and will thus be resurrected. It thus simply means 'the essence of human nature' or 'true human nature', and this text, as well as many others, argues that blood belongs to the inalienable part of the body that will be resurrected. But the formulation nevertheless once more connects blood with 'the truth'.

The argument that blood proves the incarnation of Christ, like that about transubstantiation, presupposes belief in scripture. The Bible says Christ bled; and because bleeding means being human, the logic goes, Christ must have been human. But whoever believes the Bible's claim that Christ bled presumably believes the Bible's claim that Christ became flesh anyway. The argument thus only works to give the already converted a further case in point of the Bible saying that Christ did become human. For some reason, medieval exegetes think that it would have been possible for Christ to have only an appearance of a body, until the blood shows that he has a true, fully human body. The conviction that the blood could not have also been simulated rests solely again in the truth value ascribed to blood, and its being shrouded in secrecy. If God could have given himself a simulated human body, surely he could have included some replicated blood. But because the previously concealed blood appears from the wound in the side, and is explicitly mentioned in the text, this has the ring of truth about it. Like the doubting Thomas, medieval exegetes believe it would have been impossible to fake bleeding wounds; they are incontrovertibly true, and again prove the existence of Christ's body.

The secrets of women

Karma Lochrie argues that the main function of surrounding knowledge with an air of mystery is to create a hierarchized boundary between the object of the secret and those who share it, those who *are* the secret and those who *have* it. Because any rhetoric of secrecy, independent of its object, creates this hierarchy, 'the activity of secrecy is always more important than the secrets themselves'.[35] This is not so much true for blood miracles proving the existence of Christ's body, because the omniscient God is here always party to all secrets as well as their object. But Lochrie applies this instead to the relation between different human agents. She analyses, for example, the *Secreta secretorum*, a thirteenth-century mirror of princes ascribed to Aristotle, which shows precisely a distinction between those 'in the know' – Greek male philosophers including the narrator himself, who understand the hidden meanings of texts – and those constructed as their ignorant opposites: the female and Persian characters in the text as well as any simple-minded readers. Lochrie writes:

Knowledge/ignorance is another one of the binarisms based on the subjective practice of secrecy. What Aristotle protects through the elaboration of secrecy is not only knowledge *and* ignorance, but the multiple binarisms dependent on them both, such as masculine/feminine, Greeks/Persians, philosophers/vulgar readers, and figurative/literal reading.[36]

Which knowledge is exchanged among the privileged, according to Lochrie, is relatively unimportant, as long as it keeps the elite circle intact and distinct from the ignorant. As another example, she cites the *Secreta mulierum* (*The Secrets of Women*, c.1300), a natural philosophical treatise falsely ascribed to Albert the Great, but probably written by someone in his circle.[37] This text, Lochrie claims, never makes clear exactly which secrets it contains – knowledge about women's bodies, nature, female sexuality, reproduction or embryology. Lochrie reads this as part of the text's strategies, still in place in sensationalistic descriptions of sexuality today, of deliberately obscuring its relatively bland content in order to arouse curiosity, and of indefinitely postponing the revelation of knowledge that would presuppose empathy with the Other.[38] By vaguely promising to reveal secrets from male narrator to male audience, the *Secreta mulierum* reaches its aim of forging an exclusive male community without ever having to get to the bottom of this covert information.

I suggest, however, that it is worth paying more attention to the content of the secret of the *Secreta mulierum*, which will add a whole new dimension to Lochrie's binaries: knowledge is not just opposed to ignorance, and both are not simply personified in knowledgeable or ignorant human subjects; rather, knowledge is also contrasted with and at the same time reliant on blood and the body. What Lochrie calls the 'dark matter' of secrecy in this case is indeed material.[39] For at least the anonymous fifteenth-century Southern German commentary to the *Secreta mulierum*, however shiftily and ramblingly, does spell out what the *Secreta's* secrets are about: menstrual blood.[40] After an index and a prologue, in which the treatise's topic is, as in most versions, no more specifically defined than as 'several things about the secrets of women, and the things that are secret and hidden in the nature of women', the first chapter proper begins with this added comment:[41]

Das erst Capitell yn diesem Buch anzufahen wirt von der geburt Embrionis Glosa Embrionis ist Ein flaischen Stuck zusamen gesamelt von dem Samen des mans Vnd von dem Samen der Frawenn. Vnd haist der frauen Samen menstrum. Vnnd wirth das Selb Cappitel vonn der yetz genanten matery Jn dem muterlichen leybe, vnd von der Selben matery geburt vnd bewegung werden vil dinck bekannth die da bey der natur der frauen verporgen Sindt. Hie spricht der maister, Seint ein mal das vnser vorrede ist uß gesagt von den dingen die das gemut des horers Spitzig macht Vnnd naigt nach der matery Vnsers Suns, So zimpt vns wol das wir komen zu der matery des wercks. Vnnd wirt nach der glaß ditzs buchs yn tzwelff Cappittell getailt.[42]

The first chapter in this book begins with the generation of the embryo. Gloss: 'Embryo' is a piece of flesh gathered together from the seed of the man and from the seed of the woman. And the seed of the woman is called menstruum. And this chapter will be about the aforementioned matter in the maternal body; and many things about this matter's generation and movement that are hidden in the nature of women will become known. Here the master says: now that our prologue, which makes the listener's mood keen and inclines it towards the matter in our sense, has finished talking about these things, it is appropriate that we come to the matter of the work. And following the glossary, this is divided into twelve chapters.

So it is revealed that the 'many things' that are 'hidden in the nature of women' are characteristics of the 'aforementioned matter', menstruum. The secret truth, disclosed in this chapter, is thus about menstrual blood.

Even in the versions of the *Secreta* where this is not stated explicitly, most topics covered in the treatise directly or indirectly do relate to menstrual blood, to such an extent that Monica H. Green has described the text as 'focused obsessively on menstruation'.[43] This is partly due to the central role that menstrual blood was ascribed in medieval theories of reproduction, which is the main aspect under which women's bodies are discussed in the *Secreta*. Menstrual blood is a specially processed form of blood and a woman's contribution to the generation of the embryo, which finds its male equivalent in semen. Menstruum also nourishes the embryo in the womb and, after it has been further concocted into breast milk, also the baby. Conception, pregnancy and breast-feeding are precisely the main topics of the *Secreta*, although a surprising amount of further situations and characteristics are also discussed in relation to menstruum. Menstrual blood thus defines women to such an extent throughout all chapters that the *Secreta's* description of menstruum as 'the nature of women' is apposite.[44]

The secret of this blood is again the integral body. This time, blood not only confirms this conception of the body as true or proves the existence of a particular body, but is also believed to be what actual bodies are made of. Immediately after introducing the mysterious blood, the anonymous Southern German *Secreta* states that human bodies are produced from blood:

> Von der geburt Embrionis. In dem ersten capittell ist zu Sagen von der geburt Embrionis. Von der matery Jst zu wissen vnd fleyßlich deynnem Sune Vnnd gedanckenn zuempfelhen das ein iglicher mensch der naturlich geborn wirt von dem Samen Seins vaters Vnd dem fluß Seynner muter das da menstruum haist Der wirt geborn nach dem Sinn der naturlichen meister Vnd nach dem synn der ertzt.[45]

> Of the generation of the embryo. The first chapter is about the generation of the embryo. Of this matter one should understand and remember well that every human being who is naturally generated from the seed of his father and the flow of his mother, which is called menstruum, is generated in this way according to the opinion both of the natural philosophers and of the physicians.

So the embodied human is made out of menstrual blood and the father's seed, both of which are processed forms of blood, as the accepted medical theory states (see chapter 3, pp. 91–3). Every human body thus originates from blood, and body is here again defined as a bounded entity unique to each individual, despite its origin from mixed fluids (an aspect I shall come back to in chapter 3). This assertion is especially reassuring in light of the preceding prologue, which was devoted to the eternity of the species, presenting every individual human being as part of a continuum rather than a unit unto him- or herself. The secret of menstrual blood that the treatise revolves around and circumnavigates is how it miraculously produces the body.

However, in terms of secrecy and knowledge, this view of the body as produced from blood is gendered. The *Secreta* presents the human being's emergence from blood as a secret of women's blood and bodies, about which men exchange medical knowledge. Men are almost disembodied in this text, firmly placed on the side of abstract, written knowledge and of all that transcends the body, while women are attributed bodies, but not knowledge. This adds a whole dimension to Lochrie's distinction between knowledge and lack of knowledge: the difference between knowledge and body. The knowledge conveyed in the *Secreta* is accessible only to an elite community of men. The anonymous Southern German version sets itself up as an exclusively male system of written communication: it begins as a letter from a mysterious 'town called A.' from a 'master' (in the commentary identified as the 'great lord', Albertus Magnus) to his 'dearest companion called . . .' or 'apprentice' and 'friend'; and then addresses a fellowship who commissioned the *Secreta*.[46] The ending presents the treatise as an open, incomplete entity, a work-in-progress that would benefit from extensions and contributions from 'brothers', which it invites in an appeal for further male-to-male communication.[47] As evidenced by the various commentaries accompanying different manuscript versions of text, this request was accepted by a number of actual recipients. Both beginning and end urge the readers and listeners to hide the secrets divulged here, from childlike minds; or, in a spoof papal decretal affixed to French manuscript versions of the treatise, from women. The book sets its 'enlightened' recipients apart from all others, who are likened to people who do not know the way.[48]

The unproblematic inclusion and juxtaposition of references and extensive quotations from diverse centuries-old traditions of male-authored texts extends the exclusive community of written knowledge into the past as well. The fact that it is a translation is not even mentioned in the German *Secreta*, denying any hiatus between Latin and the vernacular. The perspective from which the text is told is also consistently that of a man explicating women to other men. There is not a single claim treating women as anything but objects of distanced or hostile description, showing some empathy or understanding. Even the reference to menstrual pain is made not out of consideration of the feelings of women, but to explain the etymological origin of the word 'pain' (*schmertzen*) as a synonym for menstruation; and a recommendation to gratify women sexually is only mentioned in the same sentence as its sole aim: to increase their reproductive capability.[49]

Women are granted some knowledge in the *Secreta*, but only of their own bodies: women know when they are about to give birth, how to feign virginity, how to induce a miscarriage, how to conceal pregnancy and how to wound the penis in the vagina.[50] Among the 119 references to authorities that Margaret Schleissner has counted in the Southern German variant, 118 are to male doctors and scholars, like Aristotle, Avicenna and Galen; and one to 'several women' who allegedly told the narrator, sensibly, that it is beneficial if a baby's head comes out first during birth.[51] The mere physicality of women's knowledge is stressed when they are denied an understanding of the soul, metaphysics and orthodox Christian faith. It is dismissed as 'deception' and perhaps even 'heresy' if old women claim knowledge of extra-bodily experiences of the soul.[52] In the description of the disease 'suffocation of the womb', where trapped menstrual fluid is believed to make the womb wander through the body and thus to cause the breath to squeeze together the *gaistlichen ding* in the upper body, menstrual matter can again be read as opposed to the spirit, because *gaistlich* means not only respiratory, but also spiritual.[53] Women advising young girls verbally – which indicates that women transmit knowledge orally rather than in writing – are even called 'old sorceresses'.[54] The fact that women's secret knowledge about their bodies is unwritten makes it harder for men to uncover.

Women usually employ knowledge of their bodies to deceive and harm men (and children), according to the *Secreta*. As frequently in later texts, women are suspected of consciously misleading men when falsely claiming to be virgins.[55] They are also supposed to deliberately conceal pregnancies. Elaborate struggles for information can ensue, when men devise secret pregnancy tests, which women can again see through and undermine. One of the suggested tests is to make a woman drink water with honey; if this causes stomach pain, she is pregnant. But since the woman might be suspicious, it is recommended to wait until she feels ill, and then pretend to offer her the honeyed water as medicine. Even then, however, she might still conceal the telling pain, in which case men will fail to find out more, as the text resignedly admits.[56] So the *Secreta* here explicitly builds up a common enemy, a female community of secret, dangerous, orally transmitted knowledge about women's bodies. Paradoxically, men are imagined as knowing more about women's bodies than women themselves do, and as sharing these facts in an exclusive male exchange of written information.

Peggy McCracken in *The Curse of Eve, the Wound of the Hero* has shown that women's blood in Old French courtly romances is similarly presented as always suspect and excluded from positive public valuation. In romances such as the *Queste del Saint Graal*, the *Roman de Florence de Rome* or Chrétien de Troyes's *Le chevalier de la charrette*, McCracken has found that women's blood, which is paradigmatically menstrual blood, is usually hidden from view and cannot signify, like men's blood, a heroic wound or cause for revenge. Menstruation and heroism are mutually exclusive. This distinction between men's public and important bleeding and women's shameful, secret bleeding enforces the gender difference. But in German medical texts like the *Secreta*, such an attempted neat gendering of blood usually breaks down as soon as women's blood becomes a topic of male discourse rather than hidden, and a substance necessary for reproduction rather than insignificant. The 'secrets of women', their sexual functions that have to be modestly hidden, become the *Secreta mulierum*, a body of male knowledge that is equally esoteric and must be concealed. The distinction made in the *Secreta* between male knowledge and female boundedness to bodies is thus highly unstable: women do have some knowledge precisely of the matters discussed in the *Secreta*; and, for all its attempts at distinction, the elite male community mainly relates knowledge about the body, that is, exactly the kind of knowledge it has vilified as dangerous, female intelligence. Even the claim of literary communication from writer to reader as opposed to female orality is undermined when, in the initial statement quoted above, a listener is addressed.[57] In fact, like women's own knowledge of their bodies, the natural, physical matters that the treatise defines as its subject clash with spiritual, ethical and theological issues. An example is the conflict between the 'natural' belief in predetermination through stars and the 'religious' belief in being able to appease God through sacrifice. The main text decides to remain silent on this matter, claiming that it would need lengthy explanations, but goes on to discuss predetermination anyway. The commentary justifies this by arguing that, despite talking like the heathen natural philosophers, Albertus Magnus can still 'believe like a Christian'.[58] Similarly, the *Secreta* refuses to take a stand in the conflict between the physiological idea of sex as beneficial to women and social sexual constraints: 'this has nothing to do whatsoever with this matter'.[59] Evelyn Fox Keller projects such a tension between a wish to uncover the secrets of nature through science, and a respect for the unfathomable secrets of God and his moral prohibitions onto a timeline, locating scientific curiosity firmly in modernity and Christian reluctance to probe too deeply in the Middle Ages. But both are clearly simultaneous in thirteenth-century texts, and rather than, like Lochrie, suggesting that the *Secreta secretorum* must therefore be a premature modern text, I believe that both medieval and modern periods negotiate different levels of scientific and religious knowledge, and that a difference between medieval lack and modern wealth of knowledge cannot be upheld.[60]

While the distinction between men's knowledge and women's bodies blurs, knowledge and blood themselves also strikingly converge in the initial quotation from the beginning of the first chapter (see above pp. 32–3). This passage shows a telling shift in the meaning of the term *matery*, matter, from referring to menstrual blood to referring to the topic of the treatise, by the end of which menstrual matter *is* the subject matter. The first use of the word *matery*, announcing that this chapter will be about the 'matter in the maternal body just mentioned', stands for the menstrual blood initially described. The following claim that the text will reveal this *matery*'s origin and movement probably still refers to the physiological production and processes that menstruum undergoes, and that the first chapter as well as the rest of the text discuss. The third usage, claiming that the prologue incites the desire of the listeners for the '*matery* in our sense' is the least clear; the matter that the recipient is meant to hanker after could still be menstruum as a sexual fluid, or, more likely, the knowledge about menstrual blood divulged in this treatise. In its last appearance, as 'subject matter of the work', *matery* has made the transition from denoting menstrual matter to denoting the content of the book. *Matery* can mean subject matter as well as menstrual blood throughout the book.[61] Blood itself, not one of its characteristics or its further disclosures, thus *is* the secret truth that is revealed. Indeed, the same oscillation between a physical and an epistemological meaning is found in the word *secreta* itself, which implies both secrets and secretions, in so far as both stem from the root *secernere*, 'to set apart'.

Moreover, men also have bodies, of course, whose description creeps into the text, undermining the location of bodies exclusively on the side of women as the object of the treatise. To chapter 1, on the physiology of menstruation, a critical question is appended about the reasons why the superfluous food flows out of women, in the form of menstrual fluid, but not out of men, in the form of semen, which is then explained by men's warmer nature.[62] The last chapter also discusses semen as part of men's physiology. So the distinction between men's knowledge and its object, women's matter, subverts itself in the *Secreta* at almost every point: women do have some knowledge, men do have some matter, and knowledge and matter often blur into one. Despite its impressive air of secrecy, blood proves to be an unreliable anchor for gendered truth claims.

Blood and the text

The *Secreta* reveals matter that is both blood and knowledge. A surprising number of texts similarly use the truth value credited to blood by claiming to transmit blood-related knowledge as well as actual blood in various ways. The mystical text *Das fließende Licht der Gottheit* (*c.*1250–82) by Mechthild von Magdeburg, for example, maintains no less than that it spreads the blood of God. The *Fließendes Licht* is a collection of poems, narratives, visions and dialogues, which in some passages purports to be based on the autobiographical experiences of the narrator, a mystic named Mechthild, and to relate directly what God said to her or to 'a soul' in various conversations. For example, God tells the soul that her book is one of his messengers and that his heart's blood is written in it:

'Dis buoch sende ich nu ze botten allen geistlichen lûten, bedû den boesen und den guoten, wan swenne die sûle vallent, so mag das werk nit gestan. Ich sage dir werlich', sprach ûnser herre, 'in disem buoche stat min herzebluot geschriben, das ich in den jungesten ziten anderwarbe wil giessen.'[63]

'I am now sending this book as a messenger to all clerical people, both the bad and the good, for when the columns come down, the work cannot remain. I tell you verily', our Lord said, 'that in this book, my life-blood is written, which I will shed again in the last days'.

If God's innermost blood is written in the book, this suggests a blurring of the text with its content, blood, similar to the double meaning of matter in the *Secreta* as both 'blood' and 'subject matter'. Rather than describing God's blood, the writing *is* God's blood.[64] This is confirmed by the second image used here, that of the book as a messenger, like the saints and martyrs that God describes as his other messengers in this chapter, for example, 'my messenger of blood', St Peter Martyr (d. 1252).[65] The bleeding of martyrs imitating Christ's passion is a way of bearing witness to the truth of Christian faith, and renews the redemption for all sinners achieved through Christ's sacrificial death (see my chapter 4). The *Fließendes Licht* now claims to fulfil the same function as a person's martyrdom, even to be a more direct form of participation in the divine, since it sends out God's blood directly rather than imitating this.[66] So writing blood has taken on the truth-affirming and redemptive functions that only the actual bleeding of Christ and the martyrs used to have. It is hard to imagine a more urgent and wide-ranging appropriation of the truth value given to blood in discourse in order to authenticate writing than that in the *Fließendes Licht*. In comparing writing to physical suffering, Mechthild has overcome the limitations of the medium of writing: like a body, it can now carry the substance that holds a body's innermost secrets, blood.

From here, a link can be made to the fact that writing in the Middle Ages did happen on skin, the dead skin from which parchment was fashioned. This skin itself can be seen as revealing truths, as a bleeding body would. The topos that the skin of parchment brings hidden truths to the surface and makes them dangerously accessible is used in the *Secrets* literature. The Franciscan scholar Roger Bacon (d. *c.*1294) in his Latin version of the *Secreta secretorum* writes:

> Preterea quod interrogasti et scire desideras est archanum tale quod humana pectora vix poterunt tollerare; quomodo ergo possunt in mortalibus pellibus depingi?[67]

> Furthermore what you have asked and desire to know is so secret that human breasts are hardly able to bear it; in what manner is it thus possible for such secrets to be depicted on mortal skin?

The secrets mentioned here are so great that they can hardly be endured by the interior of the body, the human breast, let alone by the skin as the mere mortal surface of the body. Without mentioning blood, Bacon thus invokes the truth value of that which is hidden in the body, and can only be dragged out with great difficulty and under a veil of secrecy. In his *Opus Majus*, he employs this trope again:

> Quoniam secundum sententiam Aristotelis libro secretorum et Socratis magistri sui, secreta scientiarum non scribimus in pellibus caprarum et ovium, ita quod a vulgo valeant aperiri.[68]

> Hence according to the view of Aristotle in his book of secrets, and of his master, Socrates, the secrets of the sciences are not written on the skin of goats and sheep so that they may be discovered by the multitude.

Because parchment has brought to the surface previously arcane knowledge, the whole manuscript now needs to be hidden from the masses.

Not only can the book be a body, but also the body a book, for example, in the widespread comparison of a Christian's body to a parchment into which God can be inscribed, or in the predominantly English tradition of the Charter of Christ, where Christ's body is depicted as a piece of writing, marked with his blood.[69] Both book-as-body and body-as-book come together with blood in the extraordinary manuscripts of the mystical vita of Heinrich Seuse (Henry Suso) in his *Exemplar* (*c.*1362/63).

He attempts to transmit not God's, but his own blood on the skin of parchment. According to the text, the narrator scratches the name of Christ, IHS, into his heart and 'into the living blood of my heart's fluid', so that blood flows onto his chest, and keeps this wound 'secret', only ever showing it to his confidant.[70] The *Exemplar* was conceptualized together with its illustrations, and folio 7r of the oldest and best of the manuscripts – a fourteenth-century volume from Strasbourg – not only contains this passage in writing, but also an image of the letters IHS, written in blood-red ink on parchment, with ink dripping down into the margins (Fig. 2). While Jeffrey Hamburger points out that the text here becomes a performance of devotion, and Urban Küsters emphasizes the mnemonic and certifying function of scars and body inscriptions, this is also an authenticating strategy for the text: by revealing blood, it appears to show forth a hidden truth.[71] Where the *Bartholomäus*, the *Secreta* and the *Fließendes Licht* unveil blood in a linguistic performance, by writing blood or revealing the secrets of blood, the *Exemplar* adds a visual performance that shows rather than writes blood.

The voice of blood

Blood could also function within legal discourse as instant incontrovertible proof. A good example of this is the *jus cruentationis cadaveri*, or *Bahrprobe*, the belief that the body of a murder victim will bleed once more in the presence of the perpetrator.[72] From the fifteenth century onwards, this appearance of blood was used as legal proof to reveal a murderer, in particular in inquisition trials. It is unclear to what extent it was part of earlier legal practice, but it certainly appears in earlier fiction, for example, in the *Nibelungenlied* (c. 1200). This famous heroic epic is the story of the young knight Siegfried's marriage to the Burgundian princess Kriemhild, and his murder at the hands of her brothers and of the powerful vassal Hagen, and, in the second half, Kriemhild's second marriage to Etzel, king of the Huns, and her genocidal revenge. At a pivotal point between the two linked murder plots, when Siegfried's corpse is carried to the church, Kriemhild demands that Hagen submit himself to the *Bahrprobe*:

2 Monograph of Jesus Christ incised on Heinrich Seuse's heart (fourteenth century). Strasbourg, Photos et Coll. de la Bibliothèque Nationale et Universitaire, MS 2929, fol. 7r. By permission.

'swelher sî unschuldec   der lâze daz gesehen!
der sol zuo der bâre   vor den liuten gên.
dâ bî mac man di wârheit   harte schiere verstên.'

Daz ist ein michel wunder   vil dicke ez noch geschiht:
swâ man den mortmeilen   bî dem tôten siht,
sô bluotcnt im di wunden,   als ouch dâ geschach.
dâ von man die schulde   dâ ze Hagene gesach.

Di wunden vluzzen sêre   alsam si tâten ê.
die ê dâ sêre klageten   des wart nu michel mê.
do sprach der künec Gunther: 'ich wilz iuch wizzen lân.
in sluogen schâchaere,   Hagene hât es niht gctân.'

'Mir sint di schâchaere',   sprach si, 'wol bekant.
nu lâze ez got errechen   noch sîner friunde hant.
Gunther und Hagene,   jâ habet ir ez getân.'[73]

'Whoever is innocent shall let it be seen. He should approach the bier in front of everyone. In this way the truth can very quickly be ascertained.' It is a great miracle, and still happens a lot: if one secs the murderer near the dead, his wounds bleed, as happened then. So one could see Hagen's guilt. The wounds bled strongly again, as they had done before. People had lamented profusely beforehand, this became even stronger now. Then Gunther said: 'I will let you know. Robbers killed him; it wasn't Hagen.' 'I know these robbers very well', she said. 'May God give that his friends will yet avenge this. Gunther and Hagen, of course you have done it.'

Horst Wenzel describes the bleeding of Siegfried's wounds at the sight of his murderer as the last reliable sign, a 'natural' sign, in a text in which everything else becomes a matter of perception and deception.[74] Kriemhild also stresses that this test shows the truth ('In this way the truth can very quickly be recognized'), and the narrator agrees. But in fact, even the truth spoken by blood is not unambiguous and open to interpretation. While the narrator thinks that the bleeding proves Hagen's guilt, Kriemhild claims that it makes Gunther and Hagen the murderers; Gunther denies that it means anything and blames robbers; and the crowd's reaction is ambiguous. The recipients know that Hagen killed Siegfried with Gunther's consent, and so might also subscribe to the narrator's or Kriemhild's view. In fact, the question of who can be justly held accountable for Siegfried's murder and should therefore pay a price is a key question in the second half of the text, and is raised rather than answered by the bier test.

Blood also shows that a violent deed has been committed in other examples in the *Nibelungenlied*. That this is no guarantor of the 'truth' being told is clear in the many instances of wrong conclusions being drawn: when Dankwart turns up in the doorway of Etzel's hall with bloody clothes and a naked weapon to tell Hagen that the varlets have been killed, Hagen mistakes the red blood on his shirt as a sign of Dankwart being wounded.[75] Kriemhild later wrongly interprets the blood on Hagen's armour from his wound as indicating his defeat.[76] The sign of blood can also be actively manipulated, for example, when Hagen denies any violence after Gunther and several other knights have noticed the ferryman's blood in the boat, or when he persuades the rearguard not to mention the bloodshed in the battle with the Bavarians as long as it cannot be seen in the dark.[77] Similarly, the blood that Siegfried spits in the competition with Brünhild is probably deceitfully hidden by Siegfried's magic cloak, and the blood he sheds in the wedding bed is concealed by the darkness (in the morning, it might be mistaken for the blood of defloration).[78]

Such a questioning of the automatic truth value of blood is found in many texts from the allegedly so irrational Middle Ages. Many eucharistic miracles were challenged and either exposed as fakes or natural phenomena or carefully tested and verified by papal commissions, while a number of theological controversies erupted about blood miracles in general, for example, debating whether any of Christ's blood could have remained on earth.[79] The *Bahrprobe* was also much discussed and seems to have been more widely accepted in the later period now usually counted as early modernity.[80] The other famous example of a fictional *Bahrprobe* in Hartmann von Aue's Arthurian romance *Iwein* (c. 1190–1200) also gives two views of its precise truth value. *Iwein* tells of the adventures of the eponymous knight, which begin with his killing of the lord of a magic fountain, Askalon, who flees, mortally wounded, into his castle. Iwein follows him and is hidden by the maid Lunete. The narrator mentions the belief that a corpse begins to bleed if its killer approaches or touches it as 'something we have been told is true', when he describes how Askalon's dead body newly bleeds when it is carried past the hidden Iwein.[81] Blood thus reveals the secret presence of Iwein's body. But for Askalon's widow Laudine, who has no idea that Iwein is holed up in the castle, the 'truth' disclosed is instead the erroneous idea that he has bewitched them:

er ist zewâre hinne
und hât uns der sinne
mit zouber âne getân.[82]

He truly is here and has magically deprived us of our senses.

Laudine thus mistrusts her senses, but in doing so shows that even the 'natural sign' of the *jus cruentationis* is not a simple visual proof, but open to interpretation. Again, perception, loss of senses and verification are major issues throughout *Iwein*, in particular as regards the knight's relationship to Laudine.

One fictional bleeding which leads to intense deliberation about which kind of truth it reveals is Tristan's bleeding in Isolde's bed in Gottfried von Strassburg's *Tristan* (*c.*1200–10). One of the ruses set up by Isolde's husband, King Marke, to establish whether his wife is having an affair with Tristan is to spread flour on the floor between the beds in which they have been resting after a joint bloodletting. But rather than any disturbed flour on the floor, it is blood that makes their secret encounter visible: when Tristan jumps across to Isolde's bed, his vein opens again, and the blood soils the bed linen. Because Marke only sees the blood in both Tristan's and Isolde's bed, but the flour shows no footsteps, he is confused, and the lovers' secret is still somehow contained in the blood, as the narrator puts it:

iedoch ir beider tougenheit
unde der wâren geschiht
der enwiste er anders niht,
wan alse er an dem bluote sach.
diu bewaerde diu was aber swach . . .
hie mite was ime diu wârheit
beidiu geheizen und verseit.[83]

Yet he did not know more about the secrets of the two and about the true story than that which he saw from the blood. But that was weak proof . . . In this way, he was both told and denied the truth.

The narrator launches into long musings about the paradoxical truths of the blood and the flour. The recipients know that the blood, not the flour, speaks the truth in so far as Tristan and Isolde are having an affair, and he in fact deflowered her on a previous occasion, although it is not made explicit whether they have sex rather than a 'mere' tête-à-tête in Isolde's bed this time. Again, Marke's futile attempts to find out the truth about the relationship are a major concern in this romance.

Blood reveals secrets usually by showing that which is normally inside a body. In many cases, as in the eucharistic and crucifix miracles, it thus uncovers a violation of the body. This should logically be proof *against* the idea of the body as an integral unit, but the latter is safeguarded when the violation is then punished. This is what happens in the *Nibelungenlied*: Siegfried's bleeding in the presence of his murderer makes Kriemhild swear revenge, with the bloodbath of the second half of the story as its consequence (see my chapter 2). The notion that bloodshed will automatically reveal itself and be avenged also appears in the idea of sins crying to heaven for vengeance. Like the seven deadly sins, the sins crying to heaven are a subgroup of sins, which can comprise in various changing line-ups the 'silent sin against nature', that is, sodomy; the oppression of the poor, of widows and orphans; the withholding of salaries; usury; stealing from the Church; raping virgins; and almost always bloodshed. The idea that spilt blood cries to heaven comes from Genesis 4: 10, which states that Abel's blood, shed by Cain, cries to God for vengeance. This notion of blood crying out thus suggests not only that it cannot be hidden, but also that it always has to be avenged.[84]

This need to take revenge for any revelation of blood is dramatized in Paolo Uccello's *predella* of the *Profanation of the Host* (1467–8), a long narrow panel intended to be situated underneath Joos van Ghent's altarpiece of the *Communion of the Apostles* in the church of the Confraternity of Corpus Domini in Urbino.[85] This *predella* depicts the story of a host desecration which supposedly happened in Paris in 1290, one of many cases in which Jews, thieves or women are alleged to have stolen and profaned a host, which then miraculously begins to bleed and reveals itself, and in the end the perpetrators either convert or repent, or are punished or killed.[86] The Paris story is here broken down into six key images: a woman selling the host to a Jew, the discovery of the bleeding host, the procession with the recovered host to the altar, the hanging of the Christian woman, the burning of the Jewish family, and angels and devils fighting over the soul of the dead woman. The image that interests me here is the second one, in which the host is desecrated and simultaneously discovered (Fig. 3). While the written accounts of the story, such as Giovanni Villani's *Nuova Cronica* (before 1348), describe how Christian customers in the Jew's shop notice the host jumping up on the table or the blood filling the courtyard, blood here

3 Bleeding host. Second panel from Paolo Uccello, *Profanation of the Host* (1467–8), Urbino, Palazzo Ducale © 1990, Photo Scala, Florence. By permission.

flows out of the house to show that a body has been attacked.[87] We see the host in a frying pan on the fire, bleeding so profusely that the blood runs across the tiled floor to the other side of the room, where it gushes out of a hole at the bottom of the wall. There, it must have been spotted by the townspeople, as they have already gathered in arms and are trying to break into the locked door, while the Jewish family inside have retreated in horror to the opposite wall. The viewer is asked to suspend disbelief here not only as regards the representational techniques – the cut-away wall, which allows the viewer to see inside the house, and the simultaneity of perhaps successive events – but also as far as the narrative level within the picture is concerned. Why would the host bleed rather than fry or burn, if it is meant to behave like a human body would? Why would the blood run purposefully to the other side of the room?

Why would there happen to be a hole in the wall in the first place?[88] Such inconsistencies appear in many of the desecration stories, in which the hosts nearly always bleed, even if this is logically motivated only in those cases where the thieves, Jews or women stab the host – witness the host of Brugg that apparently bleeds from mere contact with water. However, the bleeding does make sense in so far as it capitalizes on the power of blood to reveal a secret truth, in a visually impressive and incontrovertible manner. If anyone had doubted how terrible it is to disrespect the eucharistic wafer, this is now abundantly clear: it means blood, violence, injury. This also confirms once more the truth of the doctrine of transubstantiation, and the alleged wickedness of the Jews.

Also noteworthy is the automatic chain of revenge that bloodshed sets into motion. Not only does the host become a bleeding body, but in the *predella*, the house itself also takes on characteristics of a body, its wall peeled open like skin in medical drawings (such as the woundman), and blood flowing out as if from a wound in this skin. But this wound in the body of Christ and the body of the house is always already being avenged, as the community is breaking in from the other side: one violation of the body is being made good by another. If we read the house as a body, then the same body is here the one that is being wounded from two sides, once in an injury and once in its punishment or revenge. This seeming paradox can be understood as a foreshortening of the idea that any violation of a body is a violation of 'the' body, inasmuch as it shows that the body is not always a fully enclosed entity. The doubt that any violation casts on the concept of a bounded body can only be erased if the violation is marked as a transgression, and accordingly punished. Paradoxically, this often means a repeat violation of the body, but this time usually of the offender's body, with which the Jew's house can also be connected. This is precisely what happens in the next pictures of the *predella*, after the skinwall has already been attacked, in the actual hanging and burning of the desecrators. Blood will cry out to the heavens for vengeance, and here, it flows out of the house into the open in a visual 'cry'. The miraculousness of this appearance makes clear that blood causes its own revenge, without having to rely on human agency.

A similar shorthand of the logic by which blood reveals the violation of a body, and is inevitably made good, is the grail question in Wolfram von Eschenbach's Arthurian romance *Parzival* (c.1200–10). The young knight Parzival happens upon the grail castle and is made witness to a strange procession, during which a bloody lance is carried forth, to the visible and audible distress of the assembled grail community. He later finds out from his hermit uncle Trevrizent that this lance is bloody because it is periodically laid (or, on this particular occasion, pressed) into the grail king Anfortas's bloody groin wound in order to alleviate his pain.[89] Anfortas, as grail king, should have waited for the grail to allocate a wife for him, but instead had chosen a girlfriend, Orgeluse, on his own, and had received his injury from a heathen while illegitimately fighting in her service. Trevrizent interprets the wound that will not heal as a divine punishment for Anfortas's transgression. It certainly has done irreparable damage not just to the king, but to the whole grail community, which remains paralysed in mourning. Only a new king is able to redeem Anfortas and renew the society. As Trevrizent explains, Parzival was meant to somehow understand that the blood on the lance was the sign of this spiritual, physical and social suffering, and he was meant to ask what caused this bleeding: 'Lord, what is your affliction?'[90] The answer to this would in the first instance have been the bloody wound, and secondly the wider issue of transgression of the rules of the grail community.[91] The blood on the lance should have revealed to Parzival that Anfortas's body, and thereby the body of the grail clan that depends on its king for survival, had been violated, and in uncovering this, the wound would have healed. Parzival fails to ask the crucial question at the grail castle, and spends much of the further plot trying to find his way back. When he finally returns and asks the question, 'uncle, what is troubling you?', disclosure of the violation and healing indeed fall together, as had been predicted by Trevrizent.[92] Asking the question seems to be enough: as soon as the blood, the violation of integrity, is revealed, the wound heals – Anfortas is cured, and the genealogical body is reinstated as Parzival becomes king. This is, then, another case of blood disclosing itself with little human agency and being necessarily made good, here not so much through revenge as through healing. The magical power that is attributed to the mere asking after blood results from the power of blood, once made public, to effect a payment by itself.

Blood is, then, an epistemological concept: the ultimate proof of superior power and knowledge, of guilt, of violation, but above all of the notion of a body as a distinct, integral entity. Keeping knowledge of blood secret and then divulging it empowers the narrator and characters in many of the texts discussed in this chapter. Etymologists have argued that the word 'blood' itself has arisen from a taboo of speaking about blood, since *blōdi- in Germanic languages replaced the older proto-Indo-European terms *ĕ-r and *kreu-, whose invocation was seen as

too powerful and dangerous.[93] This fits in with the prevalent construction of blood as a secret observed in this chapter. Taboos, however,
surrounded not just talking about blood, but also shedding blood and
touching blood, and such taboos equally enforced the idea of an enclosed
body. In the next chapter, I will turn my attention to these other taboos
against blood.

2

Blood Taboos

I am a Jew. Hath not a Jew eyes? hath not a Jew hands, organs, dimensions,
senses, affections, passions? Fed with the same food, hurt with the same
weapons, subject to the same diseases, healed by the same means, warmed
and cooled by the same winter and summer as a Christian is? – if you prick
us do we not bleed? If you tickle us do we not laugh? If you poison us do
we not die? And if you wrong us shall we not revenge? – if we are like you
in the rest, we will resemble you in that.

(William Shakespeare, *The Merchant of Venice*)

Bounded bodies and the bond of flesh

Usually seen as a compelling plea for human equality across religious and racial boundaries, Shylock's famous 'I am a Jew' speech
from William Shakespeare's *The Merchant of Venice* (*c.*1594–7) relies on
an invocation of physical similarities to make its point.[1] What unites
Jews and Christians here is that they have the same bodies in all respects
that are important to medieval and early modern physiology, in their
parts and temperaments and in relation to food, injury, disease and cli-
mate – most of Shylock's list could be less impressively summed up as
'do we not have a body?' This shared body is a fragile construction, a
conglomerate of parts (eyes, hands, organs), indistinguishable from
mind and feeling ('senses, affections, passions') and under attack ('hurt
with the same weapons, subject to the same diseases', pricked, poisoned).
Moreover, it is outside conscious control: it automatically bleeds, laughs

and dies when so stimulated. Who could deny such a pitiful common denominator to anyone, and thus doubt that Jews share it with Christians? But Shylock's last question – 'and if you wrong us, shall we not revenge?' – changes the focus from vulnerability to aggression and includes revenge in the list of physical, uncontrollable reflexes to pricking, tickling and poisoning. Shylock in this way presents revenge as an equally uncontrollable bodily response and gives it an inevitability and justification it otherwise lacks. Suddenly, biological proof no longer serves to demonstrate the sameness of Jews and gentiles, but to justify their mutual hatred. From Shylock's list of common human features, it is his observation that everyone bleeds when wounded that has become almost proverbial as an incontrovertible statement of human equality. Shylock's cascade of rhetorical questions thus rests again on the truth game with blood and the body, on the appeal to biological facts as irrefutable proof for the social construction of the difference or sameness of Christians and Jews. That this appeal can be read both as confirming their equality and their inequality again shows how unstable and malleable the 'biological facts' of blood are.

Shylock's speech is part of the plot strand in which the Christian merchant Antonio pawns a pound of his own flesh to Shylock, and the latter is prevented from cutting it out at the last minute through the intervention of the heiress Portia. Jew and Christian are not granted the same degree of integrity in this dramatic development; they do not bleed, eat and hurt in the same way. While the Christian's body is protected from the threat of incision, the Jew is left a broken and defeated man, even robbed of his 'own flesh and blood', his daughter, and saved from the gallows only by the Duke's mercy. This anti-Semitic view of Jews as lacking a fully integral body will concern us further in chapter 3, but first, I want to show that the pound of flesh motif, which was popular throughout the Middle Ages, is a tale of a body being established as a bounded entity through prohibitions against bloodshed, a fantasy of affirming this body by showing that it cannot be penetrated. Versions of this tale appear, most famously, in Johannes de Alta Silva's Latin story cycle *Dolopathos* (c.1200), in the Middle English world history *Cursor mundi* (c.1300) and in the exempla collection *Gesta romanorum* (c.1300–40), which adds the motif of a pact written in blood.[2]

A German translation of the *Gesta romanorum* is the *Märe* 'Kaiser Lucius' Tochter' from the early or mid-fifteenth century.[3] Its plot is as follows. A knight serving Emperor Lucius is in love with his lord's beautiful daughter and begs her to let him sleep with her for one night.

She allows him to do so for a thousand guilders. But as soon as the knight is in her bed, he falls asleep and is sent away in the morning without having had sex with her. The same happens the next night. The knight has now exhausted his funds, and borrows the money for his third attempt from a rich burgher, in return for a bond written in the knight's blood and sealed by him. This bond promises the burgher a portion of the knight's body weighing as much as the thousand guilders, if the money is not returned by an agreed deadline. The knight then seeks advice from a learned man, a natural philosopher, who tells him that the emperor's daughter has hidden a magic sleep-inducing letter between her sheets. That evening, the knight secretly removes the letter and forces the surprised maiden to have sex with him. She begins to enjoy this; and the couple spend so much time in bed together that the knight forgets his deadline. The burgher demands his payment in flesh; the knight refuses; and the case is brought before the local judge. The lady dresses up as a young lawyer and appears incognito at the court in order to defend her partner. He/she ascertains that the burgher can neither be swayed to accept double or even more of his money back, nor to be merciful and cancel the debt, and instead intends to kill the knight by taking the weight in flesh from his chest 'where the heart is'. She/he then tells the burgher that it is his right to have the lump of flesh, but that if he sheds the knight's blood, he must by law pay for this with his own blood. Since it is impossible to cut out the lump of flesh without spilling blood, the burgher declines to take his due and humbly asks for his money back. But as he had previously insisted on a payment in flesh rather than money, his demand is refused, and he is left with nothing: he is outwitted and the knight acquitted. Back home, the lady reveals to the grateful knight that it was she who saved him; the emperor marries her to the knight; and the couple later die in peace.

Despite the scholarly attention lavished on *The Merchant of Venice*, the central story about the pound of flesh still puzzles critics. Neither in the play nor in the medieval sources of this motif is the creditor's demand for a bond of flesh motivated in terms of character psychology or plot logic. What does the burgher gain from such a forfeit? He shows no interest in the flesh itself, which is probably worthless to him once it is cut out. Nor is he interested in financial gain, since he does not charge interest (which was prohibited by the Church) and does not accept the offer of more money. If he just wants to kill the knight, as he admits to the lady/lawyer, why did he not simply ask for the knight's life as a bond? This would be no more absurd than asking for the pound of flesh in medieval legal practice. According to Joseph Kohler's major study, body parts as well as the whole body, its life and labour, would have been possible forfeits in the Middle Ages and Renaissance, based on the idea that the debtor will have to pay back with his whole person.[4] Other scholars, like William Chester Jordan, believe that medieval courts would have allowed forfeits of bodies neither in parts nor whole, which would be tantamount to injury or killing.[5] In either case, a bond granting the burgher the right over the knight's body would have the same legal status as one granting the right over a part of that body, illegal or legal. Yet, no version of the 'pound of flesh' tale describes a bond simply giving the right to kill; in each case, the forfeit grants the right to cut out a certain amount of flesh. In many variants of the tale, it is not even clear that the knight would die from the amputation. Portia in *The Merchant of Venice* implies that the removal of a piece of flesh from 'near the heart' would not be fatal if a surgeon were called in to prevent lethal blood-loss. In other variations, it is a hand, nose or eye that is to be cut out, which would be a gruesome mutilation, but not necessarily life-threatening.[6] The wording of the contract in 'Kaiser Lucius' Tochter' confirms that the bond aims to give the burgher not the right to kill as such, or even the right to possess the flesh, but the power to cut apart the knight's body:

> ob du darin woltest simig sin
> und mir nit gebest das gelt min
> ganz und gor uf das zil,
> das ich dir ufsetzen wil,
> das ich dann sol gewalt hon,
> dinen lib zu grifen an
> und daruß schniden, was ich wil:
> des frischen flaisches din als vil,
> das denn als swer mig gesin,
> das ich domit das gelt min
> mig widerwegen an der wag.[7]

If you were late in this and were not to give me all my money by the deadline that I will set you, that I then have the power to seize your body and cut from it whatever I want: a portion of your live flesh so heavy that I can balance my money with it on a pair of scales.

This power to cut to pieces (*gewalt, dinen lib zu grifen and und daruß schniden*) is also the essence of the contract as the knight sees it:

so hat er vollen gewalt zwor
an minem lib ganz und gar
allenthalb, wo er wil,
das flaisch daruß schniden als vil,
das das gelt mig widerwegen.[8]

He then has complete power to cut out from any part of my whole body,
wherever he likes, as much of my flesh as balances the weight of the money.

The argument that the lady/lawyer uses to repeal the bond also aims
precisely against this intended cutting. Again, she does not simply invoke
the prohibition against injury or murder, which would have befitted a
simple bond for the life of the knight, but instead argues with a hair-
splitting technicality that exactly parallels the wording of the bond:

Sit dem nun also ist,
so beger ich zu der frist,
das ditz gesatz volbraucht werd,
des der ritter hie begert,
das vor menger wil und zit
ist gehalten ver und wit
und des gemainen lands sit:
quicumque sanguinem alicuius effuderit,
sanguis eius effundetur.
das betüt in tüscher ker:
wer vergüßt des andren plut
in zorns wis und unmut,
des glich im auch geschech,
das man sin plut fliessen sech . . .
der burger sol nun vachen an
zu schniden, wo er wil, den man.
doch sol er sich hieten eben,
das das plut nit fließ doneben . . .
wann wie das plut rint domit,
so muß nauch des lands sit
und nauch alten gesatzt und bot
der burger liden solich not,
sam der ritter liden muß.[9]

Since this is so, I demand now that the law which the knight wants to be
applied here will be applied, a law which has been upheld near and far for a
long time now and is the custom of our common land: 'whoever sheds

another's blood shall have his own blood shed'. This means in German translation: whoever sheds another's blood in anger and ill-will should suffer the same, so that one sees his blood flow . . . Let the burgher begin to cut the man where he will. But he must take care that no blood is spilled . . . For if the blood flows, according to the custom of the land and to old laws and commandments, the burgher will have to suffer the same as the knight suffers.

So the lady/lawyer interprets the law against bloodshed literally as a law not against killing or injury, but against spilling the bodily fluid. Shakespeare scholars have frequently argued that this argument, which characterizes all versions of the motif, is meant to illustrate the early modern triumph of equity over common law, and of justice over the letter of the law. But not only does this ignore the medieval roots of the tale, and the fact that such sophistry would be a hypocritical way to refute the burgher's insistence on the letter of the bond, but also that this could have been equally well demonstrated by showing that the prohibition against injury and killing overrides the contract, rather than by finding a technicality that renders the contract null and void.[10] Yet, in all adaptations of the motif, including 'Kaiser Lucius' Tochter', the bond is annulled through the prohibition not against injury or killing as such, but against spilling of someone's blood. Despite the seeming sophistry of the disguised lady's defence, there is no further discussion; it is immediately obvious to all involved and to the recipients of the tale that the dispute has been resolved, that no further proof is necessary to show that the burgher has no right to injure the knight. The burgher realizes at once that he has lost, and does not further insist on his piece of flesh. The judge can only spell out what the lady/lawyer's argument had been based on:

> es ist der ritter ganz und gar
> nun ledig von dem burger,
> als ich das offenlich bewer,
> wann das flaisch mag von der hüt
> mit nichten werden ußgerit,
> es müß das plut fliessen domit.[11]

The knight is completely freed of any obligations to the burgher, as I maintain publicly, since flesh cannot be ripped from skin without blood flowing.

To cut out a lump of flesh may theoretically be legal, but since this is practically impossible without bloodshed, and bloodshed is illegal, the cut is in practice illegal.

So while both the contract and the legal argument might seem absurd to modern and perhaps even medieval and early modern recipients, it was clearly the core of the story. This is not so much a tale about equity or murder, but about a threat of bodily mutilation, which is averted through recourse to blood. Blood guarantees the cohesion of the body here. The judge's conclusion is that if a body is cut to pieces, it bleeds – 'flesh cannot be torn from the skin without blood being shed' – and since shedding blood is not allowed, mutilation is not allowed either. What is affirmed, therefore, is the indivisibility and spatial boundedness of the embodied subject. The body is viewed as a container of blood, like a gourd, which gushes forth when pricked, and therefore must not be pricked. This role of blood – as seemingly connecting all the parts and running out if the system is violated at any point – is why bloodshed is invoked here rather than injury or killing as such. Blood is given the enormous value of confirming that the body is an inseparable whole.

The emphasis on enacting the indissolubility of the body is also evident in the additional arguments against the bond that appear in several versions. One objection is that it would not be allowed for the creditor to take out more or less than the exact amount stated in the bond, as argued, for instance, in *The Merchant of Venice*, in the *Dolopathos*, the early modern 'Ballad of Gernutus' and in Giovanni Fiorentino's novella cycle *Il Pecorone* (1378).[12] This is an argument that would have no legal credibility – a creditor is free to take less than his due any time – but again, the point seems to be the impossibility of separating one part of a coherent whole from another; of parcelling up the unified body. As the creditor in the *Dolopathos* says: 'there is no man, only God, who could control his hand so as to take neither more nor less'.[13] Only God has the ability to divide up the body, thus confirming once more its inseparability in human interaction. In the *Cursor mundi* and in *The Merchant of Venice*, it is also argued that the debtor had only sold his flesh, not his blood, again asserting that both are inseparable.

If we accept that 'Kaiser Lucius' Tochter' is centrally concerned with the threat of mutilation and its prohibition, which in the end confirms that the body is bounded, the burgher's insistence that the pact be written in blood also begins to make sense. Logically, this request is again superfluous, as the bond is already sealed with the knight's seal, and secured against his flesh. But the desire to have power to injure and make bleed offers again a possible motivation. In order to be able to use his blood as ink, the knight must wound himself or be wounded. This is thus an instance of the knight's body already having lost its self-evident status as a coherent, separate unit. In the shape of the letter, the burgher already holds something that can be considered a part of the knight's body, although it later turns out that it does not give him any power over the knight. It is also another recourse to blood as an appeal to authenticity; the vain wish that a pact written in blood may be more true, authentic, powerful than any other.

A similar pre-Faustian story about a pact written in blood appears in some versions of the popular legend of Theophilus, who in order to further his career as a bishop sells his soul to the Devil in a pact written in his blood, but regrets it in his dying days and is redeemed by Mary descending into hell to tear the contract apart.[14] This is another story of the coherence of the body being endangered and this threat then being neutralized through the interference of a lady. Here, the signing of the pact is explicitly already a transgression of the outer contours of the body, the skin, and a spiritual transgression, a sin. The version of the legend inserted into Brun von Schönebeck's extensive commentary on the Song of Songs, *Das Hohe Lied* (1276), stresses this physical and moral violence involved in writing the pact:

> der tubel twank in also harte,
> daz her gewan blut uz siner swarte
> und schreib durch der rede urhaf
> eine hantveste und gaf
> si deme leidigen tubel Sathan.[15]

The devil put him under so much pressure that he obtained blood from his skin, and he documented their contract in writing and gave this bond to the evil devil Satan.

The fact that this letter has to be brought up from hell to make the contract invalid suggests again that possession of a person's blood gives a hold over that person, like having any other part of her or his body would. But as Mary is able to retrieve the bond in the end, it turns out not to give the Devil any more power over Theophilus than the burgher's bond gave him over the knight. Interestingly, the process of restoring Theophilus' physical and moral integrity involves a revaluation of blood itself, too. The redemption begins when the remorseful Theophilus tears his hair and fingernails out and scratches his face until it bleeds, so that blood here becomes the product and visual sign of repentance rather than of sin.[16] Blood is fully turned into an agent of nourishment and support, not violence, when Mary buttresses her appeal to Christ to help Theophilus for her sake with a reference to her breast-milk (which was believed to be processed blood): 'remember, son, I am your mother, you have sucked my breast-milk'.[17] As the bloody pact is neutralized, so blood itself is revalued, and Theophilus' physical integrity restored.

Many of the stories accompanying the pound of flesh narrative in larger works show a common concern with bodily boundedness and with blood as its counterpart. In the stories collected in the *Dolopathos*, for instance, characters frequently find their physical integrity under threat unexpectedly. The frame narrative here is that of a young prince, Lucinius (of which Emperor Lucius may well be a variation), whose evil stepmother accuses him of rape, using the blood from self-inflicted wounds on her skin and clothes as (false) proof against him in another deceptive appeal to blood as automatically establishing the truth. Lucinius relies on seven wise men from Rome to each tell a story about similar situations, which finally make his father, the king, reconsider the death sentence he had rashly passed over his son. The denouement reports the reinstated Lucinius' extensive discussions with a Christian missionary about the creation of the body and Christ's redemption. When the missionary finally resurrects a dead boy through prayer, Lucinius and many others convert to Christianity, convinced apparently by the Christian guarantee of bodily integrity and continuity.

Two more of the embedded stories tell of an escape from threats of mutilation: in 'Polyphemus', a giant tears apart, cooks and eats a group of men. The last man manages to blind him, but then accepts a ring from the giant, which magically makes him call out where he is; and he can only narrowly escape the giant by tearing off his own finger with the ring still on it. In 'Striges', the same man comes across three hanged bandits, and then a mother and her son. He protects the son from being torn apart and eaten by witches by substituting the middle bandit for him. The witches suspect the sham and ask for a piece of flesh from each of the three dead bandits, which they can apparently tell apart from each other by their taste. The man cuts a piece from the remaining two bandits' buttocks and one from his own thigh, shedding much blood. The witches then demand to eat more of the tasty middle bandit, in whose place the man hangs himself from the tree. He is almost about to be eaten when the witches are suddenly scared away by an unexplained noise, and the humans all survive. By ascribing the desire to cut apart bodies to the monstrous giant and witches only, both stories enforce the idea that such wishes are monstrous in themselves, a violation of all rules of human interaction. The threat of mutilation is, however, in both cases taken further than in the pound of flesh tale, in so far as the man does lose two parts of his body – a finger and a portion of the thigh – in a successful attempt to prevent being cut up completely. The comforting message is that it is possible to survive even loss of limbs with one's identity intact.

Miracle tales also often demonstrate how bodily integrity is restored when the threat of bloodshed is averted, even if this necessitates divine intervention. As harm done to the victim's body is implicitly harm done to the conceptions of an integral, unbroken body, any perpetrator shoots himself or herself in the foot, as it were. Those who refrain from shedding blood in miracles therefore often have their own bodies restored as well as leaving those of their victims intact. This is apparent, for example, in the miracle tales in which a bath in blood to cure leprosy is prevented, as in many versions of the legend of St Sylvester. In the extensive German verse variant (c.1260–75) by Konrad von Würzburg, for instance, Constantine's doctors advise him to bathe in children's blood in order to be healed. But on seeing the grieving mothers, he renounces the slaughter, converts to Christianity and, as God's reward, gains a beautiful new body in the bath of baptism, 'cleansed and released from sin and disease'.[18] Constantine's body and soul are renewed and healed because he respects the prohibition against shedding the blood of others. Like the *Dolopathos*, the legend of Sylvester ends with a long disputation primarily about issues relating to Christ's body and its spatial and temporal boundedness, like his virgin birth and resurrection, followed by a miraculous resurrection.[19] Again impressed by these verbal and visual demonstrations of the Christian guarantee of bodily integrity, many Jews convert. In Hartmann von Aue's *Der arme Heinrich* (c.1190–1200), a virgin is similarly about to be killed to provide blood for a bath curing Heinrich's leprosy, but at the last minute, Heinrich puts a stop to the execution; his recognition of the taboo against bloodshed again miraculously restores his bodily health and integrity.[20] A satire on such tales of wonderfully regained bodies is Der Stricker's *Pfaffe Amis* (c.1200–50), whose eponymous hero tells a group of diseased people that bathing in the blood of the worst afflicted will heal them all.[21] Of course, for fear of being sacrificed, nobody admits to being sick anymore, and all declare themselves cured. This is another truth game played with blood: the 'truth' of health here is produced not through a show of blood, but through the overriding wish to avoid bleeding, a threat so menacing that it blinds the sick people to the fact that they could easily have exposed Amis's sham. The sick bodies are here only seemingly cured through an avoidance of a bloodbath.

Stories such as 'Kaiser Lucius' Tochter' or the legends of Theophilus and Sylvester thus aim at giving reassuring examples of how the body is protected through prohibitions against bloodshed. They thereby also safeguard this *concept* of the body: by staging a drama in which what normally counts as the body is threatened, they affirm that bleeding would be a danger to such an integral body, because it would traverse the skin. The body is affirmed in a double sense – defended against an attack on the level of the plot, and confirmed as ending at the skin on an implicit level.

In the disputation with the Jews, Konrad's Sylvester uses a striking image in which blood affirms the inviolability of the body even when the prohibition against bloodshed is violated. He compares the fact that Christ's divinity remains intact even as he hangs wounded on the cross to the way that blood acting as dye on wool cannot be affected, even if the wool is spun:

> nû man von erst die wolle span,
> dâ bi was diu varwe rôt,
> dô leit diu wolle dâ die nôt
> und was diu varwe ân allen pîn.[22]

When the wool was now spun, together with the red dye, then the wool suffered the pull, but the colour did not suffer anything.

The wool is compared to Christ's humanity, and the blood to his divinity, which is not violated even as he suffers on the cross. In this daring image, blood appears as an unenterable totality again, a guarantor of invulnerability, as in the pound of flesh tale.

A similar representation of Christ's body remaining miraculously intact even though submerged in blood is a crucifixion scene found on a striking devotional ink drawing usually ascribed to an anonymous fourteenth-century Rhenish woman (Fig. 4).[23] This shocking image presents the viewer with Christ's body on the cross completely covered in blood – seemingly an extreme example of a body utterly dissolving into blood. And yet, Christ's body actually stays fully bounded in this

4 Crucifixion (fourteenth century, Rhineland). Cologne, Schnütgen Museum, Inv. Nr. M340. By permission.

image: the continuous black contour of Christ's body is clearly visible around the red ink, which fills the space encircled by this contour and only crosses the line in clearly defined individual brushstrokes. There thus appears to be a coherently enclosed body underneath the streams of blood, despite the prohibition against bloodshed having been violated. The two spectators under the cross, an unknown nun and St Bernard, founding father of the medieval devotion to Christ's passion, are likewise untouched by the blood flowing around them; their hands remain clear of it even as they touch the cross, their bodies are encircled by an unbroken black outline. Although imitation of the passion, compassion and mystical identification with Christ are encouraged in this devotional image, the bodies here remain firmly separated and bounded in space and time. Christ's indivisible blood reaffirms the body rather than dissolving it.

Prohibitions against bloodshed and the integral body

Outside fiction and devotion, medieval laws against bloodshed not only aimed at avoiding violence, but surprisingly were also concerned with stopping blood-flow through the outer bodily boundaries for its own sake. To a contemporary reader without specialist knowledge in legal history, this would seem counterintuitive: laws against bloodshed surely serve primarily to keep human beings alive and uninjured and thereby form a fundamental tenet of social order. But as in 'Kaiser Lucius' Tochter', spilling of blood was often defined as an offence not because it would involve injuring or killing somebody, but because it made blood flow. Murder and bodily harm were of course prohibited, but making someone bleed was singled out as a severe transgression independent of any actual damage caused. As Ekkehard Kaufmann points out, many German law codes prescribe that injuries which cause blood-flow must be more harshly punished than any others, irrespective of the fact that internal injuries without visible bleedings may be a lot more harmful and painful than, say, a bloody scratch on the arm, and that in some circumstances, blood-flow was considered not only harmless, but even medically beneficial to regulate the balance of the humours.[24] The influential early medieval law of the Salic Franks, the *Lex Salica*, for instance, distinguishes between 'bleeding wounds' (*cusfredum*) and 'bruises' (*widifalt*), and declares that a beating with a stick 'so that blood does not flow' (*sanguis non exierit*) is to be punished with a fine of a mere six shillings, whereas a beating where 'blood flows' (*sanguis exierit*) is punished like a blow with an iron weapon.[25] According to the vernacular Swabian law code *Schwabenspiegel* (*c.* 1275), if a beating remains 'without bloody wounds', it should receive no more punishment than an insult.[26] The sentences based on such distinctions between bloody and non-bloody offences would thus by modern Western standards seem unfair.

Similarly, there is a distinction between punishments necessitating further bloodshed and all others. The *Schwabenspiegel* decrees that only those crimes whose punishment will make the offender bleed require that the king or ruler himself be consulted, whereas in all other cases, the judge can be a deputy.[27] The mention of bleeding is again not a metaphor for any physical punishment, since those marginal penalties which could be carried out under the authority of a deputy were also administered physically, 'on hide and hair' (*ze haut und ze hare*), which would include not just shameful haircutting, but also beatings. The only clear difference between a severe punishment and a marginal one, then, was the presence or absence of bloodshed. The fact that the non-bloody chastisements are referred to as only superficial, affecting the outer contour of skin and hair, suggests that again the integrity of the body was at stake: once an offender had pierced the body and thereby called into question its inviolability, his or hers had to be pierced in return. The same distinction between bloody and non-bloody punishments betraying a concern with blood and the coherence of the bodily contours underlies the Fourth Lateran Council's ruling on the activities of clerics. Only those castigations which make an offender bleed are declared taboo for them:

> Sententiam sanguinis nullus clericus dictet aut proferat, sed nec sanguinis vindictam exerceat aut ibi exercetur intersit . . . Nullus quoque clericus rottariis aut balistariis aut huiusmodi viris sanguinum praeponatur, nec illam chirurgiae artem subdiaconus, diaconus vel sacerdos exerceant, quae ad ustionem vel incisionem inducit.[28]

> No cleric may decree or pronounce a sentence involving the shedding of blood, or carry out a punishment involving the same, or be present when such punishment is carried out . . . Moreover no cleric may be put in command of mercenaries or crossbowmen or suchlike men of blood; nor may a subdeacon, deacon or priest practise the art of surgery, which involves cauterizing and making incisions.

As the context of the second prohibition against contact with 'men of blood' makes clear, this is again not a taboo against partaking in any severe or physical violence that may only be metaphorically bloody, but rather aims at avoiding an involvement in the shedding of blood. As the prohibition against surgery shows, this is not because of any harm that may be done to the bleeding person, but because this would mean 'making incisions', thus disturbing the coherence of the integral body.

Even the fifth commandment was often interpreted in medieval texts not as an interdiction against killing as such, but against shedding blood and thereby endangering human physical integrity. A brief fifteenth-century explanation of the Ten Commandments, for example, summarizes:

> Das fünft gebot ist: Dw solt nicht tötten. Da wirt verpoten, unschuldigs pluct zu vergiessen und auch pose ewenpild, wart und werich, da durich der mensch seinen nachsten tötten möchte an leib oder an der seel.[29]

> The fifth commandment is: Thou shalt not kill. This forbids shedding innocent blood and also its evil equivalents in words and deeds, by which the human might kill his neighbour in body or soul.

Rather than against killing as such, the catechist warns not only against evil intentions towards one's neighbour in general – which would have had the greatest practical pastoral relevance – but also against spilling blood. Actions that threaten moral and physical integrity are here seen as analogous. Berthold von Regensburg similarly interprets the fifth commandment primarily as an interdiction against 'drinking blood' rather than directly against killing.[30] Even the original murder, that of Abel by Cain, was frequently reinterpreted as being a transgression not so much because it was a killing, but because it involved bloodshed. This is the case, for example, in the hermit Trevrizent's account of original sin in Wolfram's *Parzival*:

> Kâins vater was Adâm:
> der sluoc Abeln umb krankez guot.
> dô ûf die reinen erdenz bluot
> viel ir magetuom was vervarn:
> den nam ir Adâmes barn.
> dô huop sich êrst der menschen nît:
> alsô wert er immer sît.[31]

Cain's father was Adam. He killed Abel for worthless gains. When blood
fell on the pure earth, her virginity was lost: Adam's offspring took it from
her. This was when the hatred amongst human beings started. It has lasted
ever since.

In contrast to the Bible, Trevrizent here presents not the eating of the
apple, and not even the murder as such as the original sin from which
all evil started, but the fact that blood flowed to the ground, and thereby 'deflowered' the virgin mother earth. This understanding of Cain's
murder was widespread in medieval religious and secular writing.[32] In
his explanation of the events Parzival witnessed at the grail castle
Munsalvaesche, Trevrizent subsequently links blood and sin again,
when describing the blood on the lance as a sign of Anfortas's transgression of divine laws when he fought for Orgeluse, rather than
waiting for the grail's allocation of a wife.[33] The information about the
illegitimacy of Anfortas's fighting precedes the mentioning of blood, so
that blood only occurs in the context of sin here. This is repeated in a
very similar second explanation of the bloody lance as indicating
Anfortas's sin.[34] Blood thus in every case appears as the result of the
violation of a prohibition.

Touching blood

That any practical advantages of taboos surrounding blood are of
secondary concern is even more obvious when it comes to prohibitions
not of shedding, but of touching, consuming or in other ways coming
into contact with blood. In *Purity and Danger*, Mary Douglas argues
against what she calls medical materialism, which explains religious
taboos like those against eating pork or heterosexual intercourse with
menstruating women by a practical desire to maintain hygiene. Instead,
as I discussed in the introduction, she details how such interdictions
subtly serve to protect socially constructed categories and behaviours,
like the distinctions between men and women, one people and another,
human and animals. Taboos are applied to whatever violates the
categories, for example, sexual relations between different ethnic or social
groups, and their transgressions can be defined not only religiously and
legally as sin or crime, but also 'hygienically' as pollution. I suggest that
the same applies to taboos against bloodshed, touching blood and
drinking blood. They do not only serve an immediately transparent

function, that of protecting against injury and killing, but also help to uphold the conception of the body as a bounded entity. Touching blood in particular is not so much defined as a sin or a crime but as polluting, thereby conceptualizing the bounded body not only as a legal or religious category, but also as a pure entity.

For instance, the common practice of bloodletting was regulated through numerous prohibitions, detailed at great length by medical manuals, regarding the time of the day and month, planet constellation, age and constitution of the patient, the veins to use, the quantity of blood and duration of the letting.[35] These proscriptions were believed to serve the medical function of making phlebotomy efficacious against specific illnesses, but in fact, they also buttressed the view of the body as a delicate container of blood, whose piercing should only be carried out with the utmost care. The blood itself that resulted from the letting was seen as impure, presumably because it had violated the boundary between the inside and outside of the body. Touching this substance was believed to make the person touching it impure, too, and was therefore beset with taboos like the Fourth Lateran Council's interdiction of clerics coming into any contact with blood. As Marie-Christine Pouchelle has shown, those people who had to touch blood as part of their profession, surgeons as well as butchers and executioners, themselves became suspect and were avoided.[36]

A text strongly focused on pollution, in particular through contact with blood, is Wirnt von Grafenberg's popular Arthurian romance *Wigalois* (c.1210). The narrator aims to keep the work 'unsoiled' by dirty-minded readers.[37] For the romance's protagonist, Wigalois, to be pure and stay pure under the constant threat of contamination is also established as a key issue right from the beginning of his story. Blood is one of the main antitheses to purity when it comes into contact with other substances. It is presented as soiling and discolouring pure bodies and other objects throughout the text, in expressions like 'the flowers here are becoming red and discoloured from your blood', 'that my blood may not make the bright red flowers even redder', 'one saw many a helmet redden from blood, which had previously been clear', 'then the helmets were discoloured; the swords dulled through blood' or 'her breast was black as coal with the blood having fallen onto it'.[38] Physical cleanliness, partly from blood, is also highly valued when Wigalois has 'a clean bath' before he goes to see his opponent Hojir and after his fights with the dragon Pfetan and with Roaz, when he had bled copiously.[39] Bathing is even described as 'knightly' when Gawain is bathed at the request of Joram before his introduction to Florie.[40] This representation of blood as a staining substance is complemented by its frequent description in the transitory moment of being neither inside nor outside the body, in the process of 'rushing', 'spurting', 'flowing' or 'surging' out of the body and through the armour.[41] Blood is also often depicted as clinging to bodies and other objects, as something that one can neither incorporate nor get rid of. Dried blood sticks to the hero and his opponent Roaz and stiffens the ties of Wigalois's armour.[42]

'Bleeding' always means 'dying' in this romance. In each of the thirty-one instances when blood is mentioned, death is at hand. The image of blood reddening the flowers is used as a metaphor for death by a mysterious voice and by Wigalois.[43] His blood-loss after the fight with Roaz is also described as apparent death:

> her Gwîgâlois gestriten hêt
> daz er des bluotes was ersigen;
> er hêt sich alsô gar erwigen
> daz er vür tôt ouch lac âldâ.[44]

Sir Wigalois fought until he had lost his blood; he had exhausted himself to the extent that he lay there as if dead.

That Wigalois's cheeks and hair are thus covered in blood is what makes Count Adan think that he is dead.[45] As is common in medieval fiction, the expression *des bluotes ersigen*, be drained of blood, is used as a circumlocution of 'to die'.[46] Even the colour of blood seems to signal mortal danger: Wigalois's lance is ornamented with red samite to show that he is riding into death.[47] That he is given a 'blood-red' horse for his final ride to Glois (which, after the completion of his task, to the confusion of Moral and his people, is replaced by a white one) creates another link between blood-red and death.[48] The same might be true for the blood-red ear of the stolen dog that provokes a fight, the blood-red horse of Elamie on which she leads Wigalois into another fight, and the blood-red samite cover of Karrioz's horse that rides against Wigalois.[49] Such a conceptualization of death as blood-loss meant that the body not only spatially ended where blood flowed in the sense that shed blood was defined as blood outside the body, but also that the body was understood to cease to exist when it was 'drained of blood'. Death is in this way no more than a special case of blood-loss.

Like touching blood, touching corpses is thus circumscribed by taboos. The narrator mentions four Arthurian customs to have sadly fallen into disuse since the time in which the romance is set: not to rob corpses, not to molest single female travellers, not to feign love and not to break one's oath. Their presentation as hard and fast rules to which all Arthurian knights adhered makes these four modes of behaviour central characteristics of knighthood as defined in the text.[50] As regards the custom of respecting corpses, which concerns us here, Wigalois is compared favourably to knights of the narrator's time, simply because he leaves the corpse of the knight whom he has just killed lying by his horse instead of robbing and stripping him.[51] This behaviour towards corpses is what makes an honourable knight, or rather, as the text puts it, not leaving them alone makes a man lose his status as a knight.[52] The treatment of corpses that characterizes a knight worthy of the name here not only includes a respectful distance, but usually also burial. Burial rites are important in *Wigalois* and mentioned even in very brief death descriptions: the three knights killed by Pfetan are taken to a wake; the dead from the war are duly buried; the messenger reporting Florie's death also relates that he witnessed her burial under a precious stone; the only reference to a historical event in *Wigalois* is to the funeral of the Duke of Meran.[53] Corpses that are appropriately buried are described as pure themselves. Japhite's body, which is buried in a mausoleum with two glasses containing purifying balm and a stone filled with 'pure', sweet-smelling herbs, a 'clear' glass floor and an epitaph pronouncing her 'pure', is described as a 'pure body'.[54] Liamere, who is also buried in a coffin light as the day with a 'clear glass' filled with balm, also gains the attribute 'pure'.[55] The consequences of transgressions of this rule are couched again in terms of pollution and blood. Both bodies that are touched by the living are described as bloody, not pure: that of the seemingly dead Wigalois being robbed by the evil female fisher; and that of Roaz being kissed by Japhite.[56] Not touching corpses or blood thus ensures the purity of both subjects and objects of these pollution rules.

The prohibition against bloodshed and touching blood, then, involved more than a practical prevention of bodily harm, murder or uncleanliness. As in 'Kaiser Lucius' Tochter', blood concerned people more in terms of the integrity of the body than in terms of any actual threat to life and health, to the extent that a bleeding scratch was deemed more severe than a concussion. This, I suggest, was due to the fact that bleeding meant a danger to the conception of the body as always enclosed. It had to be made clear that any bleeding was a terrible threat, that any transgression of the rigid boundaries was just that – a transgression.

The fantasy shattered

Through their fantasized happy endings, stories like 'Kaiser Lucius' Tochter' and the legends of Sylvester and Theophilus send out the comforting message that the coherent body can be maintained. But the fact that such a confirmation is necessary, and impossible to achieve without interventions by God or other characters, also implies the more unsettling conclusion that the body is not always already safely enclosed. A much more pessimistic, dystopian narrative, however, is that of the *Nibelungenlied*, where the spatially bounded body is never fully achievable, and in fact, the harder the characters try, the more at risk they are. The taboo against blood-flow is here violated, again not for any psychological reason, but as a matter of course. Even Siegfried, a man who had seemingly achieved the ideal impermeable body, turns out to be vulnerable. In other words, unlike the stories discussed so far, this epic is not about the securing of a spatially bounded body, but about its ensuing disintegration. It thus pessimistically denies the possibility of ever achieving long-term integrity.

The plot begins with Siegfried and his knights travelling from Xanten to the Burgundian court in Worms to woo King Gunther's sister Kriemhild. Gunther and his courtiers watch the arrival from the palace windows. Gunther inquires who the strangers might be, and his trusty vassal Hagen guesses that one of them must be the famous Siegfried, dragon-slayer and owner of the Nibelung treasure:[57]

> Noch weiz ich an im mêre   daz ist mir bekant:
> einen lintrachen   den sluoc des heldes hant.
> er badete sich in dem bluote;   sîn hût wart hurnîn.
> des snîdet in kein wâfen.   daz ist dicke worden schîn.[58]

I know something else about him, I know this: the hero slew a dragon with his own hand. He bathed in the blood; his skin became callous. Therefore, no weapon can injure him. This has been amply demonstrated.

So Siegfried has reached the epitome of spatial enclosure before the onset of the story; he arrives as an already bounded man with invulnerable skin.

This bounded body is again guaranteed through blood, but here, through a dragon's rather than Siegfried's own blood. Usually in medieval fictional and non-fictional writings, it is armour that can be hardened to the highest degree by immersion in blood, and especially dragon's blood. The dead King Ortnit's armour, for instance, is fortified in the blood of the dragons that had killed him, and Wolfdietrich takes on this special equipment when he slays these dragons. This armour is referred to in many versions of the Dietrich legends, for example, in the *Eckenlied* (c. 1200–50), when Seburk describes it to Ecke:

> Diu brünne ist gar stahels blos:
> die ringe guldin fingers gros
> gehert in traken bluote.
> das ich dir sage, das ist war:
> kains swertes snid ir als ain har
> gewan nie diu vil guote.[59]

The chainmail has no steel in it, but golden rings, as thick as a finger, hardened in dragon's blood. What I am telling you is true: no sword has ever cut the strong armour, not even slightly.

Alexander the Great in the medieval retellings of his adventures also often has a 'callous' hauberk, 'pickled in dragon's blood', as mentioned, for example, in Pfaffe Lamprecht's *Alexander* (c. 1150).[60] The cross-dressing wife in Dietrich von der Glezze's *Märe* 'Der Borte' (before 1296) likewise wears armour hardened in dragon's blood; and in Der Stricker's Arthurian romance *Daniel von dem Blühenden Tal* (c. 1230), a mermaid's skin has been made impenetrable by being steeped in dragon's blood.[61] Dragons were imagined both as almost impenetrable themselves, protected by their callous or scaly skin, and as a great threat to human physical integrity, since they could suck out and pierce the flesh of humans, as I shall discuss in more detail in chapter 3. If a knight who can make another bleed will seem less vulnerable than his victim by virtue of this feat and by comparison, one who can make a dragon bleed will thus appear even more unassailable. This train of thought is literalized and condensed in the motif of the dragon's blood itself providing this added protection. Siegfried, by having not just his armour, but his very skin hardened, takes this fantasy of impenetrability to its ultimate conclusion.

Nevertheless, the possibility of being penetrated and of bleeding is always already present in Siegfried's exemplary enclosed body. In the same breath as mentioning the callous skin, Hagen links it with potential aggression and with attempts to penetrate it – even if embedded in the negative form of denying their efficacy: 'his skin became callous. Therefore, no weapon can injure him.' Moreover, Hagen immediately adds that Siegfried himself could become a danger to the Burgundians:

> des snîdet in kein wâfen.   daz ist dicke worden schîn.
> Wir suln den herren   empfâhen deste baz,
> daz wir iht verdienen   des jungen recken haz.[62]

Therefore, no weapon can injure him. This has been amply demonstrated. We thus must receive the lord particularly courteously, lest we make an enemy of the young hero.

A conflict between Siegfried and the Burgundians is thus discussed as a possibility before they have even so much as exchanged greetings, and from then on a tension underlies their relationship that culminates in Siegfried's murder and Kriemhild's revenge. This clash seems to arise by itself, with the characters' intentions playing little or no part in it. As stressed by the depersonalized formulations, with weapon, skin and hands as grammatical subjects, Siegfried's fortified skin itself seems to provoke its own injury. The fantasy of being physically impenetrable shatters itself.

After Hagen's initial comment, Siegfried's invulnerable skin is not mentioned again until the murder plot begins. There is, however, another seemingly defensive layer that Siegfried puts on twice and that fore-shadows the dangers of such added protection: his magic invisibility cloak. Siegfried wears it to substitute for Gunther in the courtship of Brünhild in order to overcome her, both during the suitor's contest and during the 'wedding night'. Paradoxically, these times of presumably highest protection are the only occasions when Siegfried bleeds (even though he is not penetrated): during the suitors' test, Brünhild throws the javelin at him so that blood gushes out of his mouth; and when fighting him in Gunther's bedchamber, she squeezes Siegfried's hand so hard that the blood springs forth from underneath his fingernails.[63]

It is again paradoxically the attempt to protect Siegfried's physical borders with another covering that leads to their final disruption.

Kriemhild raises the topic of Siegfried's reinforced skin in an attempt to protect him in an allegedly imminent war. She reveals to Hagen that her husband has one vulnerable spot, a place between his shoulder blades, which had not been rendered impenetrable during his bath in the dragon's blood because it had been covered by a leaf fallen from a lime tree.[64] She marks Siegfried's cloak with a cross indicating the exact place that Hagen is meant to shield. This is another action that is not logically necessary, but makes sense within the mechanism of border enforcement causing an increased threat of penetration and bleeding. It means that Siegfried's boundaries are now doubly protected, by his skin and the cloak. Like the callous skin and the invisibility coat, however, the cloak carries within it the potential for aggression: the mark of the vulnerable place can be used not only for protection, but also for taking aim, which is precisely what Hagen does. He calls off the war, arranges a hunt instead, waits until Siegfried is isolated at a spring in the forest, and then kills him, as is described in strong terms emphasizing the penetration: 'He shot through the cross, so that blood from his heart spurted from the wound right onto Hagen's clothes'.[65] It is again not plausible within conventional plot logic that Siegfried still wears the cloak with the cross when he is murdered: he would have changed his war outfit for a hunting one; moreover, the narrator explicitly says that Siegfried wears his hunting gear when running to the spring.[66] But this is plausible within the logic of enforced physical borders automatically causing their own destruction. The double physical cover, cloak and skin, turns out to be double danger. Human intention, as so often, is thwarted: Kriemhild means to protect Siegfried, but achieves the opposite.

Such a lack of human agency, combined with a breakdown of physical coherence, is characteristic of the *Nibelungenlied* in general. The action is propelled forward not by integral, autonomous subjects, but by bodies acting largely outside conscious control, and often fragmented into parts. This impression is enhanced through a stylistic technique which often makes body parts, especially blood, the grammatical or logical subject of an action: rather than of 'Siegfried bleeding', for example, the text speaks of 'blood springing' from the wounds; that 'one saw' blood flow; or that 'flowers' are stained by the blood.[67] In the de-personalized accounts of fights, blood again seems to be brought forth by armour, weapons and body parts themselves, without human agency: the sword draws blood from wounds; there emerge bloody hands; all helmets and shields are blood-coloured from the Burgundians' hands.[68] In the murder scene, Siegfried's body and its parts, such as wounds, heart, shoulder blades and hands, are also frequently mentioned.[69] The imaginary dispassionate observer implied in the 'one saw' formula only adds to the recipient's impression of helplessly witnessing a bloodbath: 'one saw the blood flow over saddles'; 'one could see the bloody stream flow through the light helmet from Siegfried's hand'; 'one saw many brilliant shields blood-coloured'.[70] The personified hands of Siegfried especially commit many of his heroic deeds.[71] In the *Nibelungenlied*, as is common in medieval thought, hands represent agency, but there this is no longer a metaphor for the whole person, as the owner of the hands has little influence over what they do.[72] There is no such thing as a whole, active subject in the *Nibelungenlied*, and the plot is moved on anyway without human intention. Moreover, the disruption of the acting subject is paralleled by a similar broken structure of the text. The description of Siegfried looking as lovely 'as if he had been composed like a parchment' can be read as making an explicit comparison between text and Siegfried's body.[73] In any case, like its characters, the *Nibelungenlied* is not a coherent entity, but a conglomeration of various parts. It does not adhere to the same rules of narrative continuity, of logical plot development and of consistency of names, characters and objects as medieval romances and most modern narratives do, but is full of gaps and breaks.

It is in particular the attempt to buttress the contours of the body that paradoxically makes them the most vulnerable. This is suggested not just by Siegfried's fate, but also already by the frequent presentation of blood as gushing forth, seemingly of its own accord, from hard and strong armour rather than soft flesh or tender skin: 'I saw blood spurt through the helmets from the swords' blows', 'Gernot then hit the hero Rüdiger through the rock-hard helmet, so that blood flowed down', 'the brave Sigestap struck a bloody stream from hard armour', 'from three deep wounds which he inflicted upon the king through fine white armour, the sword at its edges brought forth blood from the wounds'.[74] The reinforcement of physical borders by putting on armour is also explicitly identified as dangerous rather than protective. During the famous scene when Volker and Hagen sit defiantly on the bench in Etzel's court, Volker takes the armour of the approaching Hunnish knights as a sign of intended aggression:

> Und sint ouch sümelîche   zen brusten alsô wît:
> swer sîn selbes hüete,   der tuo daz enzît!
> Ich waen si under sîden   die liehten brünne tragen.[75]

And some of them are so broad-chested: whoever wants to protect himself,
should do so in good time. I presume that they wear bright hauberks underneath the silk.

So Volker sees or suspects the armour and recommends counter-
armouring, because he feels that an attack is in the air – and he is right.
In a similar scene, the wise old knight Hildebrand who tries to mediate
between the Huns and the Burgundians initially plans to go on this
mission 'unarmed' and by himself, but eventually puts on his armour
and takes warriors with him at young Wolfhart's suggestion, an act
explicitly condemned by the narrator: 'The wise man then armed
himself at the advice of the stupid youngster'.[76] And indeed, Volker
interprets Hildebrand and Dietrich's people's armouring as a hostile
gesture:

> ich sihe dort her gân
> sô rehte vîentlîche die Dietrîches man
> gewâfent under helme: si wellent uns bestân.
> ich waene ez an daz übele uns ellenden welle gân.[77]

I can see Dietrich's men walking along there in a right hostile way, armed
and under helmets: they want to fight us. I suppose we strangers shall fare
badly now.

This sparks off a new round of fights, in which young Wolfhart's own
armour is cut through, and he dies in a pool of blood.[78]
    With the subject so powerless and borders leading to their own
destruction, blood engenders blood all by itself. The idea of blood feud
is an example of how this works – humans should avenge other humans,
but really, blood itself just 'cries out' for vengeance.[79] Kriemhild's excessive
revenge in particular can be seen as beyond her own conscious control.
After Siegfried's death, Kriemhild finds herself in one of the conflicts
of loyalties and obligations so characteristic of the *Nibelungenlied*. She
is torn between her ties to her blood relations, and blood revenge for
her husband. While neither term (blood revenge or blood relations) is
mentioned explicitly, the connection between Siegfried and Kriemhild
is depicted partly in terms of blood. Throughout the text, the physical
union between Siegfried and Kriemhild is stressed; she is described as
his body during their first 'private' meeting before the war against the
Saxons ('he carried her in his heart, she was thus his own body to him')

and as a result of their intercourse on their wedding night ('she thus became his body').[80] After he is shot through the heart and the bloody corpse is laid down at her doorstep, blood seems to create a connection between Kriemhild and Siegfried – she herself begins to bleed (the only time a woman does so), the blood gushes out of her mouth when she hears of Siegfried's death and from her eyes as she sees his dead face one last time in the coffin.[81] So his blood provokes hers. Moreover, Siegfried's wounds begin to bleed again when Hagen as the murderer approaches his body in the *Bahrprobe*, and confirm the need to make Hagen pay with his own blood. The chain of blood revenge is now irrevocably set into motion.[82]

So the body in the *Nibelungenlied* is again conceived as a bounded entity threatened by blood-flow. But the epic does not promise us that this body can be safeguarded; instead, taboos against bloodshed are broken repeatedly, and in fact, the more characters try to protect their bodies, the more easily they will be destroyed. The text thus presents not so much an alternative view to the body as a bounded entity, but shows that this conception is fundamentally unstable, that seemingly integral bodies are always already doomed to be penetrated, opened up and cut apart. That medieval recipients found such a radical criticism of the dominant understanding of the body unbearable is suggested by the addition in most manuscripts of an elegiac continuation called *Diu klage* (c.1200–50), which not only attempts to add a psychological causality and a wider Christian perspective to the bleak plot, as research has stressed, but also tries to bring the mutilated bodies back into shape and uphold the idea of a coherent individual body.[83] The *Klage* mostly consists of a report of how the survivors lift each protagonist's corpse out of the blood, identify and mourn him, cut the body out of the armour, and wash and bury it. While this cannot undo the mutilation and bloodbath, it does attempt to reinstate personal and bodily integrity.

The *Nibelungenlied* is often described as a uniquely pessimistic text in the landscape of medieval German literature, but in fact the possibility of achieving an impermeable, non-bleeding body is questioned and denied in the seemingly more optimistic romances, too. *Wigalois*, for example, makes quite clear that the constant potential for bloody destruction of the body is a constituent part of Arthurian knighthood. Like most romances, *Wigalois* gives its definition of Arthurian knighthood at the outset of the story: the requirement for becoming a member of the Round Table is here precisely risking one's life:

die muosen dicke wâgen
durch lop den lîp: daz was ir sit.
dâ muosen si verdienen mit
die stat zer tavelrunde.[84]

They often have to risk their body for fame. This was their custom. In this way, they have to earn the seat at the Round Table.

That risking one's life is the essence of knighthood is confirmed by Wigalois's exemplary experiences. He sets off to 'gain the praise of the best people, or die in a manly way'.[85] As both the plot and the comments of narrator and characters emphasize, all of Wigalois's fights are matters of life and death, for example, those with his rival Schaffilun, with the dragon Pfetan, with the wild woman Ruel, in Korntin, and particularly the encounter with Hojir, presented as Death himself.[86] Uncharacteristically for a romance hero, Wigalois even kills most of his opponents, rather than just accepting their submission and sending them back to Arthur's court.[87] The threat of a loss of the body, which, as we have seen, is strongly associated with bleeding in *Wigalois*, is thus an integral part of a knight's life even in this idealized fictional world; a fully enclosed body is never achieved once and for all.

The attempt and ultimate failure to achieve an integral body is explored even more extensively in Der Stricker's Arthurian romance *Daniel von dem Blühenden Tal* (c.1230). Physical penetration is the key threat faced by the knight Daniel and his associates. In his adventures as an individual character, rushing ahead of Arthur's court, Daniel encounters three main opponents, all of whom challenge him primarily with bodily, bloody intrusion. Daniel's first antagonist, the dwarf Juran, possesses a sword with amazing penetrative powers, which he uses to terrorize the whole Country of the Dark Mountain in pursuit of the love of the duke's daughter. Juran's blade can cut through twelve layers of armour, through otherwise impenetrable skin and through stone as if it were wood.[88] Juran has also threatened to destroy the duke's daughter's physical integrity by flaying her skin until it bleeds, and even by skinning her alive, as she tells Daniel in no uncertain terms:

so welle ez mich ane gân
mit birkînen ruoten
unz ich beginne bluoten;

swaz ich iendert hûte habe,
die slahe ez mir gar abe
über allen mînen lîp.[89]

So he was going attack me with birch rods until I bled; he was going to flay whatever skin I have, all over my body.

The following adventure presents the challenge of 'belly-less' monsters who possess a kind of Medusa-head that kills the courtly inhabitants of the Country of the Bright Fountain by violating their physical integrity through the eyes: whoever looks at the head dies.[90] These creatures also commit another bloody intrusion: after their leader has killed someone with the magic head, they suck out their victims' blood to sustain themselves like vampires, as the Lady of the Bright Fountain describes:

swem er den tôt getuot,
dem sûgent sie ûz daz bluot.
daz habent sie in ir munde
eine kurzen stunde
und lânt ez wider ûz vallen.
alsô lebent sie mit in allen,
anders pflegent sie keiner spîse.[91]

Whoever he has killed has his blood sucked out by them. They keep it in their mouths for a short while and let it flow back out again. So they all live. They are not accustomed to any other food.

Finally, Daniel confronts a bald 'red' man, who has put the Country of the Green Meadow under his spell.[92] He slaughters more than one hundred hypnotized men every week and bathes in their blood, as he has been told that doing so for a year at the most is the only way in which his unspecified disease can be healed. Torsten Haferland notes that baldness and redness could be symptoms of leprosy, and the bloodbath thus might be one of the literary cures for leprosy that we encountered in *Silvester, Der Pfaffe Amis* and *Der arme Heinrich*.[93] But whereas in those stories, the slaughter is avoided by virtue, divine intervention or cunning, *Daniel* presents a negative outcome: the cure does not seem to have worked even after a year of treatment; the blood-bather shows no intention of giving up; and Daniel has to kill the sick man to put an end to the bloodbath.

This mass killing is again described in terms of a physical stripping of protective boundaries and intrusion; the daughter of this country's duke, Sandinose, speaks of the men being 'cut to pieces', and the narrator reports in graphic detail how the sick man strips the victims naked and then 'digs' into them:[94]

> nu ergreif der sieche zwâre
> den naechsten bî dem hâre
> und zôch im abe sîn gewant
> unz er wart blôz als ein hant:
> der muose der êrste sîn.
> den begunde er stechen als ein swîn.
> über die bütenen er in huop,
> gegen dem herzen er im gruop
> mit einem mezzer unsuoze.[95]

Now the sick man regrettably picked up the nearest person by his hair and stripped him of his clothing, until he was as naked as a hand. He was to be the first. He slaughtered him like a pig. He lifted him above the tub and plunged a bitter knife into his heart.

In this episode, blood-thirst becomes a defining characteristic of the usurper, whose name is not given, but who is instead referred to simply as 'the one bathing in blood'.[96] His hypnotic glance and voice physically intrude into the subject as well, through the eyes and ears. The extraordinary golden statue of an animal also has a deafening mechanical voice, which functions as an alarm signal in Cluse; Daniel uses it again to incapacitate the victims until they are killed.[97] So, as in the other texts discussed in this chapter, the emphasis in all three descriptions of Daniel's opponents is on the danger less of death than of penetration and bleeding.

But as Peggy McCracken has pointed out, bleeding is not just something against which an Arthurian knight has to protect himself and his associates; it is also something he has to face in order to gain fame.[98] The danger of bleeding has to be clear and present to allow protection as well as brave and praiseworthy behaviour in the first place. Daniel, for instance, gains fame and praise by risking the blood-bather, the bloodsuckers and Juran spilling his blood.[99] In the battle scenes, not giving up while others are drowning in blood is explicitly described as a sign of praiseworthy prowess.[100] What is more, an

Arthurian knight not only has to endure the threat of bleeding; he also has to bring about others' blood to prove his skill. In *Daniel*, Arthur's sword thrusts through the helmets so that blood spurts out; Parzival causes everyone to lose their blood; and the Duke of the Bright Fountain makes the 'red juice' flow from the helmets until his sword is bloody down to his hands.[101] As this bloodshed is necessary to gain fame, 'the noble King Arthur' is highly praised for his valour and fighting skills, while he causes blood to gush out from the helmets; and 'the brave hero Parzival' and the Duke are likewise congratulated on their bloody deeds.[102]

But while McCracken believes that romances present men's blood as a solely positive currency in the encounters between knights, unproblematically buying blood for honour, so to speak, this bloodshed is by no means presented uncritically in most romances. In *Daniel*, the violence that is involved in this way of establishing fame and power is described in drastic terms that show that it is hardly justifiable. Large brutal battles replace the courtly joust as the usual form of combat. Jousting is devalued as a method of determining knightly prowess in the fight against Juran, where Daniel wins only because of his longer legs, which enable him to acquire the magic sword faster, and in all subsequent fights, where it is simply the superior magic rather than bravery and talent that wins out. Courtly fighting has become a mere prelude to murder when the Duke of the Green Meadow jousts for no other aim than to gather more victims for the sick man's bath of blood. Daniel does not even attempt a fair fight against the bloodsuckers and the blood-bather with their magic weapons, and instead slays them from behind. The suffering that such slaughter brings about is also graphically shown. Danise's grief over the loss of her husband, Matur, by Arthur's hand, is dwelt upon.[103] The father of the two giants whom Daniel has brutally mutilated and decapitated also extensively vents his anger and pain, and threatens to punish as many knights as he can by carrying them up a mountain from which they cannot return:

> dês war, sît diu erde
> mit mîner kinde bluote
> nâch iuwer aller muote
> alsô wol ist gelabet,
> die ir mir erslagen habet,
> die mir dâ beschert sint,
> die muoz aber dirre wint
> an disem berge verderren.[104]

Truly, because, as all of you wished, the earth is replenished with the blood of my children, whom you have slain, now whoever I can get hold of shall be dried up by the wind on this mountain.

Here it is implied that Daniel has shed blood in a way that is uncomfortably close to Cain's fratricide in the common image of Abel's blood soaking the earth, which we have already encountered in *Parzival*. From Genesis 6: 4, giants were often understood to be Cain's kin, that is, offspring of the man who shed the first blood; instead it is here an Arthurian knight who spills the giants' blood.[105] Similarly, Daniel invites the Duke of the Green Meadow to join him for the 'blood-bath' of the second battle after having just rescued him from the sick man's blood-bath: 'I will quickly bring you to a place where I must endure a bath'.[106] This is a battle in which many a knight slaughtered by Arthur's troops 'has to bathe in the blood until he drowns'.[107] This stark bloodiness betrays the influence of heroic epics, where fighters are often described as swimming and bathing in blood, but it here throws a distinctly negative light on the behaviour of both sides through the parallel to the blood-bathing mass-murderer.[108] The brutality of the fights is further demonstrated by cynical metaphors of healing and blessing, and negative descriptions of bleeding as poverty.[109] Moreover, no claims for a moral justification of the bloodshed are made, such as the struggle against heathens and rebels, for example, in the heroic epic tradition. Instead, the sole purpose of the battles is to give individual combatants a chance to excel. The strategic pointlessness of three days of mass killing is highlighted by the fact that Daniel finally achieves victory simply by paralysing the enemy with the help of the magic crying animal – and thus outshines all the brave knights without even fighting.

So while Arthurian knighthood means protecting oneself against intrusion, this requires seeking out such danger in order to gain fame. Moreover, a knight has to counter this threat by inflicting it upon others. The invaded, fragmented, sucked out and bleeding bodies of the romance mirror this reliance on constant danger, intrusion and aggression. *Daniel von dem Blühenden Tal*, as well as many other romances, exposes such violence and peril as intrinsic to the construction of ideal knighthood in the prologue, which states categorically that Arthurian knights strive for fame in combat, by claiming, for instance, that whoever rides out on adventure is given a new shield, which he has to bring back cut to pieces, so that one can see what he has been up to.[110] The plot likewise confirms that conflicts are part of what it means to be an Arthurian knight; they do not result from the protagonist's initial shortcomings, such as inexperience or lack of social responsibility, as they might have done in earlier romances. Daniel, like Wigalois and several other romance heroes, is already a king, a perfect knight and a member of the Round Table in full knowledge of his past before he goes on the *aventiure*-ride with which the bulk of the text deals. The threats he faces in the form of various opponents are thus risks for Arthurian knights as such; besides, they are linked with challenges to the whole Arthurian court. The plot thus describes not the process of becoming a perfect knight, but the successful survival of one of many adventures that can and must happen again and again to Arthur's knights. As violence and danger are by definition an inalienable part of knighthood, there is no harmonious resolution at the end of the plot. The adventures serve to demonstrate the Arthurian construction of male identity rather than to stabilize or change it. While all Arthurian knights and the court as a whole just about manage to stay intact as well as penetrable throughout the plot, this comes at the price of constant mortal danger.

The opponents, however, true to their role as a contrasting foil for the Arthurian knights, employ the alternative strategy of shielding their bodies against any penetration from outside. They can be divided into two types with different methods of protection. The first group are irreconcilable antagonists, Juran, the belly-less monsters and the blood-bather. They defend themselves through magically enhanced aggression, with the help of attacking weapons like the sword that cuts through any substance, the Medusa-head, the hypnotic voice and glance. They are mobile and have invaded others' countries. But such active aggression offers no lasting protection against Arthur's knights, who decapitate all these opponents. The second group are temporary adversaries who later become associates of the Arthurian court: the Duke of the Green Meadow and his country, which turns out to be beleaguered by the blood-bather, as well as the Queen of Cluse and her realm, who decides to marry into the Arthurian court after having lost the war against them. These characters use the purely defensive strategy of hardening their borders: the Duke of the Green Meadow wears a mermaid's skin, made impenetrable by being steeped in dragon's blood.[111] The giant brothers guarding Cluse are also protected by impenetrable skin.[112] But it is made obvious that neither extreme aggression nor total seclusion provide feasible alternatives to Arthurian openness. All the apparently invincible opponents are just as vulnerable as Arthurian knights. The magic weapons are turned against their owners: the dwarf's sword, the crying animal, and the Medusa-head; and all these aggressive opponents end up decapitated. As in the *Nibelungenlied*, the hardened boundaries also provoke blood-flow. On several occasions, the contrast between the hard armour and the flowing blood is made explicit.[113] The secluded inhabitants of Cluse and the Country of the Green Meadow eventually have to open up. So one is left with the necessity of physical permeability and exchange, which brings affirmation of as well as risk to Arthurian knighthood.

In the stories about the pound of flesh, the pact in blood and the healing bath of blood, as well as in law codes and in *Wigalois*, then, the enforcement of taboos against spilling and touching blood had confirmed the notion of the bounded body. In works like the *Nibelungenlied* and *Daniel*, on the other hand, such taboos prove impossible to maintain: despite all protective attempts, the ideal of a fully enclosed, impenetrable body dissolves in a stream of blood. Characters die when they focus on defending their bodily boundaries and on avoiding any kind of bleeding, while the Arthurian model of a more open body proves more successful. This raises the question as to how ethical the definition of human identity through a bounded body distinguished from a hostile exterior is – if it kills rather than protects (fictional) characters, is this a viable way of self-definition? The next part will complicate this ethical question by showing that the emphasis on separation of body from an exterior also implies the segregation of fully enclosed bodies from less perfect ones. The notion of the bounded male Christian body depended in particular on the devaluation of the bodies of women and Jews.

3

Bodies that Form

But nothing could easily be found that is more remarkable than the monthly flux of women.

(Pliny, *Natural History*)

To have a penis or not says it all in most circumstances

Every comparison contains both a distinction and an acknowledgement of similarity: to say, as the *Secreta mulierum* and many other medieval texts do, that 'man is worthier than woman', is to say both that man is unlike woman (worthy vs not so worthy) and that man is like woman (comparable to her).[1] In his influential discussion of sex and gender in pre-Enlightenment medical texts, Thomas Laqueur chooses to stress the similarity between the sexes in medieval medicine, setting the pre-modern 'one-sex model', where man and women differ only socially, not biologically, against the modern idea of two biological sexes.[2] Quite apart from the problematic distinction between the biological and the social here, I suggest that this 'one-sex model' is rather an acute awareness in medieval medicine of the fact that gender is a construct and that the sexes are not clearly distinguished by nature. What Laqueur does not see are the physicians' and philosophers' desperate attempts to distinguish men from women even on a physiological level. Though menstruation, for instance, to an extent had its equivalent in men's nosebleeds, as Laqueur stresses, it was still feared as a uniquely female pollution with evil powers that nosebleeds did not have. Moreover, femaleness is always already presented as secondary to the male paradigm, where menstruation is an exception to the rule. This continues to be the case in Laqueur's own book, whose claim that 'to have a penis or not says it all in most circumstances' really does say it all in this respect.[3] The body as conceptualized in medieval medicine and natural philosophy, then, was no less rigidly and problematically gendered than it is today.

This chapter looks at how differences, in particular gender differences, are imagined through blood and bodily integrity. The bodies of women, but also of Jews and fantasized monsters are represented as not fully integral or formed. Their uncontained bloody matter is presumed to leak out and pollute men – a fear that again persists in modern culture, as feminist scholars have often observed. Jean-Paul Sartre, for instance, in his important attempt to define substances including bodily fluids phenomenologically, that is, according to their 'inherent' qualities, sees fluidity as 'the feminine pole of the world', and viscous substances as being 'sticky like a too-possessive mistress'.[4] Feminist critics have shown how such 'inherent' qualities are of course dependent on Sartre's own essentialist preconceptions about gender rather than on the analysed substances themselves.[5] But as we shall see, apart from anxieties about women's fluidity and pollution, there are two further ways in which blood genders bodies: women are construed as draining men of their precious blood, and as sometimes retaining their own fluids in a way that makes them all the more dangerous. This conception of gender puts men in a paradoxical position: they claim both to be transcending the body, but also to have superior and indeed paradigmatic bodies. The imaginary threats to their integrity are double-edged, as by challenging the bodily boundaries, they ultimately also confirm those borders; and a crisis successfully overcome will leave the man strengthened and affirmed.

Bodies that form

In *Bodies that Matter*, Judith Butler explores how bodies are not just inscribed by gender, but unthinkable without gender and thus in some sense brought about by it. She does so by unravelling established philosophical theories, including the ancient Greek concept of 'matter', which she uses in her title. Throughout her book, however, she oscillates between two interpretations of this notion. First, she claims that within Greek philosophy certain bodies, such as those of homosexuals or transsexuals, or even women, are seen as abject and fail to count as proper 'bodies that matter' because they 'fail to materialize'; they do not matter in a double sense of not being significant and not consisting of physical matter as defined by Plato or Aristotle.[6] Butler here seems to understand matter as material as opposed to abstract form, as in Aristotle's classical distinction, according to which a body consists of both matter and a form imprinted on that matter.

But according to this theory, what constituted a body was not so much that it consisted of matter as the fact that it was formed; a body was defined not so much as that which matters, but that which forms out of the matter. The abject bodies are precisely those that do not *form*, that *are* mere matter, which has not been shaped or formed sufficiently. Butler uses this definition at the end of her essay on Aristotle, Plato and their modern adaptations: 'within Plato, there is a disjunction between a materiality which is feminine and formless and, hence, without a body, and bodies which are formed through – but not of – that feminine materiality'.[7] So here, bodies that count as proper bodies are the ones that are formed, that are not mere matter.

Butler's earlier formulation of 'bodies that matter' to represent hegemonic bodies only makes sense if she uses 'matter' not as opposed to form, as one could have assumed, but in a second, different sense: as always already attracting and striving for form.[8] This second sense of matter, *hyle*, as a material which has at the same time generative, productive powers, 'a certain capacity to originate', is also implied in Aristotelian philosophy, she explains:

> To speak within these classical contexts of bodies that matter is not an idle pun, for to be material means to materialize, where the principle of that materialization is precisely what 'matters' about that body, its very intelligibility. In this sense, to know the significance of something is to know how and why it matters, where 'to matter' means at once 'to materialize' and 'to mean'.[9]

Bodies that matter in this sense, then, are bodies that are productive and significant, that have a potentiality for form inherent in their matter. So matter is here no longer opposed to form, but participating in it.

But despite the philosophical and political advantages of interpreting matter in such a holistic way, to understand medieval concepts of gendered bodies, it is more helpful to return to opposition between form and matter and to think of form, not matter, as the key ingredient for a fully integral body. Matter is shared by both coherent and abject bodies, while only the former have form. Women's bodies are granted matter in this sense in medieval physiological theory; it is not matter that the bodies of women are lacking, but form. This is apparent in the work in which the ancient and medieval matter-form distinction is most extensively discussed in relation to gender, Aristotle's natural philosophical treatise on the *Generation of Animals* (*c.*350 BC). Matter and form are the respective contributions of male and female animals and humans to the conception of their offspring:

> The female always provides the material, the male provides that which fashions the material into shape; this, in our view, is the specific characteristic of each of the sexes: that is what it means to be male or to be female. Hence, necessity requires that the female should provide the physical part, i.e., a quantity of material, but not that the male should do so, since necessity does not require that the tools should reside in the product that is being made, nor that the agent which uses them should do so. Thus the physical part, the body, comes from the female, and the Soul from the male, since the Soul is the essence of a particular body.[10]

The carrier of this form is the cherished semen, which only men can produce, so Aristotle: 'male is that which is able to concoct, to cause to take shape, and to discharge, semen possessing the "principle" of the "form" . . . Female is that which receives the semen, but is unable to cause semen to take shape or to discharge it.'[11] The *Secreta mulierum* gives its own, more jumbled version of this:

> Wann Aristotiles maint nit das der Sam des vaters kum Jn die Substantz der frucht das verstee Ich also das die frucht die entpfangen wirt Jn muter leyb von dem Samen des vaters, nicht zuleget noch wachset, wan das sie allein geformirt wirth vnd ein geStalt ains menschen entpfecht . . . Hie spricht die gloß das nach der maynung Aristotilis der Sam des vaters hat ein gleychnuß mit dem Menstruo der muter: Also leyb vnd milich zusamen gemischt wirt, So wirth das lebsal mit dem zu milich. Vnd macht doch die milich vest vnd dick das sie gesteet Vnd hert wirth. vnd geht auch auß der milich dunstlich. Also ist der Same des vaters der birt nit zu dem Samen der muter oder zu der Frucht. Aber er macht die Frucht zu eynner form. Aber die artzt sprechent Das der Sam von dem vater der do haist Sperma, Vnd der Sam der muter der do haist menstrum miteinander werden zu dem wesen der Frucht alls vor geschrieben ist. Das mag einer den naturlichen maistern glauben ader den ertzten.[12]

For Aristotle thinks that the father's seed does not contribute to the substance of the embryo, by which I understand that the embryo that is received in the mother's body is not added to or expanded by the father's seed, but that it is only formed by it and receives the shape of a human being . . . Here, the commentary says that in Aristotle's opinion, the seed of the father is equivalent to the menstrual fluid of the mother. When rennet and milk are mixed, so rennet becomes milk, and yet, it makes the milk so set and thick that the milk curdles and becomes solid, and then evaporates from the milk. In the same way, the father's seed is not the carrier of the mother's seed or of the offspring, but it makes the foetus into a form. But the doctors say that the father's seed, which is called sperm, and the mother's seed, which is called menstruum, become together the essence of the offspring, as described above. One can believe the masters of natural philosophy or the doctors here.

Fathers thus contribute to human and animal bodies the form, the non-material shape with which it is stamped, while mothers contribute the material, the substance, the matter. No material is added to the embryo by the father's seed, simply an abstract shape, like that made by a seal. The seed itself later evaporates.[13] At the end of the quotation, the alternative Galenic theory is mentioned, which was also propagated in medieval medical theory rather than natural philosophy, and does not rely on a distinction between matter and form. The second-century physician Galen and his followers instead postulated that both mother and father have a seed, both of which contribute equally to the generation of the embryo. While ostensibly remaining neutral on this much-debated issue, the *Secreta* is clearly founded on Aristotelian thinking throughout. The matter that mothers contribute to the embryo is of course, as we have seen in chapter 1, menstrual blood. The *Secreta* does not distinguish between menstrual blood and the Galenic female seed, and the idea of a woman's seed is ultimately submerged, since it is usually simply referred to as *menstrum*. Clearly betraying the closeness to the Aristotelian hypothesis, moreover, the text frequently presents menstruum as matter. It refers to both menstruum and seed as *matery*, speaks of 'the matter called menstruum' and claims: 'About this flux one has to know that the Latin word *menstruum* in women means nothing but superfluous matter derived from the food and drink that this woman has'.[14] The matter that so much rides on, not in the least gender differences, is thus paradigmatically blood.

Aristotle continues to explain in the *Generation of Animals* that women not only contribute mere formless material to conception, they themselves are also not fully formed; a female embryo results from a botched attempt at making a formed male embryo:

> With these as our premises it may perhaps be clearer why and by what cause one offspring becomes male and the other female. It is this. When the 'principle' is failing to gain the mastery and is unable to effect concoction owing to the deficiency of the heat, and does not succeed in reducing the material into its own proper form, but instead is worsted in the attempt, then of necessity the material must change over into its opposite condition. Now the opposite of the male is the female, and it is the opposite in respect of that whereby one is male and the other female.[15]

If the father's seed is too cold to imprint a form onto the matter, the matter changes into its opposite. This does not mean that it either turns into form of its own accord or remains mere matter, a formless quantity of blood. It does, however, mean that the formed body is not fully achieved; what results instead is an impaired body, that of a female. Women are thus not formed but deformed, and in this sense monstrous, as Aristotle elaborates with callous misogyny:

> Anyone who does not take after his parents is really in a way a monstrosity, since in these cases Nature has in a way strained from the generic type. The first beginning of this deviation is when a female is formed instead of a male . . . We should look upon the female state as being as it were a deformity [αναπηριαυ], though one which occurs in the ordinary course of nature.[16]

A female thus of course has a body, but not one in which form has imprinted itself on matter as it should be, but one in which the proper form has been exchanged for a damaged, secondary, monstrous form. Again, the *Secreta* subscribes to this idea in a simplified version:

> auch will aristotiles Jn dem achtenden buch von den thiren, Das von dem Samen der wol gedait ist da wirtt ain knab auß geporen vnd von dem Samen der nit wol gedaitt ist da werden tochterlein auß geporenn.[17]

> Aristotle also maintains in the eighth book of the [*Generation of*] *Animals* that of well-processed seed a boy is generated, and of not well-processed seed a little daughter is generated.

So this kind of medieval physiology firmly aligned women with deformed bloody matter, in so far as they are both made out of this matter and pass this on to their offspring. Men on the other hand are ascribed exclusive access to non-bodily knowledge, as discussed in chapter 1, as well as to a form that exceeds mere matter, in their contribution to an embryo and in their own make-up. This opposition is formulated in terms of not just the conceptualization of a body, but of the very creation of every body in the womb.

The alignment of women with matter and blood and of men with metaphysical form was not limited to natural philosophy. Theologians extensively discussed similar respective contributions of mother and father to conception, mostly in terms of Christ's humanity. Christ was generally believed to have received his human material body and blood from Mary, and his soul and transcendental nature from God. In a thirteenth-century German verse narrative on Mary's ascension, 'Rheinfränkische Himmelfahrt Mariae', for example, Jesus is described as Mary's 'flesh and blood' twice, and said to have received this through his mother's milk.[18] Since blood, especially women's blood, was also a result and sign of human sinfulness, this was a fraught topic. Mechthild von Magdeburg, who states that blood is given to Adam and Eve in punishment for their original sin, avoids directly claiming that the blood in Jesus's veins was the same kind of blood (see below in this chapter). She mentions that Gabriel brought neither blood nor bones or flesh down from heaven for the annunciation, only the name Jesus, but that Jesus does have bones and flesh, soul and body later.[19] But it is never made explicit that he does indeed obtain blood as well as flesh, although this is evident from his subsequent bleeding. Moreover, as so often in medieval theory, it is stressed that this blood would stem from an exceptionally pure source: from a virgin who does not sin herself.[20] The doctrine of Mary's own immaculate conception by her parents ensures that Christ's blood and body could in no way be construed as tainted.[21]

As we have seen in chapter 1, the neat separation of matter and meta-matter self-destructs in the internal contradictions of the *Secreta*. This is true for the matter-form distinction in religious writing as well, for example, in the metaphor of the wax and seal that is most frequently used in ancient and medieval philosophy to explain the difference between matter and form and also occurs in the Song of Songs. Mystical commentaries on the passage where the bridegroom asks the bride to put him on her heart like a seal blur the difference between form and matter.[22]

The *Heilige Regel*, for instance, a guiding treatise for Cistercian monks, probably composed around 1250 in a Franconian cloister, writes:

Nu sprichet di brut unserez herren: 'Min gemineter rif zu mir, wez gerd an mich?'. Er sprach: 'lege mich uffe din herze als ein ingesigele.' als man daz in ein waz drucket, di wil ez warm ist, so wirt ez dem insegele gelich. also sule wir unseren herren in unse herze drucken, daz unser herze mit sime blute geverwet werde. Swer einen blutigen menschen legete zu eime anderen, daz mak kume sin er en wurde van ime och blutich.[23]

Now the bride of our lord says: 'My beloved has called me, what does he desire from me?' He said: 'Put me on your heart like a seal.' As one presses this seal into wax while it is warm, the wax becomes like the seal. Thus we should press our lord into our heart, so that our heart is dyed with his blood. He who puts one bloody human being next to another, this one will become bloody through the other; that can hardly be avoided.

In this series of jarring images for the mystical union of bride and bridegroom, interpreted as Christ and the Church, seal and blood become indistinguishable. The bridegroom being pressed into the bride's heart is compared to a seal imprinting wax, then to God's blood colouring the believer's heart, and finally to a bloody human bloodying another. The seal, not the wax, is thus compared to divine and human blood, the paradigmatic form to the paradigmatic matter.

Women, Jews and blood

In the strand of medieval misogynist thought best exemplified by the *Secreta mulierum*, women are conceptualized not only as insufficiently formed blood, but as bodies which reputedly lose such blood. Just as their father's seed at conception had been too cold to form the menstrual matter into a man, women themselves are not hot enough to process their own fluids properly. This means that their bodily fluids are runny and will easily seep out of the body. As standard physiology held, the *Secreta* believes that food was processed into blood and then into other bodily fluids in various stages.[24] Menstruum is one kind of blood separated in this way, and so is semen, but the latter is then concocted to a higher degree:

Es ist zuwissen das Etlich maister sprechent des mans same Sey plut geflossenn von dem harm. Vnd mit der hitz der hoden So wirtt der selb sam weyss[.] Annder maister Sprechent des mans Same sey ain vberflussigkait der hindristen speyss vnd zu dem hinderstenn mal verdait.[25]

One ought to know that several masters say that man's seed is blood separated from urine, and this seed turns white through the heat of the testicles. Other masters say that seed is a superfluity of food in its final state and most fully digested.

This passage presents both the opinion that semen is made from blood, and that it is the most processed food; both ideas are synthesized throughout the rest of text in accordance with prevalent views to suggest that semen is superior to menstrual blood because it is the better digested. Despite its status as a kind of blood, the *Secreta* avoids identifying menstrual fluid directly as blood, distancing it as far as possible from any fluid that men also have.[26] Menstrual blood was believed to be of a thinner and more watery moisture than men's more 'airy', viscous semen.[27] The same gendered difference in cohesion also extends to other bodily fluids. Well-digested, well-formed mother's milk is generated under the influence of a male foetus:

vnd das dick vnnd wolgestalt milich von Jren prusten gat vnd laufft dy alls dick ist So man dy Selben milich neme vnnd der sie gueß auff ain prett ader anders wo hin da es ebenn were vnnd Si doch bey ain [ander] bleybt das ist aber ain zaichen das die frucht ain knabe ist.[28]

And if thick and well-formed milk flows and runs from her breasts – milk that is so thick that if one took this milk and poured it on a board or another flat surface, it would stay together – that is another sign that the fruit is male.

This cohesive milk also 'does not part' if poured into urine.[29] It is explicitly contrasted with the 'undigested and thin', dissolving, uncontrollable milk produced for the female foetus, which 'flows apart' on a board like water.[30] Even salt in the case of a male baby does not 'fall apart' when strewn on the nipples.[31] The commentary again repeats the behaviour of the milk in very similar terms ('thick', 'well-digested', 'flow apart', 'melt') and explains it as a result of heat of the male foetus.[32] This binary of cohesion vs uncontrollability explicitly defines gender here when it is presented as a way to determine the gender of the foetus, as 'a sign that the fruit is male'. The same appreciation of thickness occurs in the description of semen, which, if coagulated (like boiled milk or pitch) produces strong – and as the commentary adds, more often male – children, whereas relatively thinner semen brings forth 'weak fruit'.[33]

But not only do the bodily fluids show a gendered difference in viscosity; women's bodies as a whole are also less coherent. Woman is presented in the *Secreta* as a human who cannot contain herself, as a not fully integral body in the sense that she is not a closed container, but a permeable, leaking one. This is explained precisely by the fact that her fluids are not as fully concocted and thus contain more residues from digestion that need to be regularly expelled.[34] This happens in the discharge of menstrual fluid, also referred to as 'flow' (*fluß*) or 'moisture' (*feuchte*). As opposed to man, who can control his seed emission, woman's cold and moist nature means that her menstruum just drips out:

> Zu dem dritten mal wirt getweyffelt, Warumb den Frauen die vorgenant matery auß fliese die do ist ein wbrige matery die do kombt von essen vnd vonn drincken Vnd der Samen auch ein wbrige matery ist von essen vnd von trincken[.] Darvmb ist zuantwortten das ein fraw von natur Feucht vnd kalt ist Vnd der man ist von natur warm vnd trucken. Nun muß alles das fliesen das fewcht ist.[35]

> The third question is why the aforementioned matter, which is a residual matter from food and drink, flows out of women, and semen is also a residual matter from food and drink. The answer to this is that woman is moist and cold by nature; and man is warm and dry by nature. Now everything moist must flow.

Nothing is mentioned about the involuntary emission of male seed, otherwise a popular topic of scholastic debate.[36] Men thus appear as fully bounded bodies with only controlled emissions, women as uncontrollably dripping. It is again blood that has defined gender difference here: women appear as non-integral bodies not only because they are not completely formed, but also because they leak fluids.

In religious discourse, menstruation was also most commonly seen as an impure leakage indicative of women's inferior bodies. Where the biblical account in Genesis 3: 16 speaks of labour in childbirth as Eve's punishment for the Fall, medieval exegetical tradition has it that menstruation is her penalty, the 'curse of Eve'.[37] This misogynistic view of menstruation was not uncontested; several theologians, such as

Hildegard von Bingen and Heloise in the twelfth century, as well as medical texts, such as the *Trotula*, emphasize either positive cleansing and generative functions of menstruation, or equivalent weaknesses of male physiology instead.[38] Mechthild von Magdeburg, for instance, echoing Hildegard, postulates a male equivalent to the polluting leakage. According to the *Fließendes Licht*, both genders receive blood as a consequence of the original sin:

> das sûndige menscliche saf, das Adam us dem oeppfel beis, das noch natûrlich allû unsrû lider durgat, und dar zuo das verfluochte bluot, das Even und allen wiben von dem oeppfel entstuont . . . Adam behielt das saf an ime und da nach alle man. Eva und allû wip behielten dis vil schemlich bluot.[39]

> The sinful human fluid, which Adam bit out of the apple, and which still naturally courses through all our limbs, and also the cursed blood that Eve and all other women got from the apple . . . Adam retained the liquid inside him, and so did all men after him. Eve and all other women retained this very shameful blood.

In a striking image, Adam 'bites' a masculine counterpart of the menstrual blood out of the apple, a fluid which now 'courses through all human's veins'. While this liquid is neutrally referred to as *saf*, which can also mean juice as well as humour, is it clear that blood is meant, especially since any food ending up in the veins must, according to medieval physiology, be blood or a component thereof. Mechthild thus balances the traditional vilification of menstrual blood with an equally sinful male blood and, while not challenging the negative view of menstruation, at least levels out the gender inequality.[40]

Another hierarchy, that between Christians and Jews, also overrides the dominant distinction in theology and natural philosophy between women leaking blood and bounded men. Like women, Jews of both genders were in several contexts presented as not being able to contain their blood and therefore as not possessing fully integral, formed bodies. Religious and biological explanations for their alleged lack of physical coherence are summarized in the fifteenth-century German translation of the *Secreta mulierum* by Johann Hartlieb, which claims that Jewish men menstruate:

> Dye juden haben den fluß gar vast, wann sy essenn kaltew vnd vnraine speysß vnd haben gar sellten guete dewïng, wan sy sind kalter vnd fewchter

natur . . . Darvmb get das selb all manet von in als von denn weyben, vnd vmb dye vnd nach geschriben sach sind gewondlich all iuden, den fluß all manet tzw haben . . . Dye ander vrsach ist, wann sy alczeyt feyern vnd gar selten arbaytten, vnd vmb des willen werden sy mit naturlicher hytz selten erwermt . . . Dye trytt sach ist, das dy juden albeg leben in grosser sorgfaltigkayt vnd in vnrainen gemachen. Darvmb wegst in jn gar vil melancolia, dye dan tzw verdewen gar schwär ist . . . Dye vierd vrsach ist, das dy kind der iuden auch enpfahen dy natur jrer vater, als dann schreybt Galyeneus in seinem buch von der complexyon . . . Dye funft vrsach ist, das von jnfluessen des gestirns vnd der planeten dye sach auch kumpt . . . Dye sechst vnd dye hochst vrsach an den iuden ist, das sy plwtflyssig sein. Das ist, daß sy Iesum Christum, den warcn got vnd menschen, nit mochten vberwinden tzw dem tod, vnd Pylatus sprach, er wolt vnschuldig sein an des gerechten menschen pluet. Do schryenn sy all: 'Sein pluet gee vbei vns vnd alle vnsere kinder!'[41]

The Jews have the flow very strongly, because they eat cold and impure food and rarely have a good digestion, because they are of a cold and moist nature . . . This is why this flow is emitted from them every month as it is from women; and for this and the following reasons, all Jews usually have the flow every month . . . The other reason is that they always celebrate and very rarely work, and therefore are rarely warmed by natural heat . . . The third reason is that the Jews always live in great danger and anxiety and in impure lodgings. So they gain a great amount of black bile, which is then hard to digest . . . The fourth reason is that Jewish children also inherit the nature of their fathers, as Galen writes in his book on complexion . . . The fifth reason is that this is also caused by the influence of the stars and the planets . . . The sixth and foremost reason is that Jews have a flow of blood. This means that they were unable to overcome Jesus Christ, true God and man, by death; and Pilate said that he did not want to be guilty of this righteous human's blood. Then they all cried: 'His blood be upon us and upon all our children.'

This belief in Jewish men's menstruation is found in a range of scientific and theological texts from the thirteenth century onwards, synthesizing fears of menstruation and of Jewish aggression.[42] The reasons cited in the *Secreta* demonstrate precisely the mixture of physiology, theology and prejudice from which this idea arose. They postulate in Jewish men a need to expel residues due to their diet, constitution, lack of hard work, melancholia and uncleanness; added to by inherited and astrological influences; but first and foremost because they 'called Christ's blood upon them' when Pilate washed his hands of it (Matthew 27: 25). The latter is a common anti-Semitic accusation and is often used to draw parallels between the Jews and Cain, since, as mentioned in chapter 1, Abel's blood calls out to God and accuses Cain in the same way that Christ's blood accuses the Jews. So religious and biological differences are here conflated to create a distinction between Jews and Christians, into something we might call ethnicity.[43]

This lack of an integral body that can contain its own blood is not ascribed to further races in the *Secreta mulierum*, although, as we shall see, they are in other ways defined through blood. Physiological theory in general held that 'Ethiopians', people living in hotter climates, had black skin because their blood was better processed. The *Secreta* avoids explicitly discussing the potential great cohesion of black men's bodies, but does refer to black skin colour in relation to mother's milk. Black women's milk is described as superior, thanks to their greater heat and therefore better processing of the blood – this also applies to black goats in comparison to white ones.[44] So prejudice against black people did not find its expression in ascribing blood leakage to them, as was the case for Jews and women.

Blood pollutes men

Judith Butler observed a distinction between bodies that are fully integral, have full status as bodies, and those abject bodies which fail to count as proper bodies, which are deemed lacking and monstrous, such as those of women. But bodies are distinguished not only from other bodies, but also from their immediate surroundings, from matter outside the body. If women leak blood, this therefore has implications for the world around them as well as for their embodied status. This is again particularly important in the medical theory of the humours, where all elements in macrocosm and microcosm were linked with one another, from the planets to humans to worms. The prime means of communication between the different parts of the cosmos are again the two basic qualities of temperature (hot/cold) and moisture (dry/moist), and their four possible combinations, especially in the four humours. This is a changeable and fluid world order, as the *Secreta* makes clear in accordance with mainstream science: the humours themselves are liquids; the human being also originates entirely from liquids, from its mother's and father's seeds, which remain fluid like milk and blood for the first fifteen days; life is pictured as a continuous consumption and replacement of fluids, with food being turned into blood to nourish the parts of the body where the heat has dried up the moisture.[45] In particular, the commentary to the *Secreta* tries to present a conclusive picture of all natural phenomena through the behaviour of the humours. Which phase of the moon women menstruate in, for instance, is determined by their humoural disposition. If a woman were relatively cold and wet, say, she would menstruate when the moon is relatively cold and wet, too: in its fourth quarter from half to new moon.[46] The smallest individual flux in such a tightly connected, fluid fishbowl of a cosmos could have consequences as far-reaching as the proverbial butterfly batting its wings to cause a storm at the other side of the world. An often-cited list from Pliny's monumental first-century compendium *Natural History* shows how far the polluting effects of menstruation were indeed assumed to affect nature:

Sed nihil facile reperiatur mulierum profluvio magis monstrificum. acescunt superventu musta, sterilescunt contactae fruges, moriuntur insita, exuruntur hortorum germina, fructus arborum quibus insidere decidunt, speculorum fulgor adspectu ipso hebetatur, acies ferri praestringitur, eboris nitor, alvi apium moriuntur, aes etiam ac ferrum robigo protinus corripit odorque dirus aera, in rabiem aguntur gustato eo canes atque insanabili veneno morsus inficitur. quin et bituminum sequax alioquin ac lenta natura in lacu Iudaeae qui vocatur Asphaltites certo tempore anni supernatans non quit sibi avelli ad omnem contactum adhaerens praeterquam filo quod tale virus infecerit. etiam formicis, animali minimo, inesse sensum eius ferunt, abicique gustatas fruges nec postea repeti.[47]

But nothing could easily be found that is more remarkable than the monthly flux of women. Contact with it turns new wine sour, crops touched by it become barren, grafts die, seeds in gardens are dried up, the fruit of trees falls off, the bright surface of mirrors in which it is merely reflected is dimmed, the edge of steel and the gleam of ivory are dulled, hives of bees die, even bronze and iron are at once seized by rust, and a horrible smell fills the air; to taste it drives dogs mad and infects their bites with an incurable poison. Moreover bitumen, a substance generally sticky and viscous, that at a certain season of the year floats on the surface of the lake of Judaea called the Asphalt Pool, adheres to everything touching it, and cannot be drawn asunder except by a thread soaked in the poisonous fluid in question. Even that very tiny creature the ant is said to be sensitive to it, and throws away grains of corn that taste of it and does not touch them again.

From the tiniest ant to bees and dogs, from bronze and iron to steel and ivory, from wine to fruit, from trees to crops, from air to bitumen, from Judaea to Rome, the whole natural world is corrupted, dissolved and infected by menstruum, finds Pliny.

Women's blood-flow potentially endangered not only the balance of the universe, but also, more immediately, men. Men's bodies were believed to come into direct contact with menstrual blood on numerous occasions, all of which are of great concern in the *Secreta*. The dangers that menstrual blood throws up for men begin at conception. Ortolf claims that 'when a child is generated and conceived from bad blood', it can contract leprosy; the *Secreta* says that this happens when children are conceived during menstruation.[48] This possibility for pollution continues during pregnancy, when a woman is imagined as a container for a male fruit. The latter idea shows in the analogies used in a discussion of how the foetus in the womb can die and the mother remain unharmed when lightning strikes. The main text compares this to how a barrel of wine can be hit without the wine being spilled; the commentary adds more parallels: a shoe around a foot, a sheath around a sword and a purse around pennies. Of course the content is in each case more valuable, 'strong and powerful', while the container is devalued as 'weak and not strong'.[49] As in the Aristotelian generation theory discussed earlier, the *Secreta* always imagines the foetus as paradigmatically male, evidenced by various gendered predictions about an unborn child's pre-determination through its star sign, for instance, about the kind of beard it will grow or what kind of manservant it will make.[50] In the questions following the passage on lightning, the embryo is also explicitly constructed as a continuation of a man's seed that is delivered into a woman's body. Changes to the father's seed at conception *are* changes to the embryo. For example, the question arises whether a man's seed that was intended to become a boy can be polluted by thunder at the moment of conception, so that it becomes a female embryo; the commentary claims that this is indeed possible.[51] This implies both that the father's seed here is the key constituent of the foetus (while female seed or matter is not mentioned), and that the offspring is male by default, unless an accident happens.

Reproduction for a man, then, is no less than a continuation of himself into eternity, as a member of his species.[52] A woman's interference in this process can only pose a risk. She fails to protect her male offspring not just against lightning, but also against her own blood. Menstrual bleeding is presented as a danger to an embryo or foetus in so far as it signals its death if it occurs during pregnancy.[53] That women might want to harm the foetus is suggested by allegations that they try deliberately to prevent conception and induce abortions, while the *Secreta* always sees pregnancy as desirable, for example, when it gives advice only on how to conceive, not on contraceptives.[54] Peggy McCracken has shown that not only conception and pregnancy, but also birth was often feared as a dangerous occasion of contact with blood, and thus surrounded with taboos. She believes that the prohibitions against the father being present and the fears of monstrous births were primarily anxieties about the blood of lineage.[55]

Even after birth, breastfeeding constitutes further potentially threatening contact with menstrual blood, of which milk was thought to be a processed form.[56] While the *Secreta* is more worried about the dangers of sex and conception, anxiety about a possible pollution of the child at the breast is voiced, for instance, by Ortolf von Baierland. The nurse should not be ill, not have unclean skin, not eat unclean food and not have sex, Ortolf recommends, out of concern not for the woman, but for the child, who might otherwise suck her diseases out of her and be infected by them:

> De amme sal nicht vere von der bort syn, vppe dat se icht to allde melych hebbe ader to ny; man de sal ouch warten, dat sye ich sych sy eder vnreyne an der hut, wente dat kynt suget dy suke von der ammen vnde wert dar von kranc. De amme sal nycht vorsalten spyse eten noch bitter; dat dut deme kynde we, vnde nycht vnreyns eszen. Se sal gueden trank drynken. Se sal sych kuez halden, wante von vnkuzheyt vorwandelt sych dy mellych. Se en sal ouch nycht to feyzt noch to mager syn.[57]

> The wet-nurse should not be far from having given birth, so that her milk is neither too old nor too young; one should also take care that she is not sick or has unclean skin, because the child sucks the sickness out of the nurse and thus falls ill itself. The nurse should not eat food that is too salty or bitter, this hurts the child; and she should not eat anything impure. She should have good drinks. She should remain chaste, because the milk changes through unchastity. She should not be too fat or too skinny either.

Even grown men are not safe from women's blood. Heterosexual intercourse was seen as a prime instance of contact with and thus anxiety about menstrual blood. That the penis during sex is an epitome of men's vulnerability is illustrated by the *Secreta's* warning to beware of women, especially whores, who conceal iron blades in their vagina, so that the penis is hurt during penetration.[58] The commentary adds that this is so dangerous because the penis is the crossroads of all veins, and thus the menstrual blood can enter the man's bloodstream.[59] The main text of the *Secreta* warns both men and (for once) sensible women that sex with a menstruating woman is generally damaging to men; the commentary specifies that, for instance, men can contract leprosy and other incurable diseases in this way.[60] Seeing that he is covered in blood up to his navel after sex is certainly enough to frighten a young friend of the speaker.[61] Menstruation itself is referred to as a 'disease' or even 'cancer' in the *Secreta* as well as in the *Bartholomäus*.[62] The poisonous vapours that are emitted by menstrual blood also cause the pathological 'suffocation of the womb'.[63] But the prime threat of menstrual fluid is not an infection of the woman, but of the men and children around her.

The polluting properties of menstrual blood are expressed not just as disease-giving, but also in a striking image of contamination. The uterus is compared to a public toilet, into which all superfluities in the blood are dumped:

> Vnd darvmb spricht Auicena das die matrix Jn den frauen ist alls ein sprach hauß das enmitten Jn eynner stat steet da dy leutt auff gannd vnnd Jren stul habennd, also alle wberflussigkait des pluts dy uberal Jnn der Frauen leyb ist dy kompt Jn dy matrix Vnd wirt da gereyniget.[64]

> And therefore Avicenna says that the uterus in women is like a toilet that stands in the middle of a town and to which people go to defecate, just as all residues of the blood from all over the woman's body go to the uterus and are cleaned there.

Even the purging function that menstruation was often believed to have for women is here presented in an image not so much of cleaning as of defecation.[65]

Even more remote contact with this polluting substance can be dangerous. Merely speaking to a menstruating woman makes men's voices hoarse, through the transmission of pollution from her breath via the 'unclean' air to the victim.[66] The strong male voice that is being threatened here is elsewhere described as a characteristic that only men are born with: in the first cry of a newborn male baby.[67] The eyes are even more sensitive channels for emission and reception of menstrual blood. Menstruating women corrupt clear mirrors with their gaze, turning them into a bloody cloud, reddening them so that they have to be cleaned:

alls Aristotiles Sprichet yn dem puch von dem schlaff, weliche Fraw den selbigen flus hat Vnd zu der zeyth yn eyn Spiegell sicht der Selbige Spigell wirt geschaffen alls ein plutiger wolck. Vnd ist der Spiegel newe So kan man die rotung gar kaum auß dem spigell bringen. Jst aber der Spigell alt So kann man gar leichtiglichen die Rotung auß dem Spigell bringen.[68]

As Aristotle says in his book *On Sleep*, if a women has this [menstrual] flow and looks into a mirror during this time, this mirror becomes like a bloody cloud. And if the mirror is new, one can hardly remove the red staining from the mirror, but if it is old, one can easily remove it.

This sets up a neat contrast between the shiny new mirror and the dirty menstrual blood, again disturbed by the latter's seepage. It is a widespread belief, found not in Aristotle's treatise 'On Sleep', but in his 'On Dreams', as well as in Pliny's *Natural History*.[69] As I shall show in more detail below, menstrual blood coming out of the eyes can not only affect mirrors, but again also men and children directly.

The idea that women's blood pollutes men is by no means limited to medical or natural philosophical discourse. Even the female characters in romances are often far from idealized pure and harmless women. The famous blood-drops episode in Wolfram's *Parzival*, rich in multiple levels of meaning, for example, can interestingly be read as a variation on the topic of a woman's blood affecting a man through his eyes. One morning during his travels, Parzival is captivated by the sight of three blood drops in the snow, which are enough to remind him of the red cheeks and chin in the fashionably pale face of his wife Condwiramurs. So Parzival interprets the blood – that of a goose just wounded by a falcon – as a woman's blood not so much in the sense of having been emitted by a woman, but as embodying a woman. This blood makes him fall into a trance, in which he dreams of his wife, and which, like any visual impression according to Aristotelian theory of sight, must have been caused by material particles sent out by the blood and received by Parzival's eyes. The blood-drops in the image of Condwiramurs thus have apparently been able to hypnotize him in the way that, as we shall see below, menstrual blood also can. That this visual link is a physical union is suggested by formulations claiming that Condwiramurs had Parzival's heart and senses and he had her body during the trance.[70] He is affected to such an extent that he loses conscious control over his body; he does not think, speak or consciously defend himself during this time, despite being attacked and instinctively raising his weapons; when he finally wakes up as the blood-drops are covered, he cannot remember what happened or at first even who he is.[71] The narrator's descriptions confirm this – Parzival is 'unconscious'; 'Condwiramurs took his consciousness'; 'he lost his reason'.[72] The narrator presents the way in which Condwiramurs enthrals her husband explicitly as representative of women and of how their love harms and violates men.[73] Although this episode is now usually interpreted as a positive event for the protagonist and a sign of his true love, most recently and extensively by Joachim Bumke, it also conveys some of disconcerting aspects of women's blood that we are familiar with from other texts.[74]

The pollution through blood that is faced by Wigalois in Wirnt von Grafenberg's romance is also to a great extent mediated by women. When he shows that he is flawless enough to be an Arthurian knight right at the beginning of his quest, he does so by sitting on a magic stone 'clear as a mirror', which only virtuous people can touch.[75] Gawain cannot reach the magic pure stone because he laid hand on a woman against her will:

> eine maget wol getân
> die greif er über ir willen an,
> sô daz si weinde unde schrê.[76]

He seized a beautiful maiden against her will, so that she cried and screamed.

What is suggested by 'seizing a beautiful virgin' here is probably a deflowering rape. That, quite apart from the issue of consent, it is any heterosexual intercourse which pollutes in this way is evident in a parallel episode in the anonymous romance *Wigamur* (c.1250).[77] A very similar stone for testing virtue is described, which becomes dull if a woman who has lost her virginity looks at it, or a man who has been polluted through recent sexual intercourse with women. The fact that the clear, mirroring stone is reminiscent of the clear, mirroring surfaces that menstruating women were supposed to stain, and that a woman's first menstrual bleeding is often imagined as coinciding with defloration, as we shall see, suggests the contamination is again caused specifically by women's blood, polluting men during sex and seeping through one's eyes.

Women's bodies are sources for pollution throughout *Wigalois*. One of the four customary modes of exemplary Arthurian behaviour is not to speak to and bother ladies travelling on their own, thereby avoiding too close a contact with them.[78] Although the narrator divides womankind into physically and morally 'pure' women (*edel* or *reine wîp*), often compared to clear mirrors and distinguished from evil women (*übel wîp*), even the perfect, pure courtly ladies retain dangerous potential.[79] Pure Larie's close physical union with Wigalois – she is 'his heart's blood', he is 'like her body to her' and gives his heart, body and senses to her, since 'true marriage' is 'one body' – may have frightening undertones, especially since it is formulated in terms of a crime: she 'captures' his heart until he dies.[80] The description of Florie's perfect, pure body also still betrays fears of her destructive power: her mouth is depicted as so pretty that if she had killed a man's entire family and brought him near death, a kiss would make him forget all that.[81] Even the 'red knight' Hojir could be interpreted as having taken on some of the impurity of women's blood through too close contact with them: Wigalois finds him lying in his girlfriend's 'lap', and he has red hair and a red beard, as the narrator emphasizes.[82] While I have not been able to ascertain in German texts Jacquart and Thomasset's claim that red hair was believed to be caused by conception during menstruation, as we shall see, both hair and the colour red were associated with menstruation in the *Secreta*.[83] Unusually for romances, there are even several female characters who attempt to take Wigalois's life, always in particularly bloody situations: the wild woman Ruel; Japhite's female companions at Glois; the evil wife of the fisher; as well as Marrien, the hermaphroditic monster with the magic blood; and Queen Elamire's amazons, who kill several men in the bloody battle of Namur.[84] The threat that blood poses to Wigalois's physical purity and integrity, as we have seen, thus turns out to be in many ways specifically that of women.

First blood

Feminist scholars have observed that the conception of women as insufficiently bounded and polluting characterizes many areas of Western thought and still persists.[85] But any coherence of women's bodies which approximated that of men was feared at least as much as their boundlessness. 'Menstrous' women, to coin a term for women who were not believed to menstruate regularly, like virginal, post-menopausal and pregnant women, and to some extent also Jewish men, were imagined as somewhat more bounded than 'normal', menstruating women, but as a consequence only dreaded for leaking, and equalling and drying out men, in even more perilous ways.

Although admired as paragons of pure and secluded womanhood, virgins were at the same time feared as rivalling men in their boundedness. Their status as non-yet-penetrated and at the same time not-yet-leaking gave female virgins an integrity otherwise granted only to men. The gender hierarchy demanded that men penetrate women, but in medieval texts, female virgins could potentially not only turn out to be impenetrable, but also penetrate men. For example, the story 'Kaiser Lucius' Tochter', which I discussed in chapter 2, appears in this context as a fantasy of warding off the threat of the knight being penetrating not only by the burgher, but also by the virgin daughter of Emperor Lucius. The knight faces this danger of being physically intruded upon by the virgin in the first part of the tale, before their first intercourse and the subsequent dispute with the burgher over the pound of flesh. At this early stage of his attempts to have sex with the lady, the knight already loses control over his body and mind twice, when the maiden puts him to sleep against his will on two subsequent nights. His physical integrity is here not threatened through injury or partitioning, but through a loss of consciousness and motor control. This is caused by the external interference of the magic letter or bond that the lady had hidden in the bed. Both this magic piece of paper and the bond with the burgher are referred to as *brief* or *brieflin*, indicating that the powers they grant over the knight's body are similar. While the lady in her virgin state is actively in control of her embodied self – we hear about her beauty and her voluptuous body, and see her moving about, getting up, dressing herself and waking the knight – the knight's only action is to come to her and lie down. As soon as he is in the bed, he does not even move his head to look at her, as she sneeringly remarks, but falls unconscious straightaway.

Since the knight's collapse comes at the precise moment when he had intended to have sex with the lady, it entails mainly the loss of his potency, which was (and still is) primarily understood to be the ability to 'penetrate' a woman. Sexual intercourse is commonly defined above all as inserting a penis into a vagina, which is seen not so much as people or body parts touching each other, but as a penetration of one body by another: the man 'enters' the woman, she 'receives' him, so that he is 'inside' her. In other words, a man's bodily contour is considered to remain intact in penetrative intercourse, while a woman's is perceived to be broken up by the insertion of a foreign object. This applies in particular to defloration, which is usually defined as the first time that a penis enters a vagina, and was in the Middle Ages expected to be accompanied by blood-flow. A number of excellent recent studies have amply demonstrated how virgins were distinguished from women in their greater physical coherence, and have mentioned in passing to what extent virginity was defined through blood: a virgin was perceived as non-bleeding and non-leaking, therefore matching men in their integrity, coherence and strength.[86] Not only was defloration expected to be accompanied by the woman bleeding, but a virgin was also imagined as not even menstruating; menarche and defloration were perceived to fall together as the moment of the 'first blood' flowing from the girls. Again, the *Secreta* can furnish us with an example of how scientific thought associates the loss of virginity with the onset of menstruation in the claim that a woman can and should be deflowered as soon as she has her first menstruation: 'so each daughter is to be slept with when she has her first period'.[87] Similarly, the flow of menstrual blood (though here not necessarily of the woman's first menses) falls together with the blood of defloration in the following retrospective chastity test:

Vnd wan die Selben heutleyn die dy matrix an ir hat zuprechen ader zuprochenn werden mit des mans Rutten so verlewrt ein Junckfraw iren magtthum. Vnd so sie also zu dem ersten zustoret wirdt So kumbt ir der Fewcht gar Stercklich der do menstrum haist. Vnnd das ist auch das aller schirst zaichen, das aine ein Junckfrawe gewesen ist.[88]

And when the little skins of the uterus break or are broken by the man's penis, a virgin loses her virginity. And when she is broken in for the first time, she gets a strong flow of what is called menstruum. And this is the clearest sign that a female had been a virgin.

Virginity is imagined here again as a secret of women's bodies that men can reveal despite women's trickery, with the help of blood. The *Secreta* devotes a whole chapter to tests of virginity, which were an important and fraught topic in medical, religious and fictional literature, and often relied on blood as proof, as Kathleen Coyne Kelly has shown in *Performing Virginity and Testing Chastity in the Middle Ages*. These tests of virginity depend on the idea that a virgin's body was more enclosed, and that smells and substances did not pass through her unruptured body so easily, while other women were more like sieves in their lack of boundedness. The *Bartholomäus*, for example, recommends a humiliating test of virginity, where the woman is made to smell some burnt celery, and 'if she is not a virgin, she will wet herself'.[89] That virgins are imagined as enclosed is clear not only in their lack of leakage, but also in the conception of a hymen, a skin closing off the vagina until the first intercourse, as described in the above quotation. While medical opinions diverged as to whether this mysterious skin existed, it remained an important concept in the numerous medical and courtly texts discussed by Kelly.

This concept of sexual intercourse as penetration, and of virginity as an unpenetrated body is shared in many other areas. In 'Kaiser Lucius' Tochter', for example, virginity is thus not only a sexual category, but also a physical one, that of an unpenetrated body, and a cross-gendered one, that of an appropriation of the male role, as signalled by the emperor's daughter's appearance in the guise of a man. Not just in sexual terms, the ability to penetrate and make bleed and to grant impenetrability is here seen as the prerogative of a man, and in particular of a knight, but as never safe from appropriation by a virgin. That intercourse is understood as penetration becomes clear when the knight finally succeeds in having sex with the lady. While bleeding is not explicitly mentioned, their sexual congress is described in aggressive terms:

> der ritter do nit enlie,
> mit der maget er do rang
> als vil, biß er si doch bezwang,
> biß sin will ward gar vollbracht,
> als er im das hett erdaucht.
> er macht uß der magt ain wib.[90]

The knight didn't delay; he wrestled with the maid until he overcame her after all, until his will was done completely, as he had imagined it. He made a woman out of the girl.

The belligerent formulations and the fact that this is a defloration suggest that penetrative intercourse indeed takes place, and is seen as the man acting on the woman – he turns her from a virgin into a woman for good, while he remains unchanged.

There is thus a gender imbalance in this tale when it comes to physical integrity: men may penetrate women and shed their blood in sexual contact, while themselves remaining intact, and women are not allowed to penetrate others, but must be penetrable by men. Physical enclosure for women is in this way qualified. In fact, this imbalance extends beyond sexual roles, as this story only confirms a man's inviolability. While the general prohibition against mutilation and bloodshed would have applied to both genders, it is only ever discussed in terms of the knight. In all versions of the pound of flesh tale, it is a man whose bounded body is threatened by the forfeit, while it is often a woman for whom he takes this risk or who otherwise brings him into such danger.[91]

What happens at the beginning of 'Kaiser Lucius' Tochter' is a levelling out, if not an inversion, of this gender hierarchy of physical integrity. The knight loses his expected ability to penetrate the lady. Moreover, in so far as the hypnotizing influence of the letter is an infringement from the outside, the knight has even become permeable. The lady, on the other hand, is protected against sexual penetration, and even able to infiltrate the knight via the magic letter. So it is she, not the burgher, who first causes the threat to the physical boundedness of the knight. Not only does she hypnotize him, but her resistance also leads him to close the hazardous deal with the burgher in the first place, just as her later enthusiasm in bed makes him miss the deadline. Such forgetfulness as regards the time limit, incidentally, is again motivated less by plot logic – it seems unlikely that even the most amorous knight would have spent three full weeks in bed with the emperor's daughter without ever remembering the large debt that bought him such pleasures – than on another level by the need to develop the threat of mutilation, and by wanting to implicate the lady in this. The knight's failure to penetrate the lady coincides with the fact that she is a virgin. Moreover, as in *The Merchant of Venice*, the lady is of higher social status than the knight: she is the daughter of the mighty Roman emperor, 'of noble birth, of distinguished pedigree', while the knight is rather unkindly introduced as the emperor's 'servant', suggesting that he might not be an adequate husband for her.[92]

But this story advocates the idea that even the lowliest man has the right to penetrate the mightiest virgin, and remain impenetrable himself. The fact that the penetration fails twice on successive nights is not only a typical fairytale structure, but also shows that the lady's magic protection is an impossible, paralysed, infertile situation that cannot abide. The further plot of 'Kaiser Lucius' Tochter' can be read as a reinstatement of the gender hierarchy in terms of bodily boundedness. By drawing on the help of two other men – the burgher who lends him money, and the natural philosopher who unselfishly tells him about the letter – the knight is finally able to enter the woman physically at his third attempt. As soon as he becomes resistant to the interference of the lady's *brieflin*, he regains his potency, and the lady loses her integrity.

Her attempt at saving her own inviolability ultimately fails, whilst she later succeeds in a similar case in protecting the knight from being cut open. In both cases, a thousand guilders are exchanged; twice she pleads for mercy; twice she offers double the money back; twice she is told that not even a kingdom would make the man withdraw his initial demand; twice she argues with a technicality – first, that 'sleep with' does not entail 'having sex with', and that she has sold thus her time rather than her body or sexual favours; then that 'cutting out flesh' does not entail 'spilling blood'. But while she successfully argues against the extraction of the knight's flesh, she is unable to defend herself against his demands. While the knight's body cannot be commodified and entered, the woman's can. The *Märe* reassures male recipients that even the most sharp-witted lady is helpless against men's sexual penetration.

But neither the sexual subjugation of the lady, nor her subsequent voluntary submission as she begins to enjoy sex, nor even her offer to return the borrowed money when she finds out about the knight's predicament, are enough to reinstate completely the knight's physical integrity, for he is now threatened with penetration by another man, the burgher. Only when she dramatically affirms the knight's physical inviolability in the court scene is he fully protected again. The danger that comes from a woman who refuses to be penetrated and made to bleed is thus demonstratively tamed when she invokes the law against penetration and bloodshed.

The second step in the return to a normal gender hierarchy in terms of sexual integrity is her marriage. The social system demands that a virgin be traded between her father and her husband. The emperor's daughter had here refused to function within such an exchange by selling the right over her body and defloration herself and acting as an independent, coherent body rather than as part of her family's larger body, also imagined to be held together by a shared blood.[93] But later, as a lawyer, she returns to invoking the country's laws, which, since her father is the emperor, means appealing to his authority. More importantly, this is followed by her own submission to his rule, when she lets herself be given away by him:

> Darnauch mit grosser wirdikait
> der kaiser gab die schene maid
> dem ritter klug zu eewib.[94]

After that, with great dignity, the emperor gave the beautiful maiden to the clever knight as a wife.

The disembodied centre of this story of gendered exchanges is, in a way, the patriarch Lucius. As is typical for the *Gesta Romanorum* tales, the emperor is the only named character, and this 'name of the father' is a seemingly stable point of reference at the beginning. But Lucius' vanishes from the story after the initial name-check and is thus reduced to a shadowy figure, a name without a body, without a graspable contour or a speaking role. Nor can he control his daughter, the continuation of his genealogical body, whose individual exploits the story traces. When the emperor finally reappears as the father of the bride, the family's body is reintegrated and brought under control.

But this happy ending is more than slightly forced. The wedding could only have been 'very dignified' if the *frou* or *wib*, as she had been referred to throughout the second half, indeed had miraculously become a maid again, by somehow regaining her virginity. Indeed, the knight would have to have suddenly boosted his intelligence, too, in order to become 'clever'. It was in fact the lady who had just appeared as a 'clever knight' to those present at the court.[95] For all we know, she did not even have time to take off her men's clothes or let her hair grow back – she is certainly still in drag when the knight kisses her in the lines immediately preceding the wedding scene. The lady's appearance as a lawyer here usurps a male role again, like her initial sexual impenetrability had done. Not just in sexual terms, the ability to penetrate and make bleed and to grant impenetrability is here seen as the prerogative of a man, and in particular of a knight, but as never safe from appropriation by women. In the end, the emperor's daughter willingly takes off her man's outfit and returns to a secure social status as a wife. Nevertheless, as her lingering in male clothes might suggest, the woman who could outwit everyone and assume male authority without difficulty is only precariously tamed by marriage. So while 'Kaiser Lucius' Tochter' clearly transmits the comforting message that the male body cannot be cut into, this can only ever be a temporary security, rechallenged and reinstituted in the safe space of fiction every time this story was retold.

A similar uncomfortable fantasy of banishing the threat posed by an unpenetrated and non-bleeding virgin is rehearsed in the *Nibelungenlied* around one of the most famous secular virgin warriors, Brünhild. It here becomes clear that it is indeed her integral state itself that poses a danger to men. Brünhild's unpenetratedness includes her country as well as her body. As the Burgundians hear in 'reports coming across the Rhine', she is a 'queen residing across the ocean', in a fort on a far-away island across the fierce North Sea, which it takes the Burgundians a lot of effort and preparation to reach.[96] She is beautiful, but keeps her suitors at bay by forcing them to compete against her in a series of physical tests that emphasize spatial distance: long-jumping and throwing spears and stones as far as possible. If the suitor wins, he wins her hand too; if he loses, he dies. Of course, no suitor has been better than Brünhild and they have all been killed. But as is usual in the *Nibelungenlied*, as we have seen in chapter 2, this attempt at becoming impenetrable ultimately only encourages penetration, and so the description of Brünhild's unattainability is enough to make Gunther want to woo her. That her impenetrability is related to her virginity is demonstrated when both end at once in the wedding bed, where Siegfried has substituted Gunther in order to tame her. The fight is set up as a battle of the sexes, when Siegfried claims that male dominance over all women is at stake:

> 'Owê', gedâhte der recke,   'sol ich nu mînen lîp
> von einer magt verliesen,   sô mugen elliu wîp
> her nâch immer mêre   tragen gelpfen muot
> gegen îr manne,   diu ez sus nimmer getuot.'[97]

'Alas', the hero thought, 'if I lose my life at the hands of a maiden now, all women who would otherwise never have done so will feel superior to their men.'

This thought of the normal gender roles gives him the strength to finally put Brünhild in her place, but at first it looks as if Brünhild is going to retain the upper hand, when she makes Siegfried bleed as she had done in the suitor's test and as normally a man should make a virgin bleed on their wedding night: she squeezes Siegfried's hand so hard that the blood flows from under his fingernails.[98] Although we are told that Siegfried does not have sex with her, he makes Brünhild lose her supernatural impenetrability and takes the tokens normally associated with a defloration, the ring and the girdle, which are later used by Kriemhild to make the never unambiguously refuted claim that Siegfried had deflowered Brünhild. This struggle thus comes very close to being another penetrative, bloody, deflowering and disempowering rape.[99]

Evil eyes, dragons and old women

Impenetrable and therefore potentially penetrating bodies are not only ascribed to virgins and men. In some *Mären* or short stories, married women are, like Emperor Lucius' daughter, able to cross-dress and gain the potential to defend men's inviolability, and to make bleed and remain impenetrable. In 'Beringer', as soon as a woman dresses up in armour, she has the power to make her husband bleed in combat.[100] Similarly, when in Dietrich von der Glezze's 'Der Borte' a wife puts on a suit of armour that has been hardened in dragon's blood, she becomes impervious to attacks.[101] But in many discourses, 'old' women in particular are seen to rival and potentially penetrate men's bodily integrity. The *Secreta mulierum*, for instance, defines old age in terms of physical integrity when it explains that young women's bodies are more permeable to thunderbolts than those of old women:

Wann sie habend kleine dunne lochlein durch iren leyb gan Vnd dy alten frauen haben der locher nit vnd darvmb so mag der doner Jn den Jungen Frauen mere geschaden wann den altten.[102]

For they [the young women] have small thin pores through their body, and the old women do not have these holes, and therefore thunder can harm young women more than old ones.

Aside from a lack of these imagined 'holes', the greater impenetrability of older women is also again described in terms of blood, when 'old' is understood to mean post-menopausal in the following outrageous claim:

Auch ist zu wißsenn vnd vleyssig mut vnd Sinn zw empfelhen das dy altten frauen dy also Jr zeytt habenn geladen Vnd auch ander frauen den ir menstrum frisch ist, So Sy ir kind an sehen So sie Jn der wigenn ligend, dy vergifften dy kinndt Alls albertus magnus spricht yn dem buch von dem Samen der frauen vnd von der vnrain matery dy da menstrum haist.[103]

It should be noted and kept in mind that the old women who thus have retained their period, and also other women whose menstrual fluid is fresh, poison the children when they are looking at their children lying in the cradle, as Albertus Magnus says in his book *On the Seed of Women and on the Unclean Matter Called Menstruum.*

It is unclear whether 'women whose menstrual fluid is fresh' refers to women whose menstrual period has just started in their life-cycle, after a pregnancy, or in their monthly cycle, or indeed to old women who still have menstrual bleedings; but post-menopausal women are clearly singled out for blame here. That these mature women do not bleed regularly anymore is not interpreted as a lessening of the dangers that they pose to men and children, but instead only means that they retain the poisonous menstrual blood in them until it will eventually seep out to even more polluting effect than normal menstruation. Such a retention of poison is also ascribed to the 'venomous virgin' in the legends of Alexander the Great, a girl who had been fed on poison from childhood to become resistant to it, but so poisonous herself that she would be lethal for anyone else to touch.[104] The *Secreta* tells us that all older women have even wider-reaching toxic effects through their retained menstrual blood: they kill children by merely looking at them with their evil eye. This is explained by the fact that their menstrual blood seeps out through the sweat holes in the women's eyes, affects the air that surrounds every subject, and then enters the children, even as they lie in the presumed safety of their cradles.[105] This is in accordance with Aristotelian theories of vision, and related to the belief that menstruating women can stain mirrors by looking at them. Interestingly, poor women are also identified as particularly polluting here, since they eat 'coarser' food and thus have less well-processed blood with more residues.[106] Like the age factor, such a consideration of wealth connects social hierarchies to those of bodily integrity.

Such vile accusations of 'menstrous' pollution – that is, pollution caused by menstrual blood shed in other ways than the monthly period – against old and poor women flowered in the fifteenth and sixteenth centuries and contributed to the idea of the witch.[107] The Dominican inquisitors Jakob Sprenger and Heinrich Institoris, in their famous witch-hunting manual *Malleus maleficarum* (1487), ascribe an evil eye to old and poor women, and compare this to the polluting effect of menstrual blood, a link that the authors seem to have borrowed from the *Secreta*.[108] The *strigae*, night-flying women of classical mythology, who were in some ways predecessors of witches, were believed to have the evil eye that kills children in their cradles, too.[109] But 'menstrous' women, that is, non-menstruating women nevertheless discharging menstrual blood, shared their polluting powers not only with witches, but also with monsters, in particular dragons.

The *Malleus maleficarum* further compares the witches' evil eye to that of the basilisk, a fabulous snake-like creature with a lethally poisonous gaze well known in ancient and medieval scientific works, Pliny's *Natural History* and Isidore of Seville's (d. 636) *Etymologies*.[110] In some Latin versions of the *Secreta*, the way in which a menstruating woman will stain a mirror is also likened to the basilisk's gaze. A 1538 version has: 'Et illo modo basiliscus inficit uidentem ipsum, quia uenenum emittit. Et si poneretur speculum, ad quod reuerberarentur humores ad locum basilisci, tunc ipsemet moriretur, uel inficeretur.'[111] Helen Rodnite Lemay translates from the corresponding passage in the commentary to a copy printed in Lyons in 1580: 'in the same way, a lizard is infected by seeing himself, because he emits poison. If you take a looking glass, which will reflect the humours back to the place where the lizard is, he will be killed or infected by them.'[112] Pliny and Isidore also mention the basilisk's poisonous breath and smell, its ability to scorch grass and the powers of its blood, known as Saturn's blood, which makes potions and prayers effective; all features characteristic of 'menstrous' women as well. Wigalois fights a basilisk, Pfetan, who does not have the evil eye, but poisonous breath described as foul-smelling enough to kill a whole army. Its red eyes might indicate that the polluting blood has risen to them, it is covered in scales, its rooster's comb is reminiscent of the crown that a basilisk is ascribed by Pliny, as well as of the belief, put forward, for instance, in the *Prose Salernitan Questions*, that a basilisk is born of a rooster's egg.[113] The sign of Wigalois's opponent Roaz, painted on his shield and adorning the top of his helmet, is the dragon, which was often conflated with basilisks, snakes, worms and lizards, all known most commonly as *wurm* in German.[114] Women introduce the threat of the basilisk, as every fight Wigalois engages in is motivated by a lady who either demands that Wigalois help her or is the reward for his actions.

Even the opponents in Der Stricker's *Daniel* share the evil eye of the basilisk and of menstruating women: the hypnotic gaze of the blood-bather and the Medusa-head of the bloodsuckers that kills with its gaze. Against the Medusa-head, Daniel employs the same technique of reflecting back the venom with a mirror that is recommended by the *Secreta* against a basilisk, as well as by some Spanish natural philosophical treatises against the evil eye of menstruating women, and also of course used in classical literature by Perseus against Medusa herself.[115] As in *Wigalois*, Daniel is indirectly endangered through women. The ladies of the Dull Mountain, the Bright Fountain and the Green Meadow all bring him into mortal danger by begging him to free their countries.[116] Against genre conventions, they have to persuade him to help in long, humiliating pleas, or even physically entrap him. At the Bright Fountain, it is highlighted that only men (Daniel and the Countess's husband) are actually at risk from the bloodsuckers, whereas the women (the Countess and her forty maids) are presented at a point when they are already safe. Daniel shows no interest in serving a lady or finding a wife, and only helps because he feels obliged to do so.[117] The conception of women as dangerous in their desires is confirmed by allusions to men who fell under the sway of prototypical evil and demanding women from the Bible, Samson and Solomon; the request for a beheading might even hint at Herod.[118]

The common threat that post-menopausal women and these basilisk-like monsters are imagined to pose is to rival men in their claims to physical enclosure, impenetrability and potential to thereby penetrate others in extraordinary ways with their poisonous bodily fluids. Unbroken and non-bleeding virgins, post-menopausal women in the *Secreta* without pores and not emitting blood, Daniel's hardened opponents and scaly and near-impregnable dragons all have in common their enclosed skin and physical contours. Their poisonous blood is thus channelled in dangerous ways through their eyes or mouth, in the evil eye or poisonous breath shared by 'menstrous' women, dragons and the blood-bather and bloodsuckers. In Konrad von Würzburg's 'Silvester', for example, St Sylvester faces a dragon enclosed in a hole in a mountain, which it cannot leave, in the same way that menstrual blood would be enclosed in the body. The monster comes up to the entrance of the cave and kills small children with its poisonous breath, just as the menstrual blood locked in post-menopausal women's bodies emits vapours that poison small children. An allusion to the menstrual cycle is also created by the fact that sorcerers bring sacrifices and food to this dragon every four weeks.[119] Sylvester overcomes the monster by locking it deep into the mountain and leaving the keys inside the earth, thus containing the source of the pollution for good.[120] Moreover, the dragon fought by St George also shares characteristics with 'menstrous' women. As Samantha Riches has observed, a significant strand of pictorial representations identifies the dragon as female through breasts, mounds and depressions in the genital area or the addition of young; and in at least one case, a painting by the German artist Leonard Beck, *St George Fighting with the Dragon* (c.1515; Fig. 5), the female dragon bleeds from between the legs in an irregular 'menstrous flow'.[121] Here, the defeated dragon in the bottom right corner of the image is feminized, according to Riches, because of the vulva-like hollow in its tail, its position on its back as if at the bottom of a sexual act, and its accompanying youngster. St George is

5 Leonard Beck, *St George Fighting with the Dragon* (*c.*1515), Vienna, Kunsthistorisches Museum. By permission.

ready to strike the final sword-blow, but has already pierced the dragon's throat with his lance and cut into the back of her neck, and the blood from those wounds has run down her body. A second stream of blood, however, flows from an invisible source between her legs, either from the navel area or from the inside of her left leg. It is thus a blood-flow from the genital area, but not directly from the vulva-like mound and orifice below the legs – not a regular menstrual bleeding, but another unusual release of more powerful long-retained poisonous blood from inside the hardened body.

In Alexander Barclay's *Life of St George* (1515), such a female dragon is linked with 'menstrous' women again in so far as it is physically hardened and instead penetrating others with poisonous blood. The text describes at length the creature's iron-hard scaly skin, almost impenetrable even to a Hercules:

> Upon hyr wynges and on hyr backe on hye
> were grene roughe scalys lyke yren of hardnes
> if Hercules for all his hardynes
> with bylle or clubbe had ron this dragon to
> he shulde forsoth haue founde ynough to do.[122]

This impermeable monster's womb is not only as insatiable as menstrual blood makes any woman's, as we shall see in the *Secreta*, but also wreaks precisely the kind of havoc on nature that Pliny ascribed to menstrual pollution in the list quoted above:[123]

> Hyr wombe infectyt inuenymyd the grounde
> that herbes and gras were brent and wexed drye
> the corne and flowers where she had passed nye
> decayed fadynge and hangynge downe theyr hede
> unto the grounde as blastyd faynt and dede.[124]

The withering of crops and plants from the womb had been blamed on menstrual blood since Pliny, so that the dragon here poses precisely the dangers that women are feared to cause with their menstrual blood: impenetrability and poisonous attacks.

Medieval zoology and fiction also knew related creatures who were half-dragon, half-woman, such as mermaids, sirens, the serpent that seduced Adam and Eve, and famously the fairy Melusine, as described in Jean d'Arras's *Roman de Mélusine* (1393) as well as in Thüring von

Ringoltingen's German *Melusine* (1456).[125] Melusine's lower half turns
into a snake every Saturday, when she hides from her husband in her
bath. The folklorist Claude Gaignebet has influentially proposed that
Melusine's weekly secret bathing is akin to a purification from
menstrual pollution, and thus marks Melusine as a menstruating,
venomous figure.[126] I suggest instead that it characterizes her as not
menstruating, not only because she is frequently cleansed rather than
tainted, but also because of her impregnable dragon's tail, which Thüring
lovingly describes in this way:

> Aber von dem nabel hinab do was sy ein grosser langer veÿntlicher vnd
> vngehewrei wurmcs schwancz von ploer lasur mit weisser silberin varbe.
> vnd darunder silberin troepfflin gesprenget vnder eÿnander. als dann ein
> schlang gemeingklich gestalt ist.[127]

> But from the navel down she was a big, long, threatening and monstrous
> dragon's tail, of blue colouring with a white-silverish hue, and speckled
> with interspersed silver dots, like a serpent commonly appears.

This serpent-like skin begins at the navel, so that there should be no
room for a vagina or other orifice in the lower half of her body from
which blood could be emitted. This smooth enclosure is evident in many
pictorial representations, too, where Melusine has a scaly tail without any
openings from the waist down.[128] In a manuscript of Thüring's version,
for example (Fig. 6), Melusine is shown sitting in the bath in her locked
room, as her husband Raymond, who has just sent his brother riding
away, attempts to peek inside. Her scaly, unruptured tail is clearly
displayed, floating above the water and even the opening in the wall.
She is thus impenetrable, and cannot emit anything. The dangers that
Melusine poses lie not in her menstrual bleeding, but precisely in her
unusual degree of integrity that threatens men's monopoly on boundedness. Many critics have pointed out the phallic, hardened nature of her
lower half, and her assumption of the traditional male role of founding
a dynasty, towns and churches.[129] She also usurps the male role of
guaranteeing the coherence of the genealogical body, which we shall
discuss in more detail in the next chapter.

There is, however, a monstrous or shadowy disruption of this physical
integrity of the family. In the revelation in the bath scene, what is
clearly uncovered is her hidden monstrous nature, that Melusine is not
a normal human, not 'of Christian blood', as Raymond had believed.

6 Raymond sees Melusine in the bath (1471). Basle, University Library, MS 0.I.18, fol. 35r. By permission.

This also calls into doubt the human nature of her children, each of which had been physically marked with a monstrous tooth, eye, or other mark.[130] Similarly, as regards Melusine's own body, a possibility for a genital source of an unusual bleeding is left open, because Melusine holds her hand over her genital region, a hand which here has been painted over and coloured in as part of the tail, but is more clearly covering her lap in other images. This hand might or might not be covering what might or might not be an opening. An interesting comparison can be made with Uccello's *Profanation of the Host*, discussed above in chapter 1, which similarly features a secret body visible to the viewer behind a cut-off wall, while a small hole in the wall gives away its secret to an armed knight breaking in from the outside. In contrast to Uccello's profuse stream of blood, there is no blood to be seen in Melusine's body and house. Whether she has extraordinary bleedings or is fully enclosed, she is a threat because she does not bleed regularly, and therefore has claims to male-gendered impregnability.

Bloodsucking

Some of these 'menstrous' monsters penetrate their male victims' bodily boundaries not only by infecting them with poisonous matter seeping out through unnatural channels, but also by sucking out their blood. Such precursors of our modern vampires have rarely been acknowledged in histories of these monsters.[131] Daniel von dem Blühenden Tal's belly-less antagonists, for example, suck blood to sustain themselves from the people they have killed with the Medusa-head. The fact that they do not imbibe the blood, but keep it in their mouths and spit it back out, highlights their impermeability, while their victims are pierced as well as ossified. In the Dietrich epics, young dragons that live in a cave in a mountain like those in the Sylvester legend also suck out King Ortnit's blood, even through his armour. This gruesome episode is summarized, for instance, by Seburk in the *Eckenlied*:

> ain wurm in slaffend zainer zit
> vant vor aines staines wende,
> der truok in in den holen berk
> und lait in für die jungen:
> die sugen in durch das werk.[132]

A dragon once found him sleeping in front of a rock-face and carried him
into the hollow mountain and laid him before its young, who sucked him
through the armour.

That it is predominantly blood that the dragons suck out is suggested
when their mother presents them with a lion, and they explicitly 'suck
the blood out of him up to the bone'.[133] Like the monsters and 'menstrous'
women, they thus manage to penetrate a man even through his strong
armour; but rather than injecting poison into him, they drain him of the
fluid essential to his survival. The fact that Ortnit falls into a paralysed
sleep beforehand, which allows the old dragon to carry off his unconscious
body, creates another parallel to the 'menstrous' women and monsters
with their hypnotizing evil eye.[134]

In medical thought, too, women are believed to suck out men's most
refined and heated blood, semen, in sexual intercourse. A gendered
economy of blood is constructed, where semen is men's life-blood, of
which they have only a limited amount. Women, too cold to produce
this precious liquid themselves, rob men of it through conception in
order to strengthen themselves. The embryo is presented as a way in
which women participate in this precious substance: as an extension of
the father's seed, that is, a part of the man that is absorbed into the
hostile mother's body. This life-threatening extraction of semen during
conception is described in the *Secreta*, from the perspective of the male
partner, as being sucked:

> Das ander zaichen ist, wan der man dy frawen helst ist dan das er entpfindt
> das ym sein zagell gezogen vnd gedonnet wirtt von ainer beschlissung vnd
> von aynner preß Recht alls ain kind ein tutlein saugt Vnd den Tutten
> Zeucht Also So der zagell gezogen wirtt von der muntzen der frauen.[135]

> The other sign [of conception] is, when the man embraces the woman, that
> he then feels that his penis is being pulled and squeezed by an enclosure
> and a press, just as a child sucks a little breast and pulls at the breast, so the
> penis is being pulled by the woman's vagina.

The choice of the term 'sucking' to describe how women drain men's
vitality expresses the force of female desire and her greed and hunger for
semen, but it also turns sexual intercourse into bloodsucking. Sucking semen
is here directly compared to drinking breast-milk, both processed forms of
blood. It is thus not so much a sexual act as a cannibalistic act of drinking,
like the bloodsucking of the dragons and of the belly-less monsters.

That it is indeed semen that is being sucked out here like breast-milk
is clarified when semen is described as one of the substances from which
women benefit in sexual intercourse:

aber das helssen ist den frauenn nutz vnd gesund Vnd von des helssenns
wegen werden die frauen gesterckt vnd wirt Jn die naturlich hitze gemertt
vmb das bewegen das der man auff ir thut So er die frauen helst Vnd auch
von des Samens wegen.[136]

But sex is useful and healthy for women; and women are strengthened by
sex; and their natural heat is increased by the man's movement on top of
the woman when he sleeps with her, and also by the semen.

While women profit from men's heat, emanating from his energetic
movements and from semen, men are usually left drained by sexual
intercourse. Frequent sex weakens men to such an extent that it shortens
their life. This is why they usually die earlier than women, although, as
the superior gender, they would of course normally live longer:

Vnd darvmb der Same der furpasser außgelassenn von den mannen kompt
der macht den leybe darauß er kombt durr. Wann der Sam der hat ein
krafftt feucht zumachen vnd warm. Wann aber der leybe durr wirtt vnd die
feuchtigkaitt auß dem leybe getzogen wirt, So wirtt ain krannckhait des
leybs vnd des lebenns. vnd also stirbt der mensch. Vnd das ist die sache das
die nicht lanng leben vnd schir sterbenn die vil vnd vast vnkeuschaitt
treybenn . . . Wann es ist gemainglichen war das dy man ains lengern
lebens wern dan dy Frawen Wern sie nit alls unkeusch. Wann das leben hat
sein wesenn Jnn hitze vnd feuchtigkait wurtzlichen.[137]

And thus the seed, being further ejected by the men, drains the body from
which it is discharged, for the seed has the power to make moist and warm.
But when the body dries up and the moisture is extracted from the body,
there occurs an illness of body and life, and thus the human being dies.
And this is why those do not live long and die early who often and
vigorously fornicate . . . for it is generally true that men would live longer
than women if they were not so unchaste, for the essence of life is rooted in
heat and moisture.

Semen is thus clearly presented as a precious good that is siphoned off
by women, and sex as women's bloodsucking that deprives men of this
life-giving fluid.

It is menstrual blood itself that causes women's cravings for sex and semen. Young women want sex because it allows them to purge themselves from an excess of menstrual matter:

> Wann dy selben Jungenn Frauen habent vil von einer sollichn matery So begern sie auch vast zuhelsen Von der uberflussigkait wegen der selben matery.[138]

> When these young women have much of this [menstrual] matter, they very much want to have sex, because of the excess of this matter.

Women's desire for sex and semen is again believed to be particularly strong in women who do not menstruate regularly. The *Secreta* gives the example of pregnant women, who cannot discharge their menstrual fluid (here referred to as matter rather than seed), which thus builds up in the body and increases their appetite for sex:

> Auch ist zuwissen das die frauen begiriger Sind bey den mannen zu schlafen So sie mit kinden gehent. Vnd das ist darvmb das ains yetlichn tags von essen Vnnd von drincken wirt ein matery. Vnd die Selb matery muß von den Frauen gan So Sie bey den mannen liegent Vnd das ist von wberflussigkait der Selben matery die do kombt von essen vnd von drincken. Vnnd darvmb so die selbig matery nit von den Frauen geht So sie eins kinds Schwanger wirt ader ist vnd alle tag gemert wirth so wirt die fraw yn unkeuschait entzundt. vnd wirt sie die matery Jucken das Sie muß begern bey den mannen zu liegen.[139]

> One should also know that women are keener to sleep with men when they are with child. And this is because every day, matter is produced from food and drink. And this matter is emitted from women when they sleep with men, and this is due to the superfluity of this matter made from food and drink. And because this matter is not expelled from women when she is or becomes pregnant, and is added to on a daily basis, the woman is incited to lewdness. And the matter will itch her so that she will desire to sleep with men.

Retained menstrual blood not only causes expectant mothers to want sex, but also changes their appetite and gives them cravings for strange food:

> Darvmb belangt ein frau mancherley Speys dy mit aynnem kind gat Wann zu der selben zeytt So wirt den frauen der mag vergifft mit vergifftigen

feuchtigkaitten Darvmb das der frauen Same verschlossen ist Jn der muter
leybe bey dem magen.[140]

This is why a woman who is with child has many kinds of food cravings,
because during this time, the women's stomach is poisoned by venomous
fluids, because the women's seed is enclosed in the mother's body near the
stomach.

The venomous menstrual blood, locked into her body, seeps into the
stomach, contaminates it and thus makes it crave certain kinds of food.
This applies not only to expectant mothers, but also to all menstruating
women, whom it stops wanting normal food.[141] This is not dangerous
to men in itself, except when women are unable to obtain what they
crave, which can often lead to men's offspring dying in the womb amidst a
renewed flow of menstrual blood. But one of the objects of their cravings
can again be men's body parts, as described in a warning example:

ains mals ains pauers weyb mit aynnem kind ging vnd die belanget sere vnd
gar fast nach des pauren hoden dy hett sie gern geessen vnd wart sie also
sere darnach belangen das ir nicht anders was, mochten ir dy hoden nit
werden zu essenn So must sie sterben. Vnd doch mochten Jr dy hoden
nicht werden vnd darvmb wartt ir we vnd vil Jn grosse kranckhait.
Darvmb soll man frembde speys nit nennen . . . der man nit gehaben mag
So die frauen mit kinden gand.[142]

Once upon a time, a farmer's wife was with child, and she very much and
very strongly desired the farmer's testicles, which she would have liked to
eat, and began to desire them so much that she felt nothing but that, if the
testicles could not be hers to eat, then she would die. And yet the testicles
could not become hers and she suffered because of this and fell very ill.
This is why, when women are pregnant, one should not mention strange
food . . . which one cannot get hold of.

To the pregnant woman are ascribed cannibalistic appetites for her
partner's testicles, as food, not as a sexual object. Testicles were believed
to be the site where the precious fluid was processed that only men can
produce, semen, which seems again to be the main target of women's
cravings.[143] So blood is both the cause of women's desires, in the form
of menstrual blood, and the object of those desires, in the refined form
of semen. Women are construed as wanting to suck out men, to drain
them through drinking their blood.

The blood-drinking and bloodsucking that has so often been observed in female mystics, most prominently by Caroline Walker Bynum, can usefully be seen in this context not as a radically new form of devotion to Christ's humanity, but as a perpetuation and revaluation of the idea of women as bloodsuckers.[144] In Mechthild's *Fließendes Licht*, for instance, the soul drinks Mary's milk and Jesus's blood:

> Do stuonden offen beide sine wunden und ir bruste; die wunden gussen, die bruste vlussen, also das lebendig wart die sele und gar gesunt, do er den blanken roten win gos in iren roten munt.[145]

> Both his [Christ's] wounds and her [Mary's] breasts stood open; the wounds gushed; the breasts poured so that the soul became alive and completely healthy, when he poured the bright red wine into her red mouth.

By presenting the feminized soul as drinking a life-giving fluid directly from the wound of her male sexual partner, the text invokes the image of bloodsucking familiar from works like the *Secreta* and *Daniel*. But here, the woman does not aggressively suck out the man, rather both the male and the female character deliberately give suck: both Mary and Jesus offer their blood freely. Unlike the men in the *Secreta*, unwilling to share their limited resources of semen, God and Mary seem to draw on an endless supply of fluid, which paradoxically increases when consumed.[146] The use of wine as a synonym for blood here, as in the eucharist, moves the image of bloodsucking even further away from a physical draining of men towards a normal drinking.[147] The female soul's desire is also reciprocated: God's growing lust is mentioned in this chapter; and their mutual yearning is a main theme throughout the *Fließendes Licht*; in fact, God has only created her out of his desire to be loved back.[148] Consequently, in another episode, the gender relations of female sucker and male victim are inverted: it is the soul here whose heart is sucked by Jesus.[149] In this text, then, a female character's desire for a man's blood is not seen as a threatening encroachment, but as reciprocated by his desire for the woman as well as his urge to give. Crucially, it is also no less than a way of becoming one with God – a complete revaluation of bloodsucking from a base attack on men to a divine union. The *Fließendes Licht* similarly reinterprets the gaze and its reflection in the mirror that in the *Secreta* and *Daniel* was a sign of one-sided threatening desire: the gaze is a way no longer just to desire, but actually to see, to understand, to reach God; and the mirror is a means to connect rather than destroy through reflection. Both looking and reflecting are now reciprocal actions, with the soul looking at God and acting as his mirror, and vice versa: the *gegenblik*, the 'returned gaze' of God makes the soul shine and approach God further.[150] Like sucking and giving suck, both are again felt to be predominantly blissful by their bearers, not one-sided wishes perceived by the male side as threats. By presenting the female soul in this way as a bloodsucker, Mechthild thus perpetuates this particular conception of femininity, as well as modifying its gendered imbalance and revaluing it as a mystical way of reaching God.

As well as women and monsters, sinners and, again, Jews were accused of bloodsucking. It was particularly greed and economic exploitation that was condemned as a form of bloodsucking in the image later made famous by Karl Marx. The thirteenth-century *Heilige Regel*, for example, promises an adequate punishment in hell to those who suck the blood of the poor:

> Alle di hie arme nagent und schindent und in ir blut uz sugent und di nit und haz dragent und ir ebencristen verraten, di sulen billichen her nach di heillesschen vurme nagen und pinichen und alle ir gelider durch slifen.[151]

> All those who gnaw on and exploit the poor and suck out their blood and who carry hatred and envy in their hearts and betray their fellow Christians shall justly be gnawed by the hellish dragons hereafter and all their limbs be ground.

Jews were also often accused of usury and in particular economic 'blood-sucking'. Hans Folz (d. 1513) in 'Jüdischer Wucher' claims that Jews 'suck and milk the poor Christians' blood and sweat like blood-hounds'; and in his 'Hausratbüchlein', that the householder who has to borrow from a Jew against a usurious interest is so tormented that 'if a bear sucked each of his hands, so that the blood sprang from the nails, he would feel better'.[152]

The Virgin Mary

In the *Fließendes Licht*'s rewriting of bloodsucking, the gender imbalance is also upset in another way: women as well as men now suck other women's blood, in particular in the processed form of breast-milk, as in the above quotation. Although not as important in the *Fließendes*

Licht as in male-authored devotional texts, Mary is here the most important, near-divine provider of blood. The soul, gendered female, desires Mary and her bodily fluids when she tells Mary that she and all Christians will see Mary's milk and breasts in immeasurable lust, and similarly when she envisages seeing the lust-inducing breasts naked on Judgement Day.[153] The emphasis is again on the liberal provision of blood, rather than its hostile extraction. In one version of the history of the world, for instance, Mary's fluids supersede those of Christ; her breastfeeding introduces, frames and dwarfs Christ's bleeding. She breastfeeds the prophets and sages even before her birth, in the period of the Old Testament, where God is disgusted by humankind and does not bleed or care for it.[154] She also seems to be even more driven to share her milk than Jesus to share his blood, since her breasts (unlike Jesus's wounds) would hurt if they did not pour.[155] Mary's breastfeeding and Christ's bleeding are again paralleled later, when Mary is seen to the left of God the Father's throne, milk flowing from her bare breasts, and Jesus to the right, 'with open wounds, bloody, not bandaged', and when, in another chapter, Christ explains how his redemptive blood comes from God's grace 'just like the milk which I sucked from my virgin mother'.[156]

But other medieval representations of Mary and blood were more sinister. The suspicion and fear with which virgins were met in medieval writing despite their ostensible idealization colours even depictions of the Virgin Mary to an astonishing and almost completely overlooked extent. Even the one woman usually exempt from the condemnation of all her sex was tainted by menstrual blood, impenetrable, aggressive and even cannibalistic towards men. Mary was paradigmatically imagined as a flawlessly pure virgin, physically and sexually bounded and un-penetrated. The enclosed garden and the closed door mentioned in the Song of Song and Ezekiel respectively were in medieval exegesis habitually interpreted as images for Mary's chaste body, which was presumed not to bleed, in particular not to menstruate.[157] On the other hand, Mary was still a woman, and therefore by definition impure, and penetrable in the conception through the Holy Spirit, in giving birth and in breast-feeding. This tension between her boundedness and her permeability posed considerable theological challenges, which Charles T. Wood has traced in 'The doctors' dilemma'.

Many of the vernacular praises sung to Mary make no attempts at papering over the contradictions inherent in her status as an impene-trable woman. The *Heilige Regel*, for instance, represents Mary's body superficially as pure and enclosed, without wounds or openings, not exceeding its limits or being entered into. Her eyes are not the sexually desirous, evil eyes of women that we have encountered above, but represent chastity.[158] As is common in medieval literature, her virginity, which implies a lack of penetration, is dwelt upon as one of her main features.[159] Unlike many other devotional texts, the *Regel* does not even mention her breast-feeding, which would mean the emission of a bodily fluid. As in the romances, maintenance of distinct physical boundaries is perceived as purity.[160] Nevertheless, this pure integral body has some cracks: Mary's body is presented as partitioned, not as a coherent whole. Her body parts are the text's main structural device: the *Heilige Regel* is divided into eight sections, each corresponding to a body part of the Virgin Mary and dealing with the virtues associated with them. Mary's ears, for example, are 'full of obedience', her nose 'full of understanding' and her mouth 'full of prayer'; obedience, understanding and readiness to pray are then described, praised and illustrated in each section. But the initially hierarchized order of parts – from top to bottom: eyes, ears, nose, mouth, hands and feet – slips to comprise the more general categories of 'body and soul', 'heart' and finally 'soul'.[161] Her last 'part', a praise of her soul, fizzles out into a long section on the angelic choirs, before the text breaks off. So even this partitioned body dissolves into the soul, the text and finally nothing. Moreover, Mary is not explicitly exempted from either the menstrual leakage (cited as a sign of abject impurity: 'Isaiah: "All our justice becomes filthier before God's judgement than any cloth of women's disease"'), or the aggressive sexual openness described as innate to her sex, endangering the integrity of the usual exemplary men, like David, Solomon and Samson:[162]

Swi junc ein wip si, swi ald si si, swi na si dir si, swi heilic si si, nicht ein wez ire ze heimelich.[163]

However young a woman may be, however old she may be, however close she may be to you, however holy she may be – nothing would be too intimate for her.

In the *Hohes Lied*, Mary's physical borders are as problematic as in the *Heilige Regel*. She has to retain her bodily integrity as well as remain open, this time for believers' prayers and requests, as well as for God's words; her ears, for example, are described as open rings, so that she can receive the angel's message.[164] Mary also needs to open up physically in order to give out food, advice, requests or comfort to her son and to the Church: her navel, for instance, is a chalice, endlessly providing sustaining drink to the whole world.[165] On the other hand, Mary must maintain her bounded integrity, especially her feminine purity. Her lips must be sewn up so that she can keep the angel's words in her heart after having received them.[166] Mary's belly is shut with seals like a book, and like an enclosed garden and closed gate, or like the chaste and pure elephant.[167] Such closure is also a sign of her courtliness and manners: the lips should be a door lock in front of the teeth, as the narrator 'heard from a courtly child'; open mouths are, according to a popular saying, a jester's bag that had better be closed, Brun claims.[168] Her body functions not just as an individual entity, but also as a protective layer for others: her belly is a castle for knights and a house for God; she is a watchful eye, protecting us from pain; a gate and a cover.[169] If some of these images, like her lips being sewn together or her belly sealed imply great violence being done to Mary, she is also feared to injure and penetrate others, as are Brünhild and Emperor Lucius' virgin daughter. In a sermon, the preacher Bernardino of Siena (1380–1444) describes Mary as violating and injuring God:

> Una mulier hebraea fecit invasionem in domo Regis aeterni; una puella, nescio quibus blanditiis, nescio quibus cautelis, nescio quibus violentiis, seduxit, decepit et, ut ita dicam, vulneravit et rapuit divinum cor, et Dei sapientiam circumvenit. Propterea conqueritur Dominus de beata Virgine dicens, Cant. 4, 9: *Vulnerasti cor meum, soror mea sponsa, vulnerasti cor meum.*[170]

> One Hebrew woman invaded the house of the Eternal King; one girl, with I do not know what caresses and promises and violations, seduced, deceived, and I might even say wounded and ravished God's heart, and overthrew God's wisdom. Therefore the Lord complains about the Blessed Virgin as he says in Cant. 4: 9: 'You have wounded my heart, my sister, my wife, you have wounded my heart.'

Bernardino does not shy away from ascribing to the Virgin the rape and injury of her lover, God, a potential for violence much too strong for modern tastes and thus often ignored or reinterpreted. Diane Spivey Ellington, for example, takes her effort to explain away such disturbingly violent imagery so far as to drop from her translation of the above passage the most awkward expressions, *nescio quibus violentiis* and *rapuit divinum cor*. But these images do fit in with the uneasiness about the penetrative potential of even the most perfect virgin.

In some passages of the *Hohes Lied*, Mary is even ascribed the blood-sucking and man-eating tendencies of some 'menstrous' women. In the context of the interpretation of the verse 'thy teeth as flocks of sheep' from the Song of Songs, her teeth are not only compared to sheep, but also to the teeth of the Devil, of carnivorous animals and of cannibalistic humans.[171] While this happens only in order to distinguish her teeth from the others, these odd comparisons nevertheless create an uncomfortable association between them. Mary is also implicitly presented as cannibalistic when her attraction of sinners seeking comfort is likened to how a whale supposedly sends out a sweet smell from its wide-open mouth to attract fish whenever it is hungry.[172] While the smell is elaborated on, it remains unexplained why a whale intending to take life should be an appropriate image for Mary's life-giving redemption. She is even associated with a thirst for blood in Brun's interpretation of the verse 'thy nose is as the tower of Solomon, that looketh toward Damascus'.[173] In an almost burlesque passage, the text explains that Mary answered Archangel Gabriel's Annunciation with her nose. This is because her nose signifies understanding (as it did in the *Heilige Regel*), which is compared to how the Devil understood in advance that God was about to be born. We can assume that Mary's understanding is here meant to be contrasted with rather than likened to that of the Devil, however, this is not made explicit. That her nose is a tower turned towards Damascus is further glossed by explaining that Damascus means 'bloodthirsty like the Devil':

> din nase ist gestellet so
> als ein torm gebowet ho
> und der sich habe gekart
> hin kegen Damaske wart.
> Damaskus der name ist nicht gut,
> her spricht zu duze durstende blut
> und bezeichent uns den tubel,
> vorswege ichz daz were ubel,
> der do menschenblut durstende is,
> daz ist der tubel daz ist gewis.[174]

Your [Mary's] nose is formed like a high-rising tower, which has turned towards the guardhouse of Damascus. Damascus – this name is not good, it means 'blood-thirsty' in German, and denotes the Devil for us – it would be evil if I were to remain silent about this – he who is thirsty for human blood is the Devil, that is for sure.

The fact that Mary's nose faces Damascus presumably serves defensive purposes, like the tower of a fortress, rather than showing sympathy. But again, this is not made clear, and the association between Mary and the bloodthirsty place remains. The matter is quickly brushed aside without the summary that normally ends each interpretation of a particular line of the Song of Songs. Moreover, the Devil's thirst for blood is likened to the blood-drinking of another prototypical virgin mother:

> in der stat Damaske sundir not
> irsluc Kain Abel tot.
> do verlos di erde ir magetum
> und trank menschlich blut sunder rum.
> durch daz heizet zu duze alsus
> als ich gesaget han Damaskus.[175]

In the town of Damascus, Cain deliberately slew Abel. Thus the earth lost her virginity and ingloriously drank human blood. This is why Damascus means in German what I said it means.

In contrast to texts like *Parzival*, where this episode is presented as Cain polluting his virgin ancestor, the earth, who is innocent except in so far as her inescapable expanse makes it impossible for Cain not to soil her, the formulation here suggests that the earth is actively and shamelessly drinking. In fact, if *Damaskus* means 'the bloodthirsty Devil', and part of the explanation of this etymology is that at Damascus, the earth drank blood, it seems as if the earth is analogous to the Devil here. In any case, not Mary, but a second virgin mother is conspicuously accused of drinking blood here. The motif of the earth swallowing Cain's blood appears frequently in medieval religious writing, often precisely in the context of the earth being a virgin mother to Adam, who is formed out of her. Konrad von Würzburg's 'Silvester', for instance, uses the Old Testamentarian precedent of the earth as virgin mother as an argument against the Jewish disbelief in the possibility of a virgin birth of Christ.[176] Even if Mary is meant to be a purer counterpart to the first, blood-drinking virgin mother, it is nevertheless uncomfortable that her closest prefiguration from the Old Testament should be so tainted.

Even when Mary emits rather than drinks fluids, when she exudes breast-milk, honey and oil for the comfort of Christ and for Christendom, as well as for mediating Jesus's redeeming and cleansing blood, this can turn into violent, bloody images.[177] For example, her breast-feeding is a result of bloody aggression when she is portrayed as a stone of stability, whose breasts are split by our wailing, so that grace and comfort flow out, like the diamond is split by a he-goat's blood.[178] Mary's mediation of her own child's flesh and blood as food is another instance of a brutalization of her maternal supply of bodily fluids:

> si git uns ouch vor hunger sat
> eres liben kindes vleisch ezzen
> vor den dorst hat si uns gemezzen
> eris kindes minniclichez blut
> daz uns git riches trostes sput.[179]

She also gives us her dear child's flesh to eat, in order to still our hunger; against thirst, she has poured us her child's lovely blood, which gives us the blessing of much comfort.

What is portrayed as a maternal, nourishing gesture towards Christendom – she gives her collective children to eat and to drink as a comfort – is also the cannibalistic distribution of the dead flesh of her son. His description as her 'lovely child' adds to the sense of his humanity and vulnerability and draws attention to the brutality of distributing this real human blood. The Virgin Mary's exchange of blood with others thus appears no less fraught with fear than that of any other virgin who has retained her menstrual fluid and will strive for men's pure blood as well as emitting dangerous blood in various ways.

Pliny had concluded in his long list of curiosities in the *Natural History*: 'but nothing could easily be found that is more remarkable [*monstrificum*] than the monthly flux of women'.[180] It should have become evident that there is a strong connection between menstrual blood and monstrosity, between the dragons, basilisks and belly-less creatures and the menstruating or 'menstrous' women whose blood has very similar effects, chiefly pollution and bloodsucking. An excess of menstrual blood as the mother's contribution to the foetus, moreover, causes the deformity that is female gender and is also one of the common explanations for 'monstrous births' quoted in the *Secreta mulierum*.[181] Even menstrual blood itself has been described as monstrous, because of its singular status as matter without form.[182] *Menstrum*, menstrual blood, is often written by scribes as *monstrum*, monster. Several manuscripts of the *Secreta mulierum*, for instance, include a Latin heading to the section on the question 'through which place [the vagina or the anus] menstrual fluids flow': *per quem locum fluant menstrua* or similar. Manuscript J, however, after a convoluted excursus on how much human females resemble animals, has the corrupted *per quem locum fluant monstruum*.[183] This monstrous fluid serves to mark out one gender – as well as Jews – as abnormal. It not only leaks out of incoherent women's, monsters' and Jews' bodies, but it also drives women to attack men, to eat them and to deprive them of their own precious blood by sucking it out and drinking it, while men's blood not only makes a boy in conception, not only defines what a male body is and keeps it together, but also makes it a target for women's attacks. The next chapter will consider how Jews' and women's monstrous bloodsucking and blood-pollution threatens not just the individual, but also the social body.

4

Bloodlines

In this chapter, Our Lady is likened to a pure body, of which all spiritual children shall be members; and the head of this body is Jesus Christ, God's son from heaven.

(Heilige Regel)

Blood relations

This chapter treats social bodies, groups of people imagined as an organic unit. 'The body can stand for any bounded system', Mary Douglas had claimed, as a 'symbol for society'.[1] Ernst Kantorowicz's classic study *The King's Two Bodies* has shown how the body was indeed used to represent society in the medieval and Renaissance concept of the 'body politic', most famously formulated in John of Salisbury's *Policraticus* (1159), which envisages the state as a body, and each part of the body as a social group or office: the prince is the head, the senate the heart, the feet the peasants and so on.[2] Kantorowicz traces this idea back to the patristic understanding of the Church as Christ's body, a collective unit comprising all believers. At the same time as being the Church and its head, Christ's body was of course also that of an individual human being and that of the eucharistic host. Of those interlinked functions, the complex idea of Christ as a collective body has received the least scholarly attention, and it is the one on which this chapter will be focusing, with particular emphasis on the essential role of blood in fashioning this body. The fact that other social groups were also imagined as a body, such as the family, the court and Mary's admirers, has been even more neglected, and I shall draw attention to those and to their constitution through blood as well.

Families, for example, were often conceptualized as one body. Vernacular German laws, such as the *Sachsenspiegel* (*c.*1220–35) and the *Schwabenspiegel* explain the concept of kinship through the body: man and wife are the head of the collective body, the children the shoulders, the grandchildren the elbows, great-grandchildren the wrists, the fifth generation is the base segment of the finger, the sixth the middle segment and the seventh and last the top segment.[3] Crucially, the social body of the clan is by no means merely an analogy to the individual body, as scholarship indebted to Kantorowicz and Douglas assumes, but held together by blood in the same way that an individual body is. In both Latin and German, 'blood relations' or 'to be of one blood' were commonly used to describe kinship in the sense of vertical lineage as well as of horizontal relatedness. For instance, the Second Lateran Council (1139) refers to lineage as blood, when it clarifies that 'ecclesiastical honours depend not on blood relationships (*sanguinis*) but on merit'; in Dietrich von der Glezze's 'Der Borte', relatives are of the 'family blood' (*sippe bluot*); Parzival and his brother Feirefiz as well as his cousin Ither are 'one blood' (*ein bluot*); and Mary and Christ are declared to be 'one flesh and one blood' (*ein fleihz vn ein blvt*) in the 'Rheinfränkische Himmelfahrt Mariae'.[4] While the idea of 'blood relations' continues to be used today as a metaphor for genetic relatives, it was much more than that in the Middle Ages. Just as blood was imagined as suffusing and uniting the individual body, so it was envisaged as connecting the members of a social body, as blood was actually believed to be passed on from parents to children and shared between members of a family. Isidore of Seville in his *Etymologies*, for example, argues that blood relations are called *consanguinis* precisely because they are 'of the same blood' in this way:

> Consanguinei vocati eo quod ex uno sanguine, id est ex uno patris semine nati sunt. Nam semen viri spuma est sanguinis ad instar aquae in scopulos conlisae, quae spumam candidam facit, vel sicut vinum nigrum, quod in calice agitatum spumam albentem reddit.[5]

> Blood relatives are so called because they are born of one blood, that is, of one father's seed. For the seed of the man is the foam of blood, like water which batters the rocks and creates a white foam, or also like red wine, which becomes a whitish foam when stirred in a chalice.

The blood of the father, battered into semen, is not just metaphorically shared by all members of a kinship group. In the same way that any organ or area suffused by the same blood was defined as belonging to an individual body, so people sharing the same blood were defined as part of the same social body. Social bodies defined in this way faced the same problems of distinguishing themselves from the outside and maintaining inner coherence as individual bodies did. If the human body was supposed to work together as a unit separate from the exterior, the family was expected to stand together against outsiders and to cooperate internally as well, and certainly never shed the blood of their own. But interestingly, in vernacular literature, the concept of relatives as united by a common blood is often invoked precisely when the ties that bind are violated, whenever the taboos against violence or disloyalty are broken. In Hans Folz's 'Adam und Eva', for example, Cain is referred to as Adam and Eve's 'own flesh and blood' only when Eve asks Adam to kill this 'worm' that has crawled out of her belly.[6] The wife in 'Der Borte' invokes her husband's 'clan's blood' at the precise moment when she welcomes an outsider into her house with whom she later commits adultery. A more extensive treatment of this link between the blood of kinship and the blood of violence is found in Wolfram's *Parzival*, which presents kinship as a key organizing principle of the fictional society. Almost every character in this romance belongs to one of two big clans: the Arthurian or the grail clan. As Walter Delabar has shown, an elaborate system of rules guides the behaviour of the clan members towards each other, the most important of which are that relatives are supposed to aid each other (*helfe-Gebot*) as well as not harm each other.[7] In both cases when relatives are referred to as 'one blood', the context is Parzival's violent attacks against his kinsmen. When Parzival reveals to Trevrizent that he has killed and robbed Ither in combat, Trevrizent declares the murder of his distant cousin a sin, and formulates the relationship between Parzival and Ither thus:

> wiltu für got die schulde tragn,
> sît daz ir bêde wârt ein bluot,
> ob got dâ reht gerihte tuot,
> sô giltet im dîn eigen leben.[8]

If you were to bring your sin before God, and if God were to judge it justly, he would take your life for it, because you were both one blood.

The text is thus constructed in such a way that this common blood is mentioned only in the context of a transgression against it. On the second occasion, the narrator similarly speaks of Parzival and his brother Feirefiz as 'one blood' only while deploring the fight between them that fails to respect this bond.[9] Parzival's sins are thus presented as offences against family members, and against the loyalty expected within a clan, even more so than against divine or courtly rules. This is also true for what Trevrizent considers to be Parzival's other sin: unintentionally killing his mother. Moreover, the original sin is also redefined as an offence against relatives, not as Adam and Eve eating the apple, but as Cain killing his brother as well as deflowering the earth, his grand-mother, as quoted in chapter 2.[10] Commenting on Cain's sin, Trevrizent highlights the kinship aspect by describing all humans as Adam's and God's children:

> von Adâmes künne
> huop sich riwe und wünne,
> sît er uns sippe lougent niht,
> den ieslîch engel ob im siht,
> unt daz diu sippe ist sünden wagen,
> sô daz wir sünde müezen tragen.[11]

From Adam's kin came regret and joy, because he whom every angel looks up to does not deny his kinship with us, and because kinship is the vehicle of sin, so that we have to carry sin.

The kinship with Adam brought all humankind both sorrow and pleasure, as everybody is held accountable for Cain's original sin, as well as able to claim family bonds to God himself.[12] Because of everyone's family ties to God and each other, Cain's sin, like all others, offends the rules of his father, God, and harms his offspring as well as being a transgression against his brother and grandmother; every sin is in this logic a sin against a relative. Indeed, for Parzival, any violence is violence against a relative, since not only is everybody related in the family of humans, but his opponents are also for the most part members of his maternal or paternal clans. The concept of blood-relations is thus inextricably linked to inevitable offences against them, just as the individual body in much medieval writing was always already under threat, too.

The idea of humankind as one large group of blood-relations was quite common. The narrator of the *Fließendes Licht*, for example, speaks of all human beings inheriting Adam and Eve's blood after the Fall as well.[13] The Church, with its ambition to encompass all humankind, was also perceived as one body united by a common blood, in so far as it was believed to be born from the water and blood flowing from Christ's side. This was Augustine of Hippo's (354–430) seminal interpretation of the Gospel verse which reports that the soldier later identified as Longinus pierced the dead Christ's side on the cross, so that blood and water flowed: just as Eve had been made out of Adam's side, now the Church flowed out of Christ's side.[14] At the Council of Vienne in 1311–12, this belief was formulated, making it even more explicit that the Church had been directly formed out of Christ's blood when he became flesh:

> Et quod in hac assumpta natura ipsum Dei Verbum pro omnium operanda salute non solum affigi cruci et in ea mori voluit, sed etiam, emisso iam spiritu, perforari lancea sustinuit latus suum, ut exinde profluentibus undis aquae et sanguinis formaretur unica et immaculate ac virgo sancta mater ecclesia, coniunx Christi, sicut de latere primi hominis soporati Eva sibi in coniugium est formata.[15]

> And that in this assumed nature the Word of God willed for the salvation of all not only to be nailed to the cross and to die on it, but also, having already breathed forth his spirit, permitted his side to be pierced by a lance, so that from the outflowing water and blood there might be formed the one, immaculate, and holy virginal mother Church, the bride of Christ, as from the side of the first man in his sleep Eve was fashioned as his wife.

Christ's bleeding here not only proves that he had truly become flesh, as discussed in chapter 1, but also makes the Church into a clan formed from the same blood of their forefather. While this is not a regular conception from the father's semen, it is clear that Christ's blood and water is what Christendom is made of. The idea of every Christian partaking in Christ's blood as a family member was also popular in vernacular German literature. In the *Hohes Lied*, the creation of Christendom from Christ's side is described in careful terms very similar to the Latin exegesis:

> als uz Adams slafende site
> Eva wart gemachet in dem paradise,
> glicher wis, jach mir ein wise,
> wart uz gotes site, so man seit,
> gemachet di heilige kristenheit;

do her an dem vronen cruze slif,
uz siner zesewen siten lif
wazzer und blut beide.[16]

Just as Eve was made in paradise from the sleeping Adam's side, so – as a
wise man told me – holy Christendom was made from God's side, it is said,
when he slept at the cross of the passion and from his right side ran both
blood and water.

The *Heilige Regel* uses the same idea to interpret a passage from Genesis
as foreshadowing this creation of the Church in a slightly confused image
that brings into play the blood of the mother as well as of the father:

Ein lant heizet Evilat und fluzet ein floz van dem paradise in daz lant. van
deme lande kumet daz beste gold. Evilat bedudet di martile di di vrowen
lident so si ir kint gebert, und di martile bezeichent daz unser herre mit
grozer qualen und mit grozer martele unz gebar an dem cruce, und daz rote
gold bezeichent daz rote blut daz er durch unz gezen wolde.[17]

A country is called Evilat; and a river flows from paradise into this country.
From this country stems the best gold. 'Evilat' means the martyrdom which
women suffer when they give birth to their children, and this pain signifies
that our Lord bore us with great suffering and great martyrdom on the cross;
and the red gold signifies the red blood that he shed for us.

Just as the best gold comes from Evilat, a stream of blood comes from
Christ, who gives birth to 'us', that is Christendom, amidst this blood-
flow. The Church here appears to be not so much made from the father's
blood like a child in conception, but born from Christ acting like a
mother. In any case, the Church is imagined as one large body, directly
stemming from Christ's body and sharing his blood just as any individual
body would be suffused by the same blood.

Blood-sacrifice

Caroline Walker Bynum has influentially argued that Christ's bleeding
made him a feminine, maternal figure in the eyes of medieval Christians.
With reference to numerous representations similar to the birth imagery
from the *Heilige Regel* just discussed, and in particular to images of the

blood streaming from the wound in Christ's side turning into eucharistic wine, she maintains that, in much of medieval devotion Christ's blood was seen as a nourishing eucharistic blood, feeding Christians like a mother would with her milk.[18] But as we have seen, there is an entire tradition of thought in medical, religious and courtly discourses in which women's bleeding was anything but productive and nourishing, and very much feared rather than welcomed. In fact, any nourishing value of women's blood was largely limited to breast-milk, but even this whitened blood was not without dangers for the infant. As mentioned, theologians saw women's bleeding as Eve's punishment for the Fall, a guilty, polluting bleeding which was never completely revalued, not even in the most idealized women's bleeding, that of Mary's breast-feeding. Aside from the fact that women's bleeding was highly ambiguous, Bynum neglects the whole sphere of men's bleeding that is heroic, controlled and public rather than nourishing or polluting, as Peggy McCracken has shown.[19] Christ's blood is much closer to this man's bleeding than to women's: it is sacrificial. According to McCracken, a fighter's blood is the basic currency in proving his prowess, gaining power and winning a lady. It is always public, shed in heroic fights in front of everyone, and relies on their witness function. It can also be sacrificed for a higher good, such as that of carrying out God's will. While the emphasis for most fighters might be on survival and inflicting harm on others, and for Christ and martyrs on passive suffering, both result in blood being used as a public value and potential sacrifice.

In a unique history of the world as a history of blood, Mechthild von Magdeburg summarizes this. While both admirers and critics often describe the *Fließendes Licht* as unsystematic in a way allegedly typical of women's writing, as a whole, it presents one of the clearest and most seamless accounts of salvation history in German, which clarifies Christian ideas of sin, redemption and blood. In the beginning, according to the *Fließendes Licht*, God created humankind as a bride, an object for his *minne*.[20] Humankind, however, acquired sinful blood in the Fall.[21] Throughout the time covered by the Old Testament, humankind (personified as a bride) remained in this bloody, sinful state, making her repulsive to God. Christ then volunteered to wash her clean, to redeem her of her sins – with his own blood. In the discussion with God the Father and the Holy Spirit preceding his incarnation, Christ begs:

Wiltu mir dinen segen geben, ich wil gerne die bluetigen menscheit an mich nemen und ich wil des menschen wunden salben mit dem bluote miner unschulde.[22]

If you give me your blessing, I will gladly take bloody humanity upon me and anoint the human's wound with the blood of my innocence.

After permission is granted, Christ indeed shed his blood for humanity on the cross, but this was only the beginning of his redemptive task.[23] At the time of writing, humankind continues to be sinful and bloody, and Jesus thus continues to bleed for his bride.[24] His followers, including martyrs and virgins, join his redemptive bleeding.[25] This bleeding will go on until the end of the world, including the reign of the Antichrist that constitutes the last phase before Judgement Day. On that day, Jesus's and innocent Christians' blood is weighed (presumably against sin).[26] After that, in paradise, Jesus's wounds will heal, his blood will stop flowing; and the resurrected will be freed of their sinful blood.[27] In hell and purgatory, on the other hand, the sinners will continue to bleed.[28]

How precisely the central sacrifice of God's son, who became human only to die for the sins of all Christians and then was resurrected, works, is expressed in a plethora of metaphors in the Christian tradition: healing and washing with blood, as we have just seen in the *Fließendes Licht*, or nourishing and giving life with it, as Bynum highlights. These are all just different aspects of this concept, for which an exchange or purchase, as in Mechthild's image of weighing, is perhaps the best – and least studied – analogy. Sacrifice is based on the logic that an offence causing suffering can be made good or paid for by the offending party's own suffering – a tit-for-tat, somewhat sadistic logic underlying medieval penal systems and the idea of blood revenge, too.[29] This applies not just to interpersonal relationships, but also to the relationships between the individual and society, and between the individual and God. Substitution, such as that of the life of an animal for one's own life, is also possible. The self-sacrifice of an innocent person produces an excess of atonement that can be transferred on to other people. Jesus's self-sacrifice theoretically produced such an excess of atonement that all Christians can be freed from their sins. (However, this also means that every person is in God's debt before ever having committed an offence, as formulated in the concept of original sin.) So this means that Christ's self-sacrifice is the equivalent of, redeems from and pays for the bad deeds of all Christians. Extending this concept of substitution, Christ is able to atone for all of

Christendom. Christ's sacrifice in medieval Christian contexts is always paradigmatically imagined as bloodshed, as one blood paying for the other.[30] The main medium of sacrifice was blood even in ancient Greek, Roman and Hebrew traditions.[31] The fact that redemption through Christ's blood is stressed in holy scripture as well granted some longevity to this idea. But this notion continues to be used and elaborated so enthusiastically in medieval thought, and was not interpreted away as a mere symbol, because it makes sense within the medieval ideas of social and individual bodies being generated and held together by blood.

The conception of Christ's body therefore differs from that of other male characters in two main points: first, he embraces bleeding in an act of self-sacrifice and thus revalues it. More than secular heroes, for whom being made to bleed is the ultimate danger, Christ embraces vilified blood and sin, and volunteers to give his blood. His consent is one of the prerequisites that make his death into a self-sacrifice; and this changes the meaning of blood to him. To him, blood is not primarily a threat, but an opportunity; the emphasis is much more on its positive effects than on the crisis. Second, Christ's body is not just his own, but also the collective body of his followers. This is thus another way in which the social body of Christendom is constituted through blood: because Christendom is the economic equivalent of Christ's blood, and because blood is traded between Christ and Christians, thereby connecting them like blood in veins would. Christ is imagined as buying us from his father with his blood. Here, the body is constituted as a monetary object of exchange, bounded because of its economic value, and partaking in Christ's blood because it is somehow equivalent to it in the economy of grace. Because Christ can pay for Christendom with his body and blood, Christendom is equivalent to his body and blood. Sacrificing one's blood for others is thus a way in which connections between individuals are created through blood.

By the Middle Ages, the Christian core belief that blood atones had been broadened to include not just Jesus's, but also martyrs' blood, and then asceticism and finally the suffering of a religious person in general, so that Christians could create social communities with their own blood, too.[32] In the *Fließendes Licht*, the blood of martyrs is valued; and martyrdom includes non-physical suffering.[33] The narrator even uses the language of martyrdom for her own experiences: she claims to be captured with John the Baptist, crucified with Peter, stoned with St Stephen, grilled with St Lawrence and so on.[34] She experiences an ordeal that closely resembles the passion of Christ, in which at one point her side is pierced so that instruction flows from it as, elsewhere in this text, instruction flows from Christ's blood.[35] She bleeds with great redemptive effects, too, and her bleeding for others creates blood-relations like those between a mother and children. For instance, she saves her 'children' as she 'bleeds' and 'ails' for them: looking at the first one, the sinners, 'with a bloody heart', she obtains God's forgiveness for them; the second one, the souls in purgatory, drink her 'heart's blood', while she suffers 'motherly pain' for them.[36] Like God, she desires and embraces these chances to redeem by bleeding and crying, which thus appear as a gift rather than a threat.[37]

Martyrdom and sacrifice are not the only ways in which blood creates physical connections between characters. In one of the earlier chapters, martyr's blood is explicitly represented as inferior to the mystical union between the soul and God, one of the lesser alternatives offered by the senses, but turned down by the soul, who wants to 'cool down' in bed with God instead:

'In der marterer bluote moegent ir uch sere kuelen.' 'Ich bin gemartert so manigen tag, das ich dar nu nit komen mag.'[38]

'You could cool down a lot in the blood of the martyrs.' 'I have been martyred so many a day that I do not want to go there now.'

The narrator's and God's blood instead become one: 'Lord, your blood and mine are one, without spot'.[39] Further bloody metaphors for the *unio* include Christ's blood having flown through the narrator's soul; the soul's love for God consuming her flesh and blood, but this purifying her and drawing her to God; and his blood colouring her feet.[40] By inversion, the absence of God is described strikingly as drying up her blood: 'when my flesh escapes me, my blood dries up, my bones freeze, my veins contract and my heart melts for your love'.[41]

Trading blood

This idea of exchanging one person's blood for a new community of people, of binding Christendom together in the shared blood of Christ, is central to the understanding of redemption in German devotional writing. Not only did Christ shed his redemptive blood for human sins, but this exchange is still ongoing: all Christians receive his blood and are thereby bound together in this body, besides, they pay him back with their own blood and bodily fluids, thus giving as well as receiving blood. This trade is often measured in business-like detail. On one occasion in the *Fließendes Licht*, for example, the soul's tears save precisely a thousand souls.[42] The *Heilige Regel* can serve as a more extensive example of the tendency to measure blood sacrifice, as it admonishes:

Mensche, wi geistlich du bist, wi heilic du sist, du enbeweinest daz blut Gotez, du mustez anderz anme jungesten dage umb einen iglichen drophen rede irgeben.[43]

Human, even if you are a cleric, and however holy you may be, if you do not cry over the blood of God, you will have to account for every single drop in the Last Judgement.

Christ's blood here has its appropriate equivalent in the tears of the believers shed in contemplation. How many teardrops one has to cry over Christ's blood is not specified, but the fact that every teardrop not shed for Christ has to be accounted for suggests a relationship of debt and payment. This is reminiscent of the way Christ's blood itself is measured and likened to a legal tender in which debts can be settled, 'the currency of his holy blood', in the words of the *Heilige Regel*.[44] Not to participate in this economy of redemption, to waste and spill his blood, is presented as one of the harmful effects of deadly sins: 'the second sin: that humans spill and spoil the holy blood that Our Lord would shed for all sinners'.[45] This economic calculation and tit-for-tat, drop-for-drop accountancy is a typical aspect of medieval spirituality. It works within the logic of inversion described by Bynum, which predicts the exact reversal of values in heaven, where the first shall be the last. As the *Heilige Regel* puts it:

So der mensche ie hoher ist, so demutige sich, stat an der schrift. Uberhebez du dich, du vellest; niderst du dich, du wirst irhohet.[46]

The higher the human is, the humbler he should be, scripture says. If you are haughty, you will fall; if you are humble, you will be elevated.

In keeping with this reversal, our suffering with and for Christ's blood on earth will bring joy in the afterlife, the *Heilige Regel* states:

Unser herre sprichet in dem ewangelio: 'Selic sint di di nu weinen und troric sint. si sulen her na lachen unde ewige vrowede haben'.[47]

Our Lord says in the Gospel: 'Blessed are those who are crying and sad now, they shall laugh and have eternal bliss hereafter'.

Every tear shed here presumably saves one from having to be shed in purgatory. This inversion, with suffering becoming joy, applies not just to Christians contemplating Christ's blood, but also to martyrs shedding their own blood. When St Elizabeth of Thuringia is beaten by her confessor until she bleeds, she proportionately climbs three angelic choirs closer to heaven.[48] Even metaphors that suggest the immeasurability of divine grace in his blood-sacrifice, such as that just one drop of Christ's blood would have sufficed to save the world, depend on such exact amounts:

Sente Gregorius sprichet, zu der irlosunge aller der werlte so were genuoc gewesen mit eime drophen blutez daz unser herre gezen wolde durch unz. darumbe gap er sin vile, daz di minne und di dugende dez geberez schiber wurde an dem uberfluze der gaben.[49]

St Gregory says that one drop which Our Lord would have shed for us would have been enough for the redemption of the whole world. He gave many of them in order that the love and the virtue of the donor would be evident from the abundance of gifts.

God's grace here is apparent precisely in the numerical abundance of his blood-drops.

That the idea of God's son paying for Christians with his blood and body was not seen as an entirely unproblematic exchange despite the smooth rhetoric is most evident in the way in which trading with blood and body was vilified in other contexts. An important component of 'Kaiser Lucius' Tochter' and several other variants of the pound of flesh tale, for example, is that the trading of the flesh is criticized, not the bloodshed as such. It is not an absolute prohibition against bloodshed that is invoked to prevent the mutilation, but rather the need for reciprocation, the idea of talion. The argument goes that the taking of the knight's flesh is not forbidden as such, but it will have to be paid for by an equivalent amount of flesh and blood from the burgher (despite the fact that he had already 'paid for' it with the thousand guilders).

Even in those versions of the story in which a direct prohibition of bloodshed is cited, there is often an element of calculated trade, of tit-for-tat in the prescribed punishment of an equivalent mutilation.[50] The commercial exchanges of the plot – a night with the lady against a thousand guilders; a thousand guilders against the bond in blood; the bond against the pound of flesh – thus find their indisputable end in the inviolability of the person. This is not only a rebuke to a commodity fetishism that treats money as if it really had equal value of flesh, and to bourgeois mercantilism, but it is also explicitly linked to Christ's sacrifice in the *Cursor mundi*, where the forfeit of flesh story is inserted into the story of the finding of Christ's cross. That the connection between these two plots is the affirmation of the integrity of the body even as it is traded is evident when the narrator compares the crucified Christ to a ransom. 'from the cross God bought the lives of our souls; he gave himself to ransom on it'.[51] That Christ buys Christian souls with his body or blood is a commodification and trade of the body not dissimilar to the one attempted by the burgher, and potentially just as threatening to Christ's physical integrity. The reaffirmation of bodily coherence provided by the pound of flesh tale might have made the idea of Christ suffering and dying in order to buy Christian souls more palatable. It also highlights that God makes the impossible possible: the trading of a body and blood actually takes place here, and yet, Christ's body remains whole.

Christ's blood is not only traded against Christians' sins, but also against thirty pieces of silver, by Judas – a deal similarly condemned, and strikingly often related to contemporary trading in the same way that Jesus's exchange of blood and tears with Christians is still deemed to be ongoing. *Christi Hort*, a narration of the New Testament, puts it this way:

> um driezic phennige verchouft er dich, suezer Christ.
> owe, was noch Judas ist,
> die dienen liechnamen unt din pluet
> verchaufent dicke um minner guet.[52]

He sold you, sweet Christ, for thirty pence. Alas, how many Judasses are still here, who often sell your body and your blood for lesser goods.

Christ's sacrificial trading of blood is not only linked to, and contrasted with, that of Judas, but also with blood-revenge. Although dependent

on voluntary submission, the concept of blood-sacrifice is based on the
same brutal logic as blood-revenge – that blood can pay for guilt, that
suffering can make good aggression. That Christ's death can in this way
be understood as a violent act is made clear, for example, in the *Hohes
Lied*. Christ's teeth are described as a harmless sheep's teeth, but are
then said to be sharp enough for the angry sheep to bite the Devil and
hellfire, turning the meek lamb into a raging predator out to kill:

> wie senftmutig ditz schaf si
> im wonet doch ein zorn na bi,
> sin zan hat einen scharfen sliz
> iz beiz dem tode einen biz
> daz her iz nimmer vorwant.
> sin biz zubizet den hellebrant.[53]

However meek this sheep may be, it has a quick temper; its tooth has a
sharp edge; it bites Death with such a bite that Death never recovered. Its
bite destroys hellfire.

While the link of death and biting was often made because these terms
were thought to be etymologically related, this here suggests the
connection between sacrificial death and violence.[54] In terms of blood,
the two are uncomfortably linked in the widespread idea that Christ's
blood needs to be avenged on the Jews, who are collectively held
responsible for spilling it. This is mentioned, for instance, in the version
of the apocryphal gospel of Nicodemus in *Christi Hort*, where Jesus
appears 'with bloody wounds' to Emperor Nero in a vision, and asks
him to tell Vespasian to avenge his blood on the Jews: 'he shall avenge
my blood on the Jews; he will be rewarded'.[55] The criticism of a blood-
trade in the pound of flesh plot similarly has anti-Semitic aspects.
Shylock's Jewishness is a prominent feature in *The Merchant of Venice*
and several earlier versions. In 'Kaiser Lucius' Tochter', the burgher's
religion is not mentioned; in fact, we do not even know if he is a
merchant (*mercator* is consistently translated as *burger*). But anti-Jewish
literature had long associated Jews with money-lending and Faustian
pacts. James Shapiro has suggested that the fear of having a pound of
flesh cut off by a Jew represents the dread of conversion, of becoming a
Jew by being circumcised, which was associated with being castrated
and feminized.[56] But it is also part of a wider fear of trading flesh and
blood, of Christian women selling and Jews buying Christ's body in the

host, of selling one's soul with one's blood to the Devil, of being saved from mutilation by not having sold one's blood, and of being redeemed by Christ's blood.

Enclosing social bodies

Because social bodies are seen as analogous to individual ones, they are also imagined as fragile containers of blood that have to be protected in the same way. The social body has to be defended and upheld because otherwise the concept of an individual body would crumble, too; and vice versa the individual body has to be imagined as enclosed so that the notion of a communal body can be maintained. This again goes beyond merely imaginary analogues: if societies fight each other, they can only do so through individual members, and a threat to individuals will weaken the whole community.

The way in which social bodies are dependent on individual ones and linked through blood is displayed at length in the *Nibelungenlied*, in particular as regards the Burgundians. As we have seen, when Siegfried arrives in Worms, he appears as an enclosed physical unit facing the collective of the Burgundians on his own. Siegfried's body is described as an individual entity: Hagen singles out Siegfried in his description of the group of strangers, and he characterizes Siegfried through his solitary adventures, as travelling 'alone, without support' when he first encounters the Nibelungs and their treasure.[57] Siegfried is the only one of the new arrivals to act and talk; the others are not even named. Siegfried's solitary position is contrasted with the Burgundians acting as a group. Gunther, Ortwin and Hagen watch and discuss the new arrivals together, ask and take advice from each other, interact and act as one political group. As the recipient knows, Siegfried's father Siegmund had shared this reliance on strength in numbers and had anticipated that Gunther would be supported by his subjects; but rather than following his father's advice to take a large group of knights with him to Worms, Siegfried had insisted on travelling with only twelve knights.[58]

All nobles in the *Nibelungenlied* rely on the help of their relatives and subjects, which constitutes the important bonds between them. As Müller has argued, the acting subject in the *Nibelungenlied* is often a group (*Personenverband*), not an individual member.[59] However, he does not discuss Siegfried's exceptional solitary position, a position which contributes to the catastrophe. For as an entirely self-reliant

entity who does not need a larger social body to share a common protection, Siegfried also does not fit into the defence system of the group
and thus constitutes a *gast*, an outsider and potential aggressor. The
clash between him and the Burgundians on his arrival can thus be seen
as a clash between different models of bodies (individual vs social)
acting as defensive units. Siegfried's claim to power is his individual
physical strength. He does nothing but act according to his extremely
solitary, impenetrable, thus aggressive status when, arriving in Worms,
he announces that he plans to take Gunther's country by force, by his
own physical strength (metaphorically speaking, his ability to shed blood):

> Nu ir sît sô küene,   als mir ist geseit,
> sone ruoche ich, ist daz iemen   liep oder leit;
> ich wil an iu ertwingen   swaz ir muget hân:
> lant unde bürge,   daz sol mir werden undertân.[60]

If you are as brave as I am told, I think that, whether people like it or not,
I will take from you by force everything that you own: country and castles
shall be mine.

This proclamation has always puzzled scholars, since the narrator had
told us that Siegfried had come to woo Kriemhild and not to declare
war. But his declaration has nothing to do with what Siegfried consciously or logically could have intended to do, and instead must be an
inevitable consequence of his physical strength and impenetrability. His
body is a walking provocation, whether he or anyone else likes it or not.
It is his physical force that he threatens to use, as Gunther also highlights in his reaction:

> 'Wie het ich daz verdienet',   sprach Gunther der degen,
> 'des mîn vater lange   mit êren hât gepflegen
> daz wir daz solden verliesen   von iemannes kraft?'[61]

'What would I have done to deserve this', Gunther the hero said, 'that we
should lose that which my father has honourably looked after for so long
because of someone's strength?'

In contrast to Siegfried's individually enclosed body, the Burgundians
function as a permeable group. Gunther perceives his own body to be
not that of a fortified individual, but the social body of the royal family,

whose genealogy (metaphorically speaking, bloodlines) he cites here as his claim to power. That he quite literally thinks of this elite group as physically joined becomes clear when he eventually decides to welcome the outsider to share their power:

> Dô sprach der wirt des landes: 'allez daz wir hân,
> geruochet irs nâch êren,   daz sî iu undertân,
> und sî mit iu geteilet   lîp unde guot.'[62]

Then, the lord of the country said: 'Everything that we have, if you treat it honourably, shall be at your service, and body and possessions shall be shared with you.'

This generous proposal is another plot twist that has caused much scholarly bemusement, but is perfectly understandable within Gunther's concept of an open social body. Gunther offers Siegfried to share their *lîp*, which means both body and life, and thus implies, if not an incorporation into a large body, at least the partaking in a community that is willing to lose their bodies for one another and is in this way physically united. His proposition makes Siegfried's aggression fall flat, and the openness of the social body thus turns out to be the superior strategy to individual physical enclosure in this instance.

But we soon find out that Siegfried remains in his own physical shell and cannot be integrated at all. The Burgundians also maintain their concept of a body that carries power as an open, social body during the first half of the text, and this serves them well against Siegfried. The conflict between their different notions of bodies, different notions of where power resides, comes to a head in the course of the murder plot, but resonates throughout the preceding episodes as well. Siegfried continues to act as a solitary figure: in the war against the Saxons and the Danes, the bride-winning trip, the suitors' contest, the trip to the Nibelungen lands, the wedding-bed, the hunt and even the murder scene. The Burgundians continue to act as a group throughout. It might be significant that Siegfried's murder is brought about through his one and only intimate exchange with the outside world: his relationship with Kriemhild. Kriemhild causes the murder both indirectly, as her courtship creates the conflict with the Burgundians, and directly through her 'betrayal' of Siegfried's secret.

The importance of physical borders of individual subjects is paralleled by the attention given to the boundaries of social bodies – geographical spaces between them, human-made fortifications like castles, and in particular the complex welcoming rituals, including messengers, special clothes, exchange of gifts and particular greetings. Since society and its members, in particular its head, are mutually dependent in their attempts at protection, it might come as no surprise that the same paradox of closure and penetration seems to apply as we observed in the individual bodies: the more a country tries to shut itself off, the likelier an invasion becomes.[63] Brünhild, for instance, seems to call violence and intrusion upon herself and her country, Iceland, not despite her attempts to make herself and her country inaccessible, but because of them. When she is introduced as an object for Gunther's wooing, her unattainability in her far-away fort and in the dangerous suitors' test plays at least as much of a role as her beauty does in attracting his attention.[64] Such border reinforcement ultimately leads to the breaking of those borders and finally her destruction: she is written out of the text, not playing any part in the story after the fight of the queens.

The second half of the *Nibelungenlied* tells the story of Kriemhild's attempt to avenge Siegfried's murder on Hagen and her brothers. She marries the king of the Huns, Etzel, and later invites her brother Gunther and his men over – in order to have them punished somehow. Again, this goes disastrously wrong as almost everyone, including Kriemhild herself, is slaughtered in the end, and again, this is described as a self-perpetuating mechanism of reinforced physical boundaries not only of individual characters, but also of countries and societies, provoking their own transgression. First of all, Etzel's realm in the East, populated by wild people and heathens, is presented as almost inaccessible. It is far removed from the Burgundian territory, as is stressed by the extensive descriptions of the long journeys there by Kriemhild, by the messengers, and later by the Burgundians. Two spheres are constructed, which are separated by Bavaria and Bechelaren as buffer zones on Etzel's side, and by the Danube, which marks the end of the Burgundians' kingdom around the Rhine, the point up to which they venture when accompanying Kriemhild to her new home.[65] The Danube is depicted as a flooded, broad, fast-flowing river, populated by mermaids. Like Siegfried's skin, the river has a single penetrable spot: one fierce ferryman, who is certain to bring across only one person, his exiled brother Amelrich, so that the country is practically unreachable by anyone but this particular man. The seclusion is a conscious effort to keep out enemies, according to the ferryman: 'My dear lords have enemies; this is why I never take strangers into this country', he says.[66]

But again, this attempt at border protection backfires and only provokes violent penetration: Hagen kills the ferryman and the Burgundians enter the country anyway. Hagen's bloodshed marks the simultaneous breaking of the individual skin and the geographical border. The main perspective from which the story is told in the second part of the *Nibelungenlied*, however, is that of the Burgundians. To them, the episode at the Danube means a dangerous border reinforcement as well: Hagen's killing of the ferryman, the breaking of the boat and the expulsion of the priest 'burns the bridges', enclosing them in a foreign country. This scene also shows the interdependence of individual and society. Hagen's actions reflect back on all of them. The enclosure forces the community together against an enemy, increasing their separation from everyone else. This dangerous entrapment of the Burgundians inside a foreign territory is intensified when the rearguard attacks the Bavarians. This is again the result of bloodshed: blood is mentioned as a result and visible proof of the fight, as a sign of the Bavarians' defeat and the success of Hagen's people in the fight.[67] The border reinforcement has provoked blood-flow. There is no return for the Burgundians, because their enemies are behind them (and so is the pugnacious Hagen, urging them on). As a community, they are held responsible communally for the actions of each of them, as is evident in the attacks by the Bavarians following the murder. Hagen knows this: 'Because *I* have made enemies on the road, *we* will surely be attacked'.[68] The insistence of several Burgundians on keeping their armour on seems to add to their boundedness and to the aggression they cause.[69]

The Burgundians' final, fatal entrapment takes place in the hall. At first, it is the Huns who are cornered there, since the only way out, the door leading to the stairway, is easily blocked by Dankwart and Volker, as the text describes at length.[70] The extensive negotiations to let some people out of the hall, with their frequent references to space and exits, highlight the sense of enclosure of the others.[71] The tables are turned when the Burgundians settle in the hall – this confinement spells the end for them. The bloody and rusty kings only realize at nightfall how dangerous it is to be hemmed in like this, and beg to be let out.[72] But this is disallowed, and Kriemhild has the hall set on fire. The fight inside continues until almost all fighters are slaughtered. Again, physical enclosure has been proven to provoke intrusion and destruction.

While in the *Nibelungenlied*, Siegfried with his individually closed body confronts the open society of the Burgundians, in *Daniel*, Arthurian bodies, individual and social, are open, and their opponents' bodies, individual and social, are closed. The threat faced by Daniel in his encounters with the dwarf Juran, the bloodsuckers and the blood-bathers, as well as by Arthur's court, is invasion: King Matur's giant messenger enters the Arthurian court with what is in effect a declaration of war that will be resolved in the course of the main plot line; his father similarly walks into the court and kidnaps King Arthur, setting off a second defensive phase of the plot. The parallel threats to society and individual subject in *Daniel* partly result from their mutual interaction: the social body becomes permeable precisely because of the vulnerability of its representatives' (and defenders') bodies; and the political conflicts present physical danger for the individual fighters. This interdependence of society and its members, especially its head, cannot only be inferred from the plot, but is also one of the main characteristics by which the Arthurian court is defined in the prologue. It is typical that Arthur is introduced into the text as the leader of a social group, as the head of a splendid 'house'.[73] Just as Arthur's fame depends on the large number of courtiers around him, his knights' fame relies on his own, which is the reason why many foreign knights become his companions.[74] Arthur's custom of refraining from eating until he has seen or heard of an adventure is also described as a system of mutual benefit, as it ensures that the knights do not by any chance 'rest too much', as, of course, Hartmann von Aue's Erec did, so that both parties gain fame.[75] The disciplining of the individual body thus serves the greater good of society, which in turn reflects back on the individual subject, as is concisely expressed in the text: Arthur 'promoted their fame in every way and gained praise for this'.[76]

Again, just like the individual bodies, the social body must protect itself and stay permeable, but also actively go out and penetrate other social bodies. Just as knights have to leave the court to go on journeys to gain fame, the whole court, including King Arthur, actually moves to face the enemy.[77] The relationship of the Arthurian society to outsiders is an open, accepting one. How welcome foreign knights are is expressed in a physical metaphor, when 'the best people from all countries' are said 'to come to Arthur's aid/become his hands' (*des quâmen ime ze handen die besten von den landen*).[78] Indeed, these knights are all integrated into the social body and given considerable political power at the Round Table, at which the king is a *primus inter pares*.[79] Moreover, the Arthurian sphere has to identify with outsiders and other countries to the extent that Arthur and his court are willing to see an attack on others as an attack on the Arthurian world. When

Daniel takes on the three challenges for the three ladies, this means that their problem, the threat to their bodies and countries, becomes his own (and his own opportunity to gain fame), as well as that the challenge to him is mediated by the women. Arthurian fame depends on this openness to foreign knights, stories and food. The intrusion of Matur's giant messenger, for instance, though a severe provocation starting a deadly war, is also a necessary and welcome adventure that allows knights to gain fame. The story of Daniel's acceptance as an Arthurian knight at the beginning of the plot exemplifies this openness to distinguished strangers: Daniel comes to court, proves his excellence by jousting, and is immediately welcomed 'like a very good friend'.[80] Permeability is not just a threat to Arthurian identity, but also an inalienable part of it, since facing physical danger constitutes Arthurian fame.

Consequently, the crisis characteristic of Arthurian romances does not occur in the middle of the hero's journey, but at the end, and affects the whole Arthurian court: the quick old man, the giants' father, intrudes into the court during its victory celebrations, and kidnaps the king and his best knight. This permeability even at the end confirms that the court can never be permanently and safely enclosed. Even after this humiliating infringement, Arthur keeps his realm open: when the giants' father asks for a completely secluded land between high and steep rocks as a fief, Arthur gladly gives it to him, since it is so inaccessible:

> mir waerc lieber ein ei
> denne der selbcn lande zwei
> dâ nieman ûz noch in mac.[81]

I would prefer one egg to two of these countries where nobody can get in or out.

The opponents, as we have seen, fall into two groups whose enforced or aggressively armed bodies contrast with Arthurian vulnerability. Their countries and social bodies are part of this pattern. Those opponents who aggressively invade other countries are destroyed at once: Juran, the bloodsuckers and the blood-bather. The temporarily antagonistic countries of the Green Meadow and Cluse, on the other hand, defensively harden their borders as much as their individual representatives do: Cluse, as the name suggests, is shut off by an insurmountable mountain range, traversed by a single narrow pathway guarded by a giant, a rock and a metal alarm statue.[82] There is no exchange with the outside world; the knights of Cluse fight only one another; anyone who tries to enter is killed immediately.[83] The country of the Green Meadow is cut off by a very similar mountain range whose single opening is protected by a gate, a rock and a waterfall.[84] Again, nobody leaves the country, as the blood-bather's spell binds them, and everyone who enters is killed for the blood-bath.[85] Correspondingly, the openness and equality that characterize King Arthur's leadership style are also lacking. Instead, the rulers have complete control over their subjects, with King Matur of Cluse, who combines his strict rule with a certain splendour, occupying the positive end of the scale of despots, and the blood-bathing man, who rules the country of the Green Meadow in conjunction with the Duke as his servant, being the cruellest type. For these temporary opponents defined by their hardened borders, the exclusion of fluidity is essential; they banish it to their borders or guard against it by incorporating it in an important, though marginal role. The sea is utilized as a border of the country of the Green Meadow; gushing water makes it even more inaccessible as it floods the one corridor leading to it, and water also drives the alarm statue that separates Cluse from the rest of the world.[86] But again, such seclusion itself is dangerous for the people of Cluse and the Green Meadow, as it prevents their escape from the crying animal and from the blood-bather. When the belly-less creatures come in from the sea, this also subverts the hardened boundaries and brings the margins, where such monsters live according to world maps and travel literature, into the centre.[87] Moreover, the opponents' strategy of seclusion means that they do not gain fame. Arthur has never even heard of Cluse, the realm rivalling or outdoing him in splendour.[88] So one is left with the necessity of permeability and exchange even on the level of social bodies.

Monstrous social bodies

Similar to the discussion of the ideal of a hardened social body in *Daniel* and the *Nibelungenlied*, the Church at the beginning of the thirteenth century attempted to fashion itself into a streamlined body politic. The Fourth Lateran Council (1215) was to a large extent concerned with organizing and consolidating the social body of Christ: clarifying its internal structure, united by the eucharistic blood as well as hierarchized; and creating a fixed boundary to the outside, to non-believers like Jews or to demons. Two of its first assertions are that the one Church is a community of communicants united in God and clearly separated from non-believers, and that God's body and blood are present in the eucharist:

Una vero est fidelium universalis ecclesia, extra quam nullus omnino salvatur, in qua idem ipse sacerdos et sacrificium Iesus Christus, cuius corpus et sanguis in sacramento alteris sub speciebus panis et vini veraciter continentur, transsubstantiatis pane in corpus et vino in sanguinem potestate divina, ut ad perficiendum mysterium unitatis accipiamus ipse de suo, quod accepit ipse de nostro.[89]

There is indeed one universal church of the faithful, outside of which nobody at all is saved, in which Jesus Christ is both priest and sacrifice. His body and blood are truly contained in the sacrament of the altar under the forms of bread and wine, the bread and wine having been changed in substance, by God's power, into his body and blood, so that in order to achieve this mystery of unity we receive from God what he received from us.

The Church is here presented as an exclusive organization of believers, all sharing Christ's eucharistic body. A more fervent exclusion of Jews was part of such streamlining, as evinced by the infamous decree ordering Jews to wear distinctive clothes in order to avoid any further confusion with Christians, as Jeremy Cohen has shown.[90]

The council also endeavoured to regulate in detail the organizational structure of the Church and its various offices. It uses the idea of the Church as a social body to argue against a deviation from a strictly linear hierarchy: if a town or diocese had two bishops, two 'heads', the council warns, it would turn monstrous, 'as if it were a body with several heads like a monster'.[91] The monstrous multiplication of heads, however, is a problem intrinsic to the imagination of the Church as Christ's body. In the collective body of the Church, Christ has to be both the Church and its head, as well as leave room for human Church leaders. From the mid-thirteenth century onwards, the pope was also referred to as the head of this body. In as early a text as Konrad von Würzburg's 'Silvester', for example, Constantine declares that the Church should be structured like a body, with Pope Sylvester as the 'head' of all priests, just as the king is the head of all judges.[92] When Pope Boniface VIII later dogmatized the idea of the Church as one mystical body in his bull *Unam sanctam* (1302), he still described this body as an unresolved anomaly, as having Christ at its head and God as Christ's head.[93]

The role of priests within this collective was singled out for attention, as they were the ones mediating the blood of Christ that made the

Church into more than a metaphorical body and instead a body united by a shared blood, just like a family. All communicants theoretically partook of the blood of Christ in the eucharist, but in practice, the chalice was withheld from the laity, so that priests were an exclusive subgroup drinking Christ's blood in a much more direct sense. The Fourth Lateran Council contributed to fashioning them into exclusive vessels for Christ's blood only, ordering them to keep away from all other forms of blood, as we have seen.[94] In the vernacular, this special status of priests in relation to blood is formulated and combined with the familiar fear of women, for example, by Der Stricker's 'Pfaffendirne', which proclaims that God has created clerics to serve as pure 'chalices' for 'his holy flesh and blood', therefore people who kill them should be punished as if for killing seven lay people; and women who kill their souls by seducing them should be punished as if for killing thirty laypeople.[95]

Christ's body thus had to fulfil the roles of being the body of an individual, the eucharistic body and the integral body of the Church in a tenuous balancing act. The function of Christ's body as both collective and individual creates daring images not just in official Church documents, but also in vernacular writing. In Brun von Schönebeck's *Hohes Lied*, for instance, Christ's skin is described thus: 'his skin was stretched at the cross, so that its width encompasses the whole world'.[96] This image works on the basis of Christ being responsible for the bodies of all Christians, but grotesquely distorts Christ's individual body. In another passage, his skin is not just stretched, but rather his whole body becomes a skin, spread out like the hide on a shield:

> wer einen turen schilt machet
> von richer kunst ungeswachet,
> der denet obir ein holz eine hut
> und slet dar in nagele min trut,
> daz her diste vaster si, alsus
> wart gedenet der hirre altissimus
> an dem heiligen vronen cruze.[97]

He who artfully makes a precious shield stretches a skin across a piece of wood and hammers nails into it, my dear, so that it becomes stronger. In this way the highest Lord was stretched at the holy cross of the passion.

Again, the individual body is extended out of all proportion. The description of the crafting of the shield (stretching the skin, hammering nails into it) as well as the fact that a shield is a defensive weapon emphasizes the strain and attacks involved in functionalizing Jesus's body in this way.

Surprisingly, Mary was also imagined as a collective body of Christians. The *Heilige Regel*, for example, presents itself as a way to become part of the same body as Mary:

> Dise helige regele theile wir in vier stucke. Daz erste: wie Gotes muter und alle die dise regele halten, ein lichame sinth in Gote und wi Jesus Cristus houbet ist des lichames.[98]

> We divide this Holy Rule into four parts: first, how the mother of God and all those who follow this rule are one body in God, and how Jesus Christ is the head of this body.

By following the rules given in the text, the recipient is assured that he or she will become one body in God, together with Mary, who adhered to the same rules as any other believer. That this collective body, however, is imagined not as Christ's, but as Mary's body, is clearer when the text urges its clerical recipients to become parts of her body:

> IN diseme capitile glichet sich unser vrowe eineme reinen lichamen, an deme alle geistliche kinder gelidert schollen sin, und dez lichamen houbet ist Jesus Cristus, Gotis sun von himelriche.[99]

> In this chapter, Our Lady is likened to a pure body, of which all spiritual children shall be members; and the head of this body is Jesus Christ, God's son from heaven.

Mary is here 'like' a collective body, consisting of Christians as her body parts, with Christ at its head. This is dangerously close to claiming quasi-divine status for Mary as embodying all Christendom.

As in the Fourth Lateran Council's idea that a diocese with two bishops would be like a monstrous body, the spectre of monstrosity is raised easily when it comes to collective bodies. As is the case for Arthur's court in *Daniel*, not just the individual body is threatened by blood-drinking monsters, but also the collective body, and both are often conjoined. The same applies to Christ's collective body, and again, blood plays an important role in imagining not just the adhesion, but also the violent disruption of this body. An example of blood-drinking monsters who disrupt and make bleed individual bodies as well as the collective body of Christ are Gog and Magog, people well known in medieval biblical exegesis as destroyers who would participate in the Antichrist's terrible reign at the end of time. As we shall see, to some extent, the threat they pose is imagined as converging with those of the Jews, who are similarly seen as disrupting the blood-flow within Christ's collective body. On the Ebstorf world map (c.1300), for example, they are represented as two seated naked men with receding hairlines, sitting in a square in the north-east corner of the earth, each biting into a severed and bleeding human foot (Figs 7 and 8).[100] Between them lies another naked person, bleeding copiously from the severed stumps of his or her hands and feet. Another bloody foot or hand floats in the background; the man to the left of the viewer also holds a bleeding hand. 'Here, Alexander has enclosed the two unclean people, Gog and Magog, who will accompany the Antichrist. They eat human flesh and drink blood', explains the caption.[101] Blood is here depicted at the moment when it exudes from the severed limbs, where it flows around the cannibals' mouths and where it clings to Christ's wound, as being neither completely interior nor completely exterior to the body. As is graphically illustrated, cannibalism constitutes an extreme 'deformation' of the victim's body, a mutilation. The cannibals' own bodies are also deformed, as they ingest and digest foreign body parts and visibly form a monstrous conglomerate with them.

But Gog and Magog also disrupt another body: the collective body of Christ. In the north, east, west and south of the orb, Christ's head, hands and feet are shown floating above the land (in the case of the head, in a separate square). This cannot be read as Christ standing behind or embracing the world, as in other *mappae mundi*, but rather seems to suggest that Christ's body has merged with the earth, as fits in with the theological interpretation of *corpus mysticum* as the Church, comprising every Christian as a member.[102] Just as Christ is both individual and collective, he also appears on the map in a double representation. In a strongly defined and visually striking square, similar to the ones surrounding Christ's head at the top and Gog and Magog on the top left, a second figure of Christ is seen stepping out from his grave in Jerusalem at the centre of the map. So on the one hand, he is shown as encompassing the world; and on the other hand, he is represented residing in his own navel, at the moment of his resurrection.[103] Gog and Magog are depicted at the very fringes of the body of Christ-as-collective. The square in which they are placed is situated so far in the north-east corner of the orb that it reaches out into the ocean surrounding the

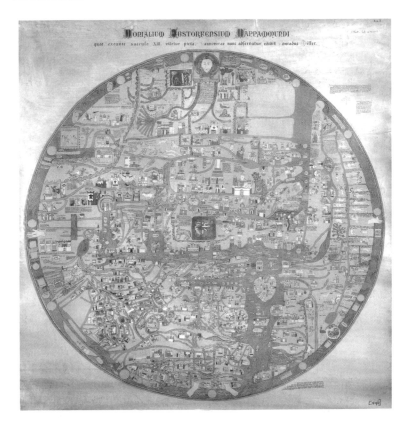

7 Ebstorf world map (*c.*1300). Reproduction from Konrad Miller (ed.), *Monialium Ebstorfensium Mappamundi/Die Ebstorfkarte* (Stuttgart: Roth, 1896). By permission of the Syndics of Cambridge University Library.

landmass and is only cut off by the lines around the whole picture (which might signify the course of the planets or the elements). Thus, they create a spatial and visual disruption in the otherwise almost perfectly round circumference of Christ's body. Indeed, it is questionable whether they are still part of Christ's body. Text and image stress Gog and Magog's enclosure and separation from the rest of the world. Their square is surrounded by mountains and walls (the latter built by Alexander the Great), and encircled by the larger country Scythia, which is home to other monsters and is depicted as fenced in by another mountain range, the Caucasus. Gog and Magog's double enclosure is not absolute,

8 Gog and Magog. Detail from the north-east corner of the Ebstorf world
map (c.1300). Reproduction from Ernst Sommerbrodt, *Die Ebstorfer
Weltkarte* (Hannover: Hahn, 1891). By permission of the Syndics of Cambridge
University Library.

however. As the text reminds the viewer, Gog and Magog will enter Christendom during the reign of the Antichrist. The visual enclosure is not complete either: one cannibal's foot reaches on to the right wall of the square; further to the right, the mountain range of the Caucasus is interrupted by the Caspian Gates. So Gog and Magog can be seen both as part of Christ's body and as separate from it. Such an ambiguous presence of monsters in or near Christ's body disrupts its integrity. Since the monsters are both part of and not part of that body, it is unclear where the *corpus mysticum* ends and the monsters begin. Any body, if it were to incorporate a monstrous part, would become a monstrous composite in itself. This precarious position, on the borderline between inside and out, is typical of monsters. As Jeffrey Jerome Cohen puts it, though without reference to bodies: 'the monster's very existence is a rebuke to boundary and closure'.[104]

But Christ's collective body is not only geographically disrupted by Gog and Magog; their mutilation of the individual human bodies is also set in the context of Christ's body-as-earth. A striking visual parallel is created between the severed and bloody hands and feet eaten by Gog and Magog, and the separate hands and feet of Christ at the 'corners' of the map, Christ's right hand showing its bloody stigma. This visual link between the fragments about to be devoured and Christ's members highlights the fragility and vulnerability of Christ's body and draws attention to the tension between Christ's body as a human, individual body and as the *corpus mysticum* of the Church. The severed head, hands and feet at the edges of the world make visual sense if read as part of the symbolic body of Christendom, but they become disturbing if read as parts of a human body. The fact that Gog and Magog drink blood and that they are part of the fringes of Christendom thus gives two expressions of the same function: the breaking of the body's integrity.

Although the Ebstorf map makes no explicit reference to the eucharist in text or image, the round orb visually resembles a host, highlighting again the function of the eucharist as forging a collective through letting every Christian share in God's sacrificial blood. Like the sacrifice, this creation of community through sharing blood as a drink has a subtext of violence, of the bloodshed of the passion. Gog and Magog show the negative aspects of blood-drinking that destroy rather than forge bodies. A secular parallel to the disruption that Gog and Magog pose through their blood-drinking is found in the *Nibelungenlied*. In courtly as well as heroic values systems, the festive communal eating and drinking in the mead-hall or the banquet-hall are central tenets of forging a community and courtly or heroic communal identity. But in the *Nibelungenlied*, this is gradually inverted into dangerous blood-drinking. While the first feast, the celebration of Siegfried's knighting, is unspoiled and unbloody, and the wedding banquet also passes without casualties and relatively little blood in the night after, the meal after the hunt contributes to Siegfried's bloody murder: Hagen 'forgets' to order drinks, so that Siegfried runs to the spring to drink, where Hagen spears him bloodily. The combination of drink imagery and blood imagery becomes even more important in the final banquet at Etzel's court, which turns into an 'anti-banquet'.[105] In the crucial scene that starts off the battle in the hall (after the news of the fighting has been carried into the hall by the bloody Dankwart), Hagen 'pays back' the wine and 'drinks to the memory' of Siegfried by decapitating Ortlieb, so that the blood runs down the sword on to his hands.[106] The *minnetrinken*, or pouring blood as a bitter drink, equates drinking with blood and vulnerability once more.[107] Finally, blood itself becomes the meal when the Nibelungs drink the blood of the dead in the hall.[108] The courtly and heroic communal celebration of drinking together has now been fully perverted into drinking one another.[109]

Another group of blood-drinkers that problematize the collective and individual Christian body at the same time are described in the sermon 'Of the Three Walls' by Berthold von Regensburg (d. 1272): weeds growing among the wheat of the field that represents Christendom.[110] Berthold addresses these weeds as 'blood-drinkers' (*bluottrinker*), an epithet he uses throughout his sermons for murderers, especially Cain; here he includes, amongst others, Judas, Esau and Jezebel, whose own blood is lapped up by dogs in hell.[111] The blood-drinkers thus, like Gog and Magog, destroy the integrity of individual bodies. But they also do the same to the contours of the collective body. The sermon deals with the biblical example of a field with a treasure, for which a man gladly exchanges all his possessions.[112] This treasure is here interpreted as the Christian's soul, the field as Christendom, which Jesus bought with his body and fertilized with his blood: 'He fertilized it with his noble lovely life-blood, because the earth was soaked with it.'[113] The equation of Christendom with Christ's body is not made explicit in this particular sermon, although the fact that Christ bought the field with his body suggests that field and body are equivalent. Moreover, the soaking of the earth with blood is awkwardly reminiscent of Cain's bloodshed, and thereby of the image of the earth as a virgin body.[114] The fact that it contains 'a soul' in the singular, like an individual body would, and that the surrounding walls could be thought of as covering individual bodies, means that the idea of the field as a body is never far away. The blood-drinkers in the field as well as Gog and Magog again are layered with anti-Semitic connotations that give them a sad political relevance. It seems to be the Jews' role as disrupting not just physical and social boundaries, but also conceptual ones, as being neither Christian nor heathen, that creates fears. Jeremy Cohen claims that Jews are entirely excluded from the Christian field: 'The Jew, states the friar emphatically, has no rightful access to this field and its treasure; at best he represents a weed planted by the devil in the field, one which will, it is hoped, be removed.'[115] But in fact, the Jews are rather ambiguously positioned both inside and outside the field, and only clearly excluded by the first of the three eponymous walls that surround the field. This first wall is made of silk and signifies the stole of the priest, clerical power. Pope and clergy teach Christians how to keep their faith in case Jews, heathens or heretics try to dissuade them; and how to act according to their faith. The second, iron wall, representing the iron sword of worldly legal authority, also protects against the same enemies of the faith, so that in case someone breaks the silk wall, 'this iron wall is still in front of it and shields the field from Jews and from heathens and from heretics'.[116] But at the same time, in a paradox that is not resolved in the sermon, Jews are themselves sheltered by it: the worldly authorities 'shall also protect the Jews' life and belongings just as they protect the Christians', since they are included in the peace'.[117] The third wall is a heavenly wall that protects each side, each patch, each ear of corn of the field, or each kingdom, duchy, diocese, town, village, cloister, farm, dwelling, castle, house and human being. These walls again surround Christians as well as Jews, heathens, heretics, Slavs and Tartars. So Jews are separated from Christians and vice versa by their individual walls, but included by the ones around each village, town and so forth. So Jews do belong to the 'field' of Christendom that is protected by the second and third walls, but also do not belong to it. Again, this seems to result from problems in the construction of Christendom itself, claiming universal status as well as exclusivity.[118] That Jews are not fully excluded here makes Berthold's preaching no less anti-Semitic; on the contrary, if Jews could be neatly excluded from the Church, mentally and logically, they would not be such a thorn in the side of medieval theologians and agitators. It is precisely because they are seen as disrupting the *corpus Christi*, as not quite heathen and not quite Christian, that they are of such concern.

Similarly, some anti-Jewish fears were projected on to Gog and Magog. Andrew Gow painstakingly traces the convergence of Gog and Magog with the 'unclean people', whom Alexander the Great had enclosed behind mountains in the far north-east, as well as with the ten 'lost' tribes of Israel, 'long believed by many Jews (and later by Christians) to be a huge army somewhere in the East in reserve against the day when God would send them out to wreak havoc on a sinful world'.[119] By the thirteenth century, Gog and Magog were thought of as Jewish and referred to as the Red Jews in a range of German texts. The men on the Ebstorf map indeed are drawn with stereotypical 'Jewish' features, as identified in medieval anti-Semitic visual art by Ruth Mellinkoff: elongated eyes and deformed noses shown in profile.[120] Cannibalism and the use of human blood were also accusations often levelled against Jews; the first recorded allegation of Jews requiring Christian blood as a cure was raised in the German town of Fulda in 1235, resulting in the mass murder of the local Jews.[121] Gow suggests that images of Gog and Magog such as the one on the map could have fuelled the belief that contemporary German Jews eat Christian children and consume their blood.[122] Indeed, most of the accusations levelled against Jews in anti-Semitic writings involve blood. Narratives of host desecration and ritual murder, rumours about the crucifixion of Christian boys and accounts describing images of Christ being attacked with knives – all partook of the anti-Semitic processes by which Jews were associated with blood.[123] Blood is usually a central element in these narratives, streaming out of hosts, images and corpses. This is because blood in these stories marks, disturbs and enforces the body of Christ, in the shape of the eucharist, the Church, the little boy, the crucified Christ and the devotional image. As in the witch-hunts, seemingly fantastic accusations of violating individual and collective bodily integrity through blood thus gained a terrible relevance for medieval Jews.

The imagining of social units as bodies, then, leads to a similar abjection of an exterior, as discussed in previous chapters in relation to individual bodies. Like an individual body is held together by blood, so is a social body united by the blood of kinship and sacrifice, and threatened by blood-loss and disruption. The ensuing attempts at dividing people and territories into inside and outside, friend and enemy, have emerged as every bit as dangerous – and ultimately futile – as those at demarcating individual bodies.

Conclusion

It was like all this despair I'd been having vanished as I concentrated on this trickle of blood. It took all this pain that I couldn't describe into something physical, something you could deal with . . . Seeing the blood reminds you you are alive . . . It brings home the fact you physically exist.

(Sophie Gill, on cutting herself, quoted in the *Observer*, 5 September 2004)

What is the alternative?

I hope to have shown that the body was not a self-evident entity in the Middle Ages, but one laboriously upheld by truth games and prohibitions against blood and bleeding, which were often discussed in disproportionate relation to what actual bodily harm they could cause. I have also indicated the ethical cost of this model: the fantasy of a completely integral body depends on being able to make a huge number of exceptions. This will automatically lead to a hierarchy between perfect and imperfect bodies, which, in the Middle Ages, as we have seen, in particular mutually reinforced the hierarchies between men and women, and Christians and Jews.

To what extent has this imagination of the body, and the resulting violence, changed over time? Twenty-first-century Western cultures still overwhelmingly conceive the body as a bounded entity, and bleeding as primarily a danger. It would of course have been impossible at any one time to completely step out of culture and language and radically rethink such essential concepts. Societies and individuals can only ever take as a starting point their position inside language, inside culture; any 'return' to a state 'before the law', where embodied subjects and bleeding are not perceived as such, is foreclosed. Any changes to such concepts must thus be gradual. Despite the fact that blood has been found to be less essential for health and procreation as well as for devotion than it was in the Middle Ages, blood has retained its imaginary value to affirm bodily boundaries. People still faint at the sight of blood emerging from the skin; blood still looms large in stories, films and language; monsters like vampires are still imagined to suck blood; families are still referred to as blood-relatives; women are still distinguished by their menstrual status; blood is still used to shock and convince. The currently endemic strategy of self-harming, for instance, seems to work on the basis that for sufferers to gain relief, blood must become visible to create an affliction that is seen as more authentic than 'psychological' pain and to reassure them of their physical, incontrovertible existence through the temporary transgression of the bodily boundary. Power struggles between nations are also still often decided through bloodshed. Moreover, the ideal body is a bounded, firm, pert body with smooth skin that does not 'spill' out of its clothes. Incontinent bodies that cannot contain their fluids, to some extent even menstruating ones, are pathologized and stigmatized. Anxieties about pollution through sexual fluids are rampant and feed into and from homophobic, xenophobic and misogynist tendencies.

Nevertheless, in several areas, the model of the body as a bounded entity was and is challenged by alternative models: in the idea of self-sacrifice, of the mystical embrace of multiple bodies, of the equality of 'deformed' and 'imperfect' bodies, in art, writing and philosophy that attempts to tweak and rethink the contours of the body. Much current forward-thinking research, in fact, has gone to the other extreme of valuing fluidity for its own sake, of proclaiming a fluid, open body as an unquestioned ideal; and judging any boundary transgression, any breaking down of taboos; any destabilization, any challenge to existing power structures to be positive. But a complete embrace of fluidity, like that of mystics and martyrs, leads to death (in a conventional, physical sense, notwithstanding beliefs in resurrection). Despite the obvious problems with the concept of the body as a bounded entity, then, it is also extremely useful. If Butler postulates that the taboo against homosexuality creates gendered bodies, most of her readers would agree that one should work against this taboo and allow for more play with gender – any gradual changes of these categories, in discourse and actuality, would almost certainly be welcome. But although bloodshed helps to maintain a rigid notion of the body, it would be very hard to argue for a legitimization of it. Even if the overemphasis on enclosure should no doubt be challenged, violence should never be condoned. Perhaps even more so than gender, the embodied subject and the bounded body are a thought pattern without which we cannot exist, a 'necessary fiction', in Butler's words. But precisely since it is as impossible to do away with as is the gender system, challenging its exclusions and rigidities is important and necessary work.

Notes

Introduction

[1] Augustine of Hippo, *Confessions*, tr. Henry Chadwick (Oxford: Oxford University Press, 1991), pp. 230–9 (11. 14–25).

[2] Shannon Sullivan, *Living across and through Skins: Transactional Bodies, Pragmatism and Feminism* (Bloomington: Indiana University Press, 2001), p. x. Various scholars have argued that, at the same time, our investment in needing the skin to be an absolute boundary has grown; for example, Claudia Benthien, *Skin: On the Cultural Border Between Self and World*, tr. Thomas Dunlap (New York: Columbia University Press, 2002 [1999]); Didier Anzieu, *The Skin Ego*, tr. Chris Turner (New Haven: Yale University Press, 1989 [1985]); Judith Halberstam, *Skin Shows: Gothic Horror and the Technology of Monsters* (Durham, NC: Duke University Press, 1995).

[3] Donna J. Haraway, 'A cyborg manifesto: science, technology, and socialist-feminism in the late twentieth century', in Haraway, *Simians, Cyborgs and Women: The Reinvention of Nature* (New York: Routledge, 1991), pp. 149–81; Gilles Deleuze and Félix Guattari, *Anti-Oedipus: Capitalism and Schizophrenia*, tr. Robert Hurley, Mark Seem and Helen R. Lane (London: Athlone, 1984 [1972]).

[4] Christine Battersby, *The Phenomenal Woman: Feminist Metaphysics and the Patterns of Identity* (Oxford: Polity, 1998).

[5] As an empirical introduction to the issue of personal identity in relation to the body, see, for example, Brian Garrett, 'Personal identity', in *Routledge Encyclopedia of Philosophy*, ed. Edward Craig, 10 vols (London: Routledge, 1998), VII, pp. 305–14.

[6] David Hillmann and Carla Mazzio, 'Introduction: individual parts', in Hillmann and Mazzio (eds), *The Body in Parts: Fantasies of Corporeality in Early Modern Europe* (London: Routledge, 1997), pp. xi–xxix (p. xvii).

⁷ Mikhail Bakhtin, *Rabelais and his World*, tr. Helene Iswolsky (Bloomington: Indiana University Press, 1984 [1965]), pp. 26–7.

⁸ Ibid., p. 29.

⁹ Norbert Elias, *The Civilizing Process: Sociogenetic and Psychogenetic Investigations*, ed. Eric Dunning, Johan Goudsblom and Stephen Mennell, tr. Edmund Jephcott, 2nd, rev. edn (Oxford: Blackwell, 2000 [1939]); Michel Foucault, *The History of Sexuality*, I, *An Introduction*, tr. Robert Hurley (Harmondsworth: Penguin, 1981 [1976]), see my chapter 1, pp. 18–20; Klaus Theweleit, *Männerphantasien*, 2 vols, 2nd edn (Munich: Piper, 2000 [1977]), I, esp. pp. 311–21; Thomas Laqueur, *Making Sex: Body and Gender from the Greeks to Freud* (Cambridge, MA: Harvard University Press, 1990), see my chapter 3, pp. 84–5.

¹⁰ For blood in the Middle Ages in general, see Francesco Vattioni (ed.), *Sangue e antropologia*, 16 vols (Rome: Pia Unione Prezissimo Sangue, 1981–9), an eclectic collection focusing on biblical and patristic writing, with references to mostly early medieval texts throughout the volumes, including on Old High German writing; Carla del Zotto, 'Il "sangue" nella tradizione evangelica germanica', in *Sangue e antropologia nella letteratura cristiana*, II, Sangue e antropologia, 6 (1983), pp. 1375–1420; Anna Maria Guerriri, 'Il sangue nella tradiozine poetica germanica', in *Sangue e antropologia nella biblica nella patristica*, II, Sangue e antropologia, 4 (1982), pp. 907–34; Carla del Zotto Tozzolli, 'Il sangue nei testi germanici medievali', in *Sangue e antropologia nella teologia*, II, Sangue e antropologia, 15 (1989), pp. 1455–1522; James M. Bradburne (ed.), *Blood: Art, Power, Politics, and Pathology* (Munich: Prestel, 2001), the beautifully illustrated catalogue to the exhibition of the same name held at the Museum für Angewandte Kunst and the Schirn Kunsthalle in Frankfurt am Main from 11 November 2001 to 27 January 2002, with essays by Miri Rubin and James Clifton particularly relevant for the medieval period; Piero Camporesi, *Juice of Life: The Symbolic and Magic Significance of Blood*, tr. Robert R. Barr (New York: Continuum, 1995 [1988]), with a strong focus on sixteenth- and seventeenth-century Italy; Michel Faure (ed.), *Le Sang au Moyen Age: Actes du quatrième colloque international de Montpellier Université Paul-Valéry 27–29 novembre 1997*, Les Cahiers du CRISIMA, 4 (Montpellier: CRISIMA, 1999); Marie-Christine Pouchelle, 'Le sang et ses pouvoirs au Moyen Age', in *Affaires de Sang: Festschrift Arlette Farge*, Mentalités, 1 (Paris: Imago, 1988), pp. 17–41; Kathleen Biddick, 'Genders, bodies, borders: technologies of the visible', *Speculum*, 68 (1993), 389–418; see also references in the following notes.

¹¹ Bynum, 'Blood of Christ', *Church History*, 71/4 (December 2002), 685–714 (pp. 706–7).

¹² Similarly, for example, in Francesco Vattioni, 'Sangue: vita o morte nella Bibbia?', in *Sangue e antropologia biblica*, II, Sangue e antropologia, 2 (1981), pp. 367–78; Angelo Penna, 'Il sangue nell'Antico Testamento', in *Sangue e antropologia biblica*, II, Sangue e antropologia, 2 (1981), pp. 379–402; Jan

Hendrik Waszink, 'Blut', in *Reallexikon für Antike und Christentum:
Sachwörterbuch zur Auseinandersetzung des Christentums mit der antiken
Welt*, ed. Theodor Klauser, 18 vols (Stuttgart: Hiersemann, 1950–), II
(1954), col. 459–73; Hans Wißmann, 'Blut I: Religionsgeschichtlich', in
Gerhard Krause and Gerhard Müller (eds), *Theologische Realenzyklopädie*
(Berlin: de Gruyter, 1977–), VI (1980), cols 727–9; Otto Böcher, 'Blut II:
Biblische und frühjüdische Auffassungen', in Krause and Müller (eds),
Theologische Realenzyklopädie, VI (1980), cols 729–36; Uli Linke, *Blood and
Nation: The European Aesthetics of Race*, Contemporary Ethnography
(Philadelphia: University of Pennsylvania Press, 1999), pp. 3–35.

13 The literature on various aspects of medieval conceptions of bodies is now
extensive; for good general starting points see Sarah Kay and Miri Rubin
(eds), *Framing Medieval Bodies* (Manchester: Manchester University Press,
1994); Darryll Grantley and Nina Taunton (eds), *The Body in Late Medieval
and Early Modern Culture* (Aldershot: Ashgate, 2000); Linda Lomperis and
Sarah Stanbury (eds), *Feminist Approaches to the Body in Medieval
Literature* (Philadelphia: University of Pennsylvania Press, 1993); Caroline
Walker Bynum, 'Why all the fuss about the body? A medievalist's perspective',
Critical Inquiry, 22 (Autumn 1995), 1–33; Alain Boureau, 'The sacrality of
one's own body in the Middle Ages', *Yale French Studies*, 86 (1994), 5–17.
Much of the older literature is listed and described in Barbara Duden, 'A
repertory of body history', in Michel Feher (ed.), *Fragments for a History of
the Human Body*, 3 vols (New York: Zone, 1989), III, pp. 471–578.

14 Caroline Walker Bynum, *The Resurrection of the Body in Western Christianity,
200–1336*, Lectures on the History of Religions, NS 15 (New York: Columbia
University Press, 1995); Miri Rubin, 'The body whole and vulnerable in
fifteenth-century England', in Barbara Hanawalt and David Wallace (eds),
*Bodies and Disciplines: Intersections of Literature and History in Fifteenth-
Century England*, Medieval Cultures, 9 (Minneapolis: University of Minnesota
Press, 1996), pp. 19–28; see also Philip Lyndon Reynolds, *Food and the Body:
Some Peculiar Questions in High Medieval Theology*, Studien und Texte zur
Geistesgeschichte des Mittelalters, 69 (Leiden: Brill, 1999); and Nicholas
Vincent, *Holy Blood: King Henry III and the Westminster Blood Relic*
(Cambridge: Cambridge University Press, 2001), esp. pp. 82–136.

15 'Das Nonnenturnier', in *Die deutsche Märendichtung des 15. Jahrhunderts*,
ed. Hanns Fischer, Münchner Texte und Untersuchungen zur Literatur des
Mittelalters, 12 (Munich: Beck, 1966), pp. 31–47; 'Gold und Zers', ibid., pp.
431–43.

16 *Moriz von Craûn*, ed. and tr. Stephanie Cain van d'Elden (New York: Garland,
1990), ll. 133–79.

17 Jeffrey Jerome Cohen, *Medieval Identity Machines*, Medieval Cultures, 35
(Minneapolis: University of Minnesota Press, 2003).

18 Judith Butler, *Gender Trouble: Feminism and the Subversion of Identity*
(New York: Routledge, 1999 [1990]), p. 164; see also her reading of Descartes
in Butler, 'How can I deny that these hands and this body are mine?', in

Tom Cohen, Barbara Cohen, J. Hillis Miller and Andrzej Warminski (eds), *Material Events: Paul de Man and the Afterlife of Theory* (Minneapolis: University of Minnesota Press, 2001), pp. 254–73; and her reading of Foucault in Butler, 'Revisiting bodies and pleasures', *Theory, Culture and Society*, 16/2 (1999), 11–20. For similar criticisms of Friedrich Nietzsche's, Alphonso Lingis's and Michel Foucault's ideas, see Elizabeth Grosz, *Volatile Bodies: Toward a Corporeal Feminism*, Theories of Representation and Difference (Bloomington: Indiana University Press, 1994), pp. 138–59.

19 Judith Butler, *Bodies that Matter: On the Discursive Limits of 'Sex'* (New York: Routledge, 1993), p. xi.

20 While Butler is concerned with the more obviously performative aspects of gender identity, intersex babies (with male and female genitalia, genes or hormones) are denied an existence according to the same mechanisms.

21 Mary Douglas, *Purity and Danger: An Analysis of the Concepts of Pollution and Taboo* (London: Routledge, 1966), p. 116. Douglas later revised her interpretation of the pollution rules in Leviticus, without giving up on her theory of pollution in general, in Douglas, *Leviticus as Literature* (Oxford: Oxford University Press, 1999).

22 Douglas, *Purity and Danger*, p. 125.

23 Ibid., p. 122.

24 Butler, *Gender Trouble*, p. 167, Butler's emphasis.

25 Julia Kristeva, *Powers of Horror: An Essay on Abjection*, tr. Leon S. Roudiez (New York: Columbia University Press, 1982 [1980]), p. 67.

26 Ibid., p. 3, Kristeva's emphasis.

27 Ibid., p. 70.

28 Ibid., p. 71, Kristeva's emphasis.

29 Heroic epics with their graphic battle descriptions show statistically a particularly high blood count, while lyrics with their focus on love and politics have the lowest, as evidenced by the 125 or so medieval German fictional texts collected in the Middle-High German Conceptual Database, published at *mhdbdb.sbg.ac.at:8000/index.html*.

30 Peggy McCracken, *The Curse of Eve, the Wound of the Hero: Blood, Gender, and Medieval Literature* (Philadelphia: University of Pennsylvania Press, 2003).

Chapter 1

1 'Die gestohlene Monstranz', in *Eine Schweizer Kleinepiksammlung des fünfzehnten Jahrhunderts*, ed. Hanns Fischer, Altdeutsche Textbibliothek, 65 (Tübingen: Niemeyer, 1965), pp. 84–6, l. 18, *dri bluottropfen klar*. There does not seem to have been an actual cult of blood in Brugg that could be related to this tale.

2 Ibid., l. 27, *mit dem lebenden gottesbluot*.

3   Ibid., ll. 37–46.
4   Caesarius of Heisterbach, *Dialogus miraculorum*, ed. Joseph Strange, 2 vols
    (Cologne: Lempertz, 1851), I, p. 2 (Prologue) *viris religiosis, finxisse*; trans-
    lation: Caesarius, *The Dialogue on Miracles*, tr. Henry von Essen Scott and
    Charles Cooke Swinton Bland, 2 vols (London: Routledge, 1929), I, p. 2.
    Caesarius' German translator Johann Hartlieb is much more pragmatic in
    his prologue, stressing didactic use rather than truth value: 'even if the whole
    text had been invented – which it is not – great and good teaching could still
    be derived from it', Hartlieb, *Übersetzung des* Dialogus Miraculorum *von
    Caesarius von Heisterbach*, ed. Karl Drescher, Deutsche Texte des Mittelalters,
    33 (Berlin: Weidmann, 1929), p. 1, *ob nuon dise geschrifft alle erdicht wäer,
    das doch nit ist, noch dann mocht daraus grosse und guotteu underweysung
    geschehen.*
5   Caesarius, *Dialogus miraculorum*, II, p. 164 (9, prologue), *cum timore*; tr.
    Dialogue on Miracles, II, p. 103. See also Miri Rubin, *Corpus Christi: The
    Eucharist in Late Medieval Culture* (Cambridge: Cambridge University Press,
    1991), pp. 108–29.
6   Caesarius, *Dialogus miraculorum*, II, pp. 165–7 (9. 1); tr. *Dialogue on Miracles*, II,
    p. 106.
7   Caesarius, *Dialogus miraculorum*, II, p. 182 (9. 23); tr. *Dialogue on Miracles*, II,
    p. 126, emphasis in originals.
8   Foucault, *History of Sexuality*, I, p. 147.
9   Ibid., pp. 147–8, Foucault's emphasis throughout.
10 Michel Foucault, 'Truth and power', in Foucault, *Power/Knowledge:
    Selected Interviews and Other Writings, 1972–1977*, ed. Colin Gordon (New
    York: Pantheon, 1980 [1977]), pp. 109–33 (p. 131).
11 Foucault, *Use of Pleasure*, pp. 6–7.
12 It is even at odds with the preceding discussion of the medieval roots of
    sexual confession, Foucault, *History of Sexuality*, I, pp. 57–73. Critical
    evaluations of this distinction are provided in relation to sexuality in Karma
    Lochrie, 'Desiring Foucault', *Journal of Medieval and Early Modern Studies*,
    27/1 (Winter 1997), 3–16; Lochrie, *Covert Operations: The Medieval Uses of
    Secrecy*, The Middle Ages Series (Philadelphia: University of Pennsylvania
    Press, 1999), pp. 12–24; Carolyn Dinshaw, *Getting Medieval: Sexualities and
    Communities, Pre- and Postmodern* (Durham, NC: Duke University Press,
    1999), pp. 191–206; in relation to blood in Kathleen Biddick, 'The cut of
    genealogy: pedagogy in the blood', *Journal of Medieval and Early Modern
    Studies*, 30/3 (Fall 2000), 449–62; and in relation to the distinction between
    body and speech in Judith Butler, *Undoing Gender* (New York: Routledge,
    2004), pp. 161–74.
13 Foucault again uses the metaphor of blood as an authenticating trope
    derived from Friedrich Nietzsche's *Genealogy of Morality* in his 'Nietzsche,
    genealogy, history', in Foucault, *Aesthetics, Method and Epistomology*, ed.
    James D. Faubion, *Essential Works of Foucault 1954–84*, II (New York:
    New Press, 1998 [1971]), pp. 369–91. Daniel Punday similarly points out

that Foucault uses the body as an authenticating trope, Punday, 'Foucault's body tropes', *New Literary History*, 31 (2000), 509–28.

14 Butler, *Gender Trouble*, esp. pp. 3–44. Despite these critical feminist studies, the recourse to the body as privileged access to truth is currently making a comeback in historical and other humanities research that appeals to physical sensations, in particular to touch, as more authentic than abstract and non-material 'knowledge' or 'learning'. In a pattern very similar to the usage of physical blood in medieval thought, the idea of physically 'touching' the past is described as a more authentic, privileged access to the past, superior to rational knowledge, for example, in Hans Ulrich Gumbrecht, *In 1926: Living at the Edge of Time* (Cambridge, MA: Harvard University Press, 1997), esp. pp. 419 and 424, and in Carolyn Dinshaw, *Getting Medieval*, esp. pp. 44 and 52.

15 See Valentin Groebner, *Defaced: The Visual Culture of Violence in the Late Middle Ages*, tr. Pamela Selwyn (New York: Zone, 2004 [2003]), pp. 108–10.

16 The eucharist itself is frequently described as a *mysterium*, too, for example, by Gerhard von Köln, who speaks of *mysteria sanguinis Christi quam corporis*, see Klaus Berg, 'Der Traktat des Gerhard von Köln über das kostbarste Blut Christi aus dem Jahre 1280', in Norbert Kruse and Hans-Ulrich Rudolf (eds), *900 Jahre Heilig-Blut-Verehrung in Weingarten, 1094–1994*, 2 vols (Sigmaringen: Thorbecke, 1994), I, pp. 435–84 (p. 460).

17 'Bartholomäus', in *Zwei deutsche Arzneibücher aus dem XII. und XIII. Jahrhundert*, ed. Franz Pfeiffer, Sitzungsberichte der österreichischen Akademie der Wissenschaften Wien, Philosophisch-historische Klasse, 42 (Vienna: Gerold's Sohn, 1863), pp. 20–51 (p. 20), *diu er versuohte, daz si wâr sint*. See Gundolf Keil, '*Bartholomäus*', in Kurt Ruh (ed.), *Die deutsche Literatur des Mittelalters: Verfasserlexikon*, 2nd, rev. edn, 11 vols (Berlin: de Gruyter, 1978–), I (1978), cols 609–15 (610–12). Walter L. Wardale's posthumously published edn of fifteenth-century versions of the *Bartholomäus* lists parallels to many other eleventh- and twelfth-century Salernitan texts which may have served as sources, particularly the treatise *De Aegritudinum curatione* and the works of Constantinus Africanus and Petrocellus Salernitanus, although in some passages Wardale seems to assume the existence of a Latin text of which the *Bartholomäus* would be a straight-forward translation, see Wardale, *The High German 'Bartholomaeus': Text, with Critical Commentary, of a Mediaeval Medical Book* ([Dundee:] Follan, 1993), for example, Introduction V, p. 1. In any case, it is not a translation of the *Practica* by the Salernitan author Bartholomew, despite Bernhard Schnell's recent claim that this has never been checked, in Schnell, 'Die deutsche Medizinliteratur im 13. Jahrhundert: Ein erster Überblick', in Christa Bertelsmeier-Kirst and Christopher Young (eds), *Eine Epoche im Umbruch: Volkssprachliche Literalität 1200–1300* (Tübingen: Niemeyer, 2003), pp. 249–65.

18 'Bartholomäus', ed. Pfeiffer, p. 20.

19 Ibid., p. 21.

[20] Excess blood, pp. 21 (twice), 22 and 39; blood (not in excess), pp. 38 and 40; unclean blood, pp. 25 and 45; other causes given are *colerica rubea* ('red bile', p. 21) and *flecmate* ('phlegm', pp. 21 and 22), which are derivatives of blood.

[21] On the problems of diagnosis and the physician's task of revealing the inner condition of the body, see William F. Bynum and Roy Porter (eds), *Medicine and the Five Senses* (Cambridge: Cambridge University Press, 1993), in particular the article by Vivian Nutton, 'Galen at the bedside: the methods of a medical detective', pp. 7–16.

[22] Reynolds, *Food and the Body*, passim; see also chapter 3, pp. 91–3.

[23] Gundolf Keil speaks of over 400 versions of the *Arzneibuch* altogether, 200 of them manuscripts, including seventy complete texts, Keil, 'Ortolf von Baierland (von Würzburg)', in K. Ruh (ed.), *Die deutsche Literatur des Mittelalters: Verfasserlexikon*, VII (Berlin: de Gruyter, 1989), cols 67–82 (col. 75).

[24] For a detailed study of Ortolf's sources, including Rhazes (ar-Rāzī), Isaac Judaeus, Gilles de Corbeil, Hippocrates and Gilbertus Anglicus, see Ortrun Riha, *Ortolf von Baierland und seine lateinischen Quellen: Hochschulmedizin in der Volkssprache*, Wissensliteratur im Mittelalter, 10 (Wiesbaden: Reichert, 1992). The sources date from 1150 to 1240 and reflect the state of the art before 1250, which leads Keil to assume that Ortolf finished his university studies before 1250 and collected practical experiences before writing his *Arzneibuch* in old age, Keil, 'Ortolf von Baierland', col. 68. Keil dates it before 1280, Riha around 1290, Crossgrove puts it before 1300. Keil, 'Ortolf von Baierland', col. 68, Riha, *Ortolf von Baierland*; William Crossgrove, *Die deutsche Sachliteratur des Mittelalters* (Berne: Lang, 1994), p. 60.

[25] Ortolf von Baierland, *Das Arzneibuch Ortolfs von Baierland nach der ältesten Handschrift (14. Jahrhundert)*, ed. James Follan, Veröffentlichungen der Internationalen Gesellschaft für Geschichte der Pharmazie, NS 23 (Stuttgart: Wissenschaftliche Verlagsgesellschaft, 1963), p. 92 (ch. 28); this edition is based on one of the oldest manuscripts, Cologne, Stadtarchiv, W 4° 24*, dating from 1398 or earlier; for a similar appraisal of bloodletting in the same text, see p. 87 (ch. 16).

[26] Blood, taken in phlebotomy or visible in urine, also helps to diagnose diseases, ibid., p. 103 (ch. 51); p. 116 (ch. 73). Sometimes, bloodletting not only serves to expel surplus blood, but also bad, poisoned blood, which seems to carry diseases, p. 93 (ch. 30); pp. 96–7 (ch. 36); p. 116 (ch. 73); p. 161 (ch. 137); p. 163 (ch. 140); p. 168 (ch. 152). On bloodletting in general, see Peter Brain, *Galen on Bloodletting: A Study of the Origins, Developments and Validity of his Opinions* (Cambridge: Cambridge University Press, 1986); Pedro Gil-Sotres, 'Derivation and revulsion: the theory and practice of medieval phlebotomy', in Luis Garcia Ballester, Roger French, Jon Arrizabalaga and Andrew Cunningham (eds), *Practical Medicine from Salerno to the Black Death* (Cambridge: Cambridge University Press, 1993), pp. 110–56; Shigesa Kuriyama, *The Expressiveness of the Body and the Divergence of Greek and Chinese Medicine* (New York: Zone, 1999), esp. pp. 195–231;

Eve Dérrien, 'Le sang et la saignée dans le roman médiéval en vers', *Lettres Romanes*, 51/1–2 (February–May 1997), 3–18.

[27] London, Wellcome Library, MS 49, fol. 35r. The Wellcome Apocalypse, probably produced around 1420 in Thuringia for an unknown audience, is a near-encyclopedic assortment of an apocalypse, an *ars moriendi*, medical instruction, moral and political allegories, held together mainly by a desire to collect and structure knowledge as well as by a *memento mori* theme. Colour microfiche reproduction and description of the manuscript in Almuth Seebohm, *Apokalypse, ars moriendi, medizinische Traktate, Tugend- und Lasterlehren: Die erbaulich-didaktische Sammelhandschrift London, Wellcome Institute for the History of Medicine, Ms. 49* (Munich: Lengenfelder, 1995); edition of the text surrounding the woundman and of the accompanying treatise on fols 34r and 34v in Boyd H. Hill, 'A medieval German wound man: Wellcome MS 49', *Journal of the History of Medicine and Allied Sciences*, 20 (1965), 334–57. Hill misreads several inscriptions: the bee near the right arm is inscribed *Vor bynen stich*; to the right side of the face, I read *Flecken oder ruden am antlitze*; in the cavity next to the stomach the word *splen* (not *flux*) appears; Hill also misses out the label *serpentes* near the snake in the stomach. On woundmen generally, see also Vivian Nutton, 'Medicine in medieval western Europe, 1000–1500', in Lawrence I. Conrad et al. (eds), *The Western Medical Tradition, 800 BC to AD 1800* (Cambridge: Cambridge University Press, 1995), pp. 139–205 (p. 181).

[28] For example, here on fol. 41r, or in London, British Library, Harley MS 3719, fols 158v–159r, reproduced and discussed in Peter Murray Jones, *Medieval Medical Miniatures* (London: British Library, 1984), pp. 120–1 (p. 120, fig. 54).

[29] Sarah Beckwith, *Christ's Body: Identity, Culture and Society in Late Medieval Writings* (London: Routledge, 1993); Caroline Walker Bynum, *Jesus as Mother: Studies in the Spirituality of the High Middle Ages* (Berkeley: University of California Press, 1982); Bynum, *Holy Feast and Holy Fast: The Religious Significance of Food to Medieval Women*, The New Historicism: Studies in Cultural Poetics (Berkeley: University of California Press, 1987); Bynum, *Fragmentation and Redemption: Essays on Gender and the Human Body in Medieval Religion* (New York: Zone, 1991); Bynum, 'Blood of Christ'; Rubin, *Corpus Christi*; Stephen Greenblatt, *Marvelous Possessions: The Wonder of the New World* (Oxford: Clarendon Press, 1991).

[30] Caesarius, *Dialogus miraculorum*, II, p. 232 (10. 19), tr. *Dialogue on Miracles*, II, p. 189.

[31] Caesarius, *Dialogus miraculorum*, II, p. 233 (10. 20), tr. *Dialogue on Miracles*, II, p. 189, emphasis in original.

[32] John 19: 34, *sed unus militum lancea latus eius aperuit; et continuo exivit sanguis et aqua.* Bible verses throughout are from the Latin vulgate and the English Douay-Rheims version.

[33] St Thomas Aquinas, *Super Evangelium S. Ioannis*, ed. P. Raphaelis Cai (Rome: Marietti, 1952), p. 455 (para. 2458); see also Berg, 'Der Traktat des Gerhard von Köln', p. 440.

34 Innocent III, 'De Sacro alteris mysterio', in Innocent III, *Opera Omnia*, ed. Jacques-Paul Migne, 4 vols, Patrilogiae Cursus Completus: Series Latina (Paris: Migne, 1855), CCXVII, cols 773–916 (col. 876, 4. 30). On the concept of *veritas humanae naturae*, see Reynolds, *Food and the Body*, esp. pp. 50–66.

35 Karma Lochrie, *Covert Operations: The Medieval Uses of Secrecy* (Philadelphia: University of Pennsylvania Press, 1999), pp. 4 and 129. See also Lochrie, 'Don't ask, don't tell: murderous plots and medieval secrets', in Louise Aranye Fradenburg and Carla Freccero (eds), *Premodern Sexualities* (New York: Routledge, 1996), pp. 137–52.

36 Lochrie, *Covert Operations*, p. 118. The persistent alignment of men with knowledge and reason and women with ignorance and folly has often been observed by feminists, see, for example, Genevieve Lloyd, *The Man of Reason: 'Male' and 'Female' in Western Philosophy* (Minneapolis: University of Minnesota Press, 1984).

37 The Latin *Secreta* has not yet been edited and is so far only accessible in modern publication as an abbreviated English translation of sixteenth-century prints, *Women's Secrets: A Translation of Pseudo-Albertus Magnus's 'De Secretis mulierum with Commentaries'*, tr. Helen Rodnite Lemay, SUNY Series in Medieval Studies (Albany: State University of New York Press, 1992). Possibly the oldest extant manuscript of this text is Munich, Bayerische Staatsbibliothek, Clm 22297 (Windberg 97), fols 21v–50v. Clm 22297 was, according to the scribe, completed in Erfurt in 1320. A scholarly debate about whether Munich, Bayerische Staatsbibliothek, Clm 22300 (Windberg 100), fols 61r–76r, might be older is not yet settled, since Christopher Ferckel dates it tentatively *c.*1300, the Munich catalogue as thirteenth-century, and Lynn Thorndike as fourteenth century, Ferckel, 'Die *Secreta mulierum* und ihr Verfasser', *Sudhoffs Archiv*, 38 (1954), 267–74 (p. 272); Thorndike, 'Further considerations of the *Experimenta, Speculum Astronomia*, and *De Secretis mulierum* ascribed to Albertus Magnus', *Speculum*, 30 (1955), 413–43 (p. 428); see also, with additional support for both views, Brigitte Kusche, 'Zur *Secreta mulierum*-Forschung', *Janus*, 62 (1975), 103–23 (pp. 104–6). In personal conversations, Tessa Webber has suggested that Clm 22230 at first glance seems to date from 1250–1350, probably from *c.*1300. Commentaries to the *Secreta*, falling into two main traditions, exist in numerous Latin manuscripts, the earliest extant one dating from 1353.

38 Lochrie, *Covert Operations*, pp. 128–9. On the shifting meaning of 'women's secrets' in this context, see also Monica H. Green, 'From "Diseases of Women" to "Secrets of Women": the transformation of gynecological literature in the later Middle Ages', *Journal of Medieval and Early Modern Studies*, 30/1 (Winter 2000), 5–39.

39 Lochrie, *Covert Operations*, p. 1.

40 The anonymous commented translation of the *Secreta* into German, dating from the third quarter of the fifteenth century and probably produced for the Southern German urban elite, is available in an unpublished critical

edition, *Pseudo-Albertus Magnus*, 'Secreta Mulierum Cum Commento, Deutsch': *Critical Text and Commentary*, ed. Margaret Rose Schleissner (doctoral dissertation, University of Princeton, 1987). The only other edited German adaptation was written *c.* 1460–5 by Johann Hartlieb, physician at the court of Duke Albrecht III of Bavaria-Munich and of his son Siegmund, Hartlieb, Secreta mulierum *mit Glosse in der deutschen Bearbeitung von Johann Hartlieb*, ed. Kristian Bosselmann-Cyran, Würzburger medizinhistorische Forschungen, 36 (Pattensen/Hanover: Wellm, 1985). The anonymous Southern German translation adds an extensive commentary only loosely based on Latin predecessors and probably written by the translator himself, but otherwise stays close to the Latin version transmitted in Munich, Bayerische Staatsbibliothek, Clm 22297 (Windberg 97), fols 21v–50v. I have compared the anonymous Southern German translation to Clm 22297, provided transcriptions of my key quotations and commented on the differences when appropriate.

41   *Secreta mulierum*, ed. Schleissner, ll. 9–10, *etliche ding . . . von den haimligkaiten der frauen, Vnnd von den dingenn di haimlich vnd verporgen Sindt, bey der nature der Frawen.*

42   Ibid., ll. 87–98.

43   Monica H. Green, ' "Traittié tout de mençonges": the *Secrés des dames*, "Trotula," and attitudes toward women's medicine in fourteenth- and early-fifteenth-century France', in Marilynn Desmond (ed.), *Christine de Pizan and the Categories of Difference* (Minneapolis: University of Minnesota Press, 1998), pp. 146–78 (p. 150).

44   *Secreta mulierum*, ed. Schleissner, ll. 2716–21, *natur der frauen dy menstrum haist.*

45   Ibid., ll. 99–104.

46   Ibid., ll. 1–10, *von eynner solichen Stat Erstlicher genant. A., maister, der gros her, Seynnem allerliebsten gesellen genandt . . . geselle, Freundt.* On men writing about women's bodies see also Carolyn Dinshaw, *Chaucer's Sexual Poetics* (Madison: University of Wisconsin Press, 1989), pp. 3–27.

47   *Secreta mulierum*, ed. Schleissner, ll. 2988–94, *Bruder.*

48   Ibid., ll. 2999–3002.

49   Ibid., ll. 163–5 and ll. 1862–9.

50   Ibid., ll. 1692–4, 2299–2309, 2115–16, 2357–60, 1405–12, 1448–55, 2110–28, 2216–35 and 584–625.

51   Ibid., ll. 1617–21.

52   Ibid., ll. 924–6 and 2449–61, *katzen glauben und Deuscherey.* For the link between 'cat' (*katze*) and 'heretic' (*ketzer*) see Georg Friedrich Benecke, Wilhelm Müller and Friedrich Zarncke (eds), *Mittelhochdeutsches Wörterbuch*, 3 vols (Leipzig: Hirzel, 1854–61), I (1854), col. 792.

53   *Secreta mulierum*, ed. Schleissner, ll. 2390–2405.

54   Ibid., ll. 1448–55, *alten zauberin.*

55   Ibid., ll. 2299–2301.

56   Ibid., ll. 2216–35.

[57] Similarly ibid., l. 2999.

[58] Ibid., ll. 908–47, *glaubt alls ein cristen man.*

[59] Ibid., ll. 2444–8, *das gat diese matery nichts nit ann.*

[60] Evelyn Fox Keller, 'Secrets of God, nature, and life' in Keller, *Secrets of Life, Secrets of Death: Essays on Language, Gender, and Science* (New York: Routledge, 1992 [1990]), pp. 56–72, Lochrie, *Covert Operations*, p. 107.

[61] *Secreta mulierum*, ed. Schleissner, subject matter, for example, ll. 950–60, 2087–8, and 2971; menstrual blood, for example, ll. 152–4, 171–2, 183, 185, 186, 187, 212, 216–17, 220, 222, 234, 236, 237 and 239.

[62] Ibid., ll. 187–214. On the tension between men transcending matter and yet being more perfectly embodied than women, see my chapter 3, pp. 85–90; and D. Vance Smith, 'Body doubles: producing the masculine *corpus*', in Jeffrey Jerome Cohen and Bonnie Wheeler (eds), *Becoming Male in the Middle Ages*, The New Middle Ages, 4 (New York: Garland, 1997), pp. 3–19.

[63] Mechthild von Magdeburg, *Das fließende Licht der Gottheit*, ed. Gisela Vollmann-Profe, Bibliothek des Mittelalters, 19 (Frankfurt/Main: Deutscher Klassiker-Verlag, 2003), p. 406 (5. 34). Part of this quotation, which is repeated in the prologue, has been much discussed, without consideration of blood; summary and references in Frank Tobin, *Mechthild von Magdeburg: A Medieval Mystic in Modern Eyes*, Studies in German Literature, Linguistics and Culture: Literary Criticism in Perspective (Columbia, SC: Camden House, 1995), pp. 134–6. On the notion of secrecy in the *Fließendes Licht*, see Marianne Heimbach-Steins, 'Gottes und des Menschen "heimlichkeit": Zu einem Zentralbegriff der mystischen Theologie Mechthilds von Magdeburg', in Claudia Brinker, Urs Herzog, Niklaus Largier and Paul Michel (eds), *Contemplata aliis tradere: Studien zum Verhältnis von Literatur und Spiritualität* (Berne: Lang, 1995), pp. 71–86; Alois M. Haas, 'Mechthilds von Magdeburg dichterische *heimlichkeit*', in Rüdiger Schnell (ed.), *Gotes und der werlde hulde: Literatur in Mittelalter und Neuzeit: Festschrift für Heinz Rupp zum 70. Geburtstag* (Berne: Francke, 1989), pp. 206–23.

[64] See also Mechthild, *Fließendes Licht*, p. 136 (2. 26), where material (parchment), signifiers (words) and signified (voice of the words) meta-phorically signify the Trinity, but the actual book is not claimed to embody it.

[65] Ibid., p. 404 (5. 34), *min botte des bluotes.*

[66] On the representation of martyrdom in the *Fließendes Licht*, see chapter 4, pp. 141–2.

[67] Roger Bacon, *Secreta secretorum cum glossis et notulis*, in *Opera hactenus inedita Roger Baconi*, ed. Robert Steele, 16 vols (Oxford: Clarendon, 1909–40), V (1909), p. 40; alternative translation and discussion in Lochrie, *Covert Operations*, p. 102.

[68] Roger Bacon, *Opus majus*, ed. John Henry Bridges, 3 vols (Oxford: Clarendon, 1897), I, p. 10 (part 1, ch. 4); translation: Bacon, *Opus majus*, tr. Robert Belle Burke, 2 vols (Philadelphia: University of Pennsylvania Press, 1928), I, p. 12. See also William Eamon, *Science and the Secrets of Nature: Books of Secrets in Medieval and Early Modern Culture* (Princeton: Princeton University Press, 1994).

[69] On Christians as parchment, see Dieter Richter, 'Die Allegorie der Pergamentbearbeitung: Beziehungen zwischen handwerklichen Vorgängen und der geistlichen Bildersprache des Mittelalters', in Gundolf Keil, Rainer Rudolf, Wolfram Schmitt and Hans J. Vermeer (eds), *Fachliteratur des Mittelalters: Festschrift für Gerhard Eis* (Stuttgart: Metzler, 1968), pp. 83–92; on the bodies of Mary and Christians as a book, see Urban Küsters, 'Narbenschriften: Zur religiösen Literatur des Spätmittelalters', in Jan-Dirk Müller and Horst Wenzel (eds), *Mittelalter* (Stuttgart: Hirzel, 1999), 81–110; on the Charter of Christ, see Mary Caroline Spalding, *The Middle English Charters of Christ*, Bryn Mawr College Monograph Series, 15 (Bryn Mawr, PA: Bryn Mawr College, 1914); Rubin, *Corpus Christi*, pp. 306–8; Laura Ashe, 'The Short Charter of Christ: an unpublished longer version, from Cambridge University Library, MS Add. 6686', *Medium Aevum*, 72/1 (2003), 32–48.

[70] Heinrich Seuse, 'Leben', in *Deutsche Schriften*, ed. Karl Bihlmeyer (Frankfurt/ Main: Minerva, 1961 [1907]), pp. 7–195 (p. 16, ch. 4), *in daz frisch bluot mins herzensafes gezeichent; in der heinlichi*.

[71] Jeffrey F. Hamburger, *Nuns as Artists: The Visual Culture of a Medieval Convent*, California Studies in the History of Art, 37 (Berkeley: University of California Press, 1997), pp. 178–81; Küsters, 'Narbenschriften', pp. 105–9; on the relationship between body and writing in these manuscripts, see also Niklaus Largier, 'Der Körper der Schrift: Text und Bild am Beispiel einer Seuse-Handschrift des 15. Jahrhunderts', in Müller and Wenzel (eds), *Mittelalter*, pp. 241–71; on the materiality of the skin of parchment, see Sarah Kay, 'Flayed skin as *objet a*: Representation and materiality in Guillaume de Deguileville's *Pèlerinage de vie humaine*', in Jane E. Burns (ed.), *Medieval Fabrications: Dress, Textiles, Cloth Work, and Other Cultural Imaginings*, New Middle Ages Series (New York: Palgrave Macmillan, 2004), pp. 193–205 and 249–51.

[72] See W. Ogris, 'Bahrprobe', in *Handwörterbuch zur deutschen Rechtsgeschichte*, I (1971), cols 283–5; Henri Platelle, 'La voix du sang: le cadavre qui saigne en présence de son meutrier', in *Actes du 99e Congrès national des Sociétés savantes, Besançon, 1974, Section de philologie et d'histoire jusqu'à 1610*, I, *La Piété Populaire au Moyen Age* (Paris: Bibliothèque Nationale, 1977), pp. 161–79; Olav Moormann van Kappen, 'Over de geschiednis van de baarproef in de Nederlanden', in Moormann van Kappen, *Lex Loci*, ed. E. C. Coppens et al., Rechtshistorische Reeks van het Gerard Noodt Instituut, 45 (Nijmegen: Gerard Noodt Instituut, 2000 [1985]), pp. 65–82; and Stuart Clark, *Thinking with Demons: The Idea of Witchcraft in Early Modern Europe* (Oxford: Oxford University Press, 1997), pp. 590–1.

[73] *Das Nibelungenlied: Mittelhochdeutscher Text und Übertragung*, ed. and tr. Helmut Brackert (Frankfurt/Main: Fischer, 1970–1), stanzas 1043–6.

[74] Horst Wenzel, 'Szene und Gebärde: zur visuellen Imagination im *Nibelungenlied*', *Zeitschrift für deutsche Philologie*, 111 (1992), 321–43.

[75] *Nibelungenlied*, ed. Brackert, stanza 1955.

76 Ibid., stanza 2055.
77 Ibid., stanzas 1566–8 and 1617–25.
78 Ibid., stanzas 458 and 675.
79 See passim Dinzelbacher, 'Blut Christi'; Miri Rubin, *Gentile Tales: The Narrative Assault on Late Medieval Jews* (New Haven: Yale University Press, 1999) for example, pp. 104–16; Vincent, *Holy Blood*; Walter Kasper, 'Der bleibende Gehalt der Heilig-Blut-Verehrung aus theologischer Sicht', in Kruse and Rudolf (eds), *900 Jahre Heilig-Blut-Verehrung in Weingarten*, pp. 377–86; Lukas Weichenrieder, 'Das Heilige Blut von Mantua', ibid., pp. 331–6.
80 On scepticism about ordeals in general and duels in particular voiced in medieval fiction and non-fiction invalidating claims of increasing rationality in the course of history, see Rüdiger Schnell, 'Rechtsgeschichte, Mentalitäten und Gattungsgeschichte: zur literarischen Autonomie im Mittelalter', in Joachim Heinzle (ed.), *Literarische Interessenbildung im Mittelalter: DFG Symposion 1991*, Germanistische Symposien Berichtsbände, 14 (Stuttgart: Metzler, 1993), pp. 401–30.
81 Hartmann von Aue, *Iwein*, ed. Georg Friedrich Benecke and Karl Lachmann, tr. Thomas Cramer (Berlin: de Gruyter, 1981 [1966]), ll. 1355–6, *Nû ist uns ein dinc geseit vil dicke vür die wârheit.*
82 Ibid., ll. 1369–71.
83 Gottfried von Straßburg, *Tristan*, ed. and tr. Rüdiger Krohn, 3 vols (Stuttgart: Reclam, 1996 [1980]), II, ll. 15232–58.
84 Examples of catalogues of sins crying to heaven in catechetic manuscripts are given in P. Egino Weidenhiller, *Untersuchungen zur deutschsprachigen katechetischen Literatur des späten Mittelalters* (Munich: Beck, 1965), pp. 22–3, such as Munich, Bayerische Staatsbibliothek, cgm 458, *Dye stym des pluetz*; Munich, Bayerische Staatsbibliothek, cgm 121, *unschuldigs pluet zu vergiessenn*; '*Eine gute peicht*', transmitted in three manuscripts, pp. 77–8, *unschuldigs plut vergiessen, todschlag (interfectio)*; see also Hans Folz, 'Beichtspiegel', in Folz, *Die Reimpaarsprüche*, ed. Hanns Fischer, Münchner Texte und Untersuchungen zur deutschen Literatur des Mittelalters, 1 (Munich: Beck, 1961), pp. 188–210 (l. 55), *Die stim des pluts, wer schuld daran hat*. Other sins frequently mentioned could also be described as wasting or sucking dry of blood: blood and money were often used interchangeably, with usury described as bloodsucking, see my chapter 3, p. 125; emitting semen for anything other than procreation is interpreted as a wasting of blood (Dinshaw, *Getting Medieval*, pp. 62–3); raping virgins meant shedding their virginal blood, see my chapter 3, pp. 103–10.
85 See Marilyn Aronberg Lavin, 'The altar of Corpus Domini in Urbino: Paolo Uccello, Joos van Ghent, Piero della Francesca', *Art Bulletin*, 19/1 (March 1967), 1–24 (esp. pp. 3–7); Stephen Greenblatt and Catherine Gallagher, 'The wound in the wall', in Greenblatt and Gallagher, *Practicing New Historicism* (Chicago: University of Chicago Press, 2000), pp. 75–109 (esp. pp. 96–104); Biddick, 'Genders, bodies, borders', esp. pp. 404–8; Rubin,

Gentile Tales, pp. 148–9. All stress the image's interlinked functions of expressing anti-Jewish sentiment while promoting the cult of the eucharist and the group's piety.

86 Although Rubin does not draw this out, the abundant evidence on host desecration accusations that she collects in *Gentile Tales* shows that the bleeding is almost always an integral part of these stories.

87 Giovanni Villani, *Nuova Cronica*, ed. Giuseppe Porta, Bibliotheca di scrittori italiani, 3 vols (Parma: Bembo, 1990–1), I (1990), pp. 616–17 (8. 143).

88 See also Greenblatt and Gallagher, 'Wound in the wall', pp. 101–4.

89 Wolfram von Eschenbach, *Parzival*, ed. Eberhard Nellmann, 2 vols, Bibliothek des Mittelalters, 8 (Frankfurt/Main: Deutscher Klassiker-Verlag, 1994), 489, l. 22–490, l. 30 (490, l. 2), *des wart daz sper bluotec rôt*, 'the lance thus became blood-red'. (*Parzival* is conventionally divided into blocks of thirty lines, so that standard references are to block and line.) This is a much-researched topic, for an overview and bibliography see Joachim Bumke, *Wolfram von Eschenbach*, Sammlung Metzler, 36 (Stuttgart: Metzler, 2004 [1991]).

90 Wolfram, *Parzival*, 484, l. 27, *hêrre, wie stêt iwer nôt?*.

91 Penelope Shuttle and Peter Redgrove in their popular Jungian book read this as indicating wonder at the mystery of menstruation, see Shuttle and Redgrove, *The Wise Wound: Menstruation and Everywoman*, 2nd, rev. edn (London: Boyars, 1999 [1978]), esp. pp. 17 and 191–3. Anfortas does bleed periodically according to the lunar cycle from a genital wound, which, like menstruation according to medieval interpretations, stems from a transgression of divine laws of chastity.

92 Wolfram, *Parzival*, 795, l. 28, *oeheim, was wirret dier?*.

93 See discussion in Linke, *Blood and Nation*, pp. 40–7.

Chapter 2

1 William Shakespeare, *The Merchant of Venice: Arden Shakespeare*, ed. John Russell Brown (London: Methuen, 1955), p. 73 (Act III, Sc. 1).

2 Main versions and further references in Hannsjost Lixfeld, 'Fleischpfand', in *Enzyklopädie des Märchens: Handwörterbuch zur historischen und vergleichenden Erzählforschung*, ed. Kurt Ranke, 11 vols (Berlin: de Gruyter, 1975–), IV (1984), cols 1256–62; see also Britta Wenger, 'Shylocks Pfund Fleisch: Eine stoffgeschichtliche Untersuchung', *Shakespeare-Jahrbuch*, 65 (1929), 92–174. Editions and translations: Johannes de Alta Silva, *Dolopathos, sive, De rege et septem sapientibus*, ed. Hermann Oesterley (Strasbourg: Trübner, 1873), pp. 57–61; Johannes, *Dolopathos or the King and the Seven Wise Men*, tr. Brady B. Gilleland, Medieval and Renaissance Texts and Studies, 2 (Binghampton, NY: Center for Medieval and Early Renaissance Studies, 1981); *Cursor mundi (The Cursur o' the World): A Northumbrian*

Poem of the XIVth Century in Four Versions, ed. Richard Morris, 3 vols, Early English Text Society, os 57, 59, 62, 66, 68, 99, 101 (London: Kegan Paul, Trench, Trübner, 1874–93), III (1874–7), ll. 21347–846 (parallel edn of four manuscripts, I here quote Oxford, Bodleian Library, Fairfax MS 14); *Gesta romanorum*, ed. Hermann Oesterley (Berlin: Weidmann, 1872), pp. 603–8.

3   'Kaiser Lucius' Tochter', in *Die deutsche Märendichtung des 15. Jahrhunderts*, ed. Hanns Fischer, Münchner Texte und Untersuchungen zur deutschen Literatur des Mittelalters, 12 (Munich: Beck, 1966), pp. 71–88, from Friedrich Heinrich von der Hagen's transcription of an unknown manuscript. While there is a large amount of literature on *The Merchant of Venice*, not much has been published on 'Kaiser Lucius' Tochter', but see Klaus Grubmüller, 'Kaiser Lucius' Tochter: Zur Vorgeschichte von Shakespeares *Kaufmann von Venedig*', in Ulrich Mölk (ed.), *Literatur und Recht: Literarische Rechtsfälle von der Antike bis in die Gegenwart* (Göttingen: Wallstein, 1996), pp. 94–137 (with a reprint and a modern German translation); Uwe Diederichsen, 'Das Fleischpfand', ibid., pp. 138–49.

4   Joseph Kohler, *Shakespeare vor dem Forum der Jurisprudenz*, 2nd edn (Berlin: Rothschild, 1919 [1883]), see also Diederichsen, 'Fleischpfand'. As regards the forfeit of body parts, however, Kohler only cites bets, and prohibitions of such practices, as evidence.

5   William Chester Jordan, 'Approaches to the court scene in the bond story: equity and mercy or reason and nature', *Shakespeare Quarterly*, 33 (1982), 49–59 (pp. 50–1).

6   Eyes, hands, tongue and nose in the *Cursor mundi*; perhaps a foot in the *Dolopathos*; eyes in Anthony Munday, *Zelauto: The Fountaine of Fame*, ed. Jack Stillinger (Carbondale, IL: Southern Illinois University Press, 1963 [1580]), pp. 113–80 (p. 179).

7   'Kaiser Lucius' Tochter', in *Deutsche Märendichtung*, ed. Fischer, ll. 139–49.

8   Ibid., ll. 323–7.

9   Ibid., ll. 469–99.

10   See also Jordan, 'Approaches', pp. 50–3.

11   'Kaiser Lucius' Tochter', in *Deutsche Märendichtung*, ed. Fischer, ll. 520–5.

12   'The Ballad of Gernutus', in *Arden Shakespeare*, pp. 153–6; Giovanni Fiorentino, *Il Pecorone*, ed. Enzo Esposito, Classici italiani minori, 1 (Ravenna: Longo, 1974); English translation in *Arden Shakespeare*.

13   Johannes, *Dolopathos*, p. 60, *nullus est hominum excepto deo, qui ita manum modificare possit, quin plus minusve auferat.*

14   Konrad Kunze and Hansjürgen Linke, 'Theophilus', in K. Ruh (ed.), *Die deutsche Literatur des Mittelalters: Verfasserlexikon*, IX (Berlin: de Gruyter, 1995), cols 775–82.

15   Brun von Schönebeck, *Das Hohe Lied*, ed. Arwed Fischer, Bibliothek des litterarischen Vereins in Stuttgart, 198 (Tübingen: Litterarischer Verein Stuttgart, 1893), ll. 6217–21. Many versions include a report of how Jews and sorcerers point the way to the Devil, see Kunze and Linke, 'Theophilus'.

Passing over the role of fluids, Hans Heinrich Weber stresses the opposition between Mary and the Devil, and her superiority, see Weber, *Studien zur deutschen Marienlegende des Mittelalters am Beispiel des Theophilus* (doctoral dissertation, University of Hamburg, 1966), pp. 40–75.

[16] Brun, *Hohes Lied*, l. 6263.

[17] Ibid., ll. 6278–9, *gedenke sun, ich bin din muter, du sogest miner bruste mamme*.

[18] Konrad von Würzburg, *Die Legenden*, ed. Paul Gereke, 3 vols (Halle/Saale: Niemeyer, 1925–7), I (1925), 'Silvester', ll. 1849–50, *gereinet unde wol getwagen von sünden und von siechtagen*.

[19] On the construction of proof in this disputation in an earlier version of the legend, see Vera Milde, '*Si entrunnen alle scentlîchen dannen*: Christlich-jüdischer Disput in der Silvesterlegende der *Kaiserchronik*', in Ursula Schulze (ed.), *Juden in der deutschen Literatur des Mittelalters: Religiöse Konzepte – Feindbilder – Rechtfertigungen* (Tübingen: Niemeyer, 2002), pp. 13–34.

[20] Hartmann von Aue, *Der arme Heinrich*, ed. Hermann Paul and Kurt Gärtner, Altdeutsche Textbibliothek, 3 (Tübingen: Niemeyer, 2001).

[21] Der Stricker, *Der Pfaffe Amis: Mittelhochdeutsch/Neuhochdeutsch*, ed. Michael Schilling (Stuttgart: Reclam, 1994).

[22] Konrad von Würzburg, *Die Legenden*, I, ll. 4198–4201.

[23] See discussion in Hamburger, *Nuns as Artists*, pp. 1–3.

[24] Ekkehard Kaufmann, 'Körperverletzung', in Adalbert Erler and Kaufmann (eds), *Handwörterbuch zur deutschen Rechtsgeschichte*, 5 vols (Berlin: Schmidt, 1971–98), II (1978), cols 1159–63 (cols 1159–60). This is the case for written law codes and may not have applied in the interpretation and enforcement of laws.

[25] *Lex Salica: 100 Titel-Text*, ed. Karl August Eckhardt, Germanenrechte Neue Folge, Abteilung Westgermanisches Recht (Weimar: Böhlau, 1953), pp. 138–40 (chs 22 and 23; here p. 140, ch. 23).

[26] *Schwabenspiegel. Kurzform*, ed. Karl August Eckhardt, 2 vols, Monumenta Germaniae historica, Fontes iuris Germanici antiqui, NS 4–5, 2nd edn (Hanover: Hahn, 1972–4), I (1972), pp. 388–9, *an plutrunsen*.

[27] Ibid., II (1974), p. 111. The terms used are: sentences which 'affect the people's lives or bloodshed', 'with a bloody hand', for 'blood-penitents', 'who shed their blood at their judgment', *den leuten an den leip oder an pluotgiezen gat, vber pluotige hant, bluotrewige, di ir pluot vor ir gerichte vegiezent*.

[28] *Decrees of the Ecumenical Councils*, ed. and tr. Norman P. Tanner, 2 vols (London: Sheed & Ward, 1990), I, p. 244 (Canon 18), tr. Tanner.

[29] Munich, Bayerische Staatsbibliothek, Cgm 121 (from the Benedictine nunnery Nonnberg near Salzburg), fols 319r–319v, in Weidenhiller, *Untersuchungen zur deutschsprachigen katechetischen Literatur*, p. 47.

[30] Berthold von Regensburg, 'Von den zehen geboten unsers Herren', in Berthold, *Vollständige Ausgabe seiner Predigten*, ed. Franz Pfeiffer, 2 vols (Vienna: Braumüller, 1862–80), I (1862), pp. 264–88 (pp. 276–8).

[31] Wolfram, *Parzival*, 464, ll. 16–22.

[32] Examples in Reinhold Köhler, 'Die Erde als jungfräuliche Mutter Adams', *Germania*, 7 (1862), 476–80. On Cain's association with blood as a man exceeding his bodily boundaries, see Lyndal Roper, *Oedipus and the Devil: Witchcraft, Sexuality and Religion in Early Modern Europe* (London: Routledge, 1994), pp. 116–17. On bloodshed as defloration, see my chapter 3, pp. 103–10.

[33] Wolfram, *Parzival*, 489–90, ll. 22–30 (490, l. 2), *des wart daz sper bluotec rôt*, 'the lance thus became blood-red', see also chapter 1, pp. 48–9.

[34] Wolfram, *Parzival*, 492, ll. 11–14.

[35] See, for example, Ortolf's *Arzneibuch*, which gives not only detailed instructions for bloodletting, but also ways of stopping any excessive bleeding, be it menstrual, from the nose or from wounds, p. 87 (ch. 16); pp. 115–17 (ch. 73); p. 129 (ch. 94); pp. 156–7 (ch. 131) and p. 165 (ch. 144).

[36] Marie-Christine Pouchelle, *The Body and Surgery in the Middle Ages*, tr. Rosemary Morris (Cambridge: Polity, 1990 [1983]), pp. 70–8.

[37] Wirnt von Grafenberg, *Wigalois der Ritter mit dem Rade*, ed. J. M. N. Kapteyn, Rheinische Beiträge zur germanischen Philologie und Volkskunde, 9 (Bonn: Klopp, 1926), ll. 8–15, 79–81 and 120–1.

[38] Wirnt, *Wigalois*, ll. 6916–17, 7123–4, 10950–1, 11088–9 and 4893–4; *von dînem bluote werdent rôt und missevar die bluomen hie; daz die liehten bluomen rôt mîn bluot iht roeter mache; man sach vil manegen helm roten von bluote der ê lûter was; dâ wurden die helme missevar diu swert von bluote erblichen; ir brust was swarz alsam ein kol, daz bluot darunder geloufen.*

[39] Ibid., ll. 2743–6, 5904 and 8382–3; *ein reinez bat.*

[40] Ibid., ll. 689–96, *rîterlîche.*

[41] Ibid., ll. 5118–19, 10962, 10599–600 and 11074–5; *dranc; spranc; flouc; gôz;* and *flôz.*

[42] Ibid., ll. 5793–4, 7014–17, 7695–6, 7993–4 and 5334–6.

[43] Ibid., ll. 6915–17 and 7122–6.

[44] Ibid., ll. 7766–9.

[45] Ibid., ll. 7993–4.

[46] Ibid., l. 10970.

[47] Ibid., ll. 6153–4.

[48] Ibid., ll. 8550 and 6246–7.

[49] Ibid., ll. 2207, 2400–2 and 6552–8.

[50] Simon Gaunt points out this pattern in Chrétien's *Le chevalier de la charrette*, see Gaunt, *Gender and Genre in Medieval French Literature*, Cambridge Studies in French, 53 (Cambridge: Cambridge University Press, 1995), p. 94.

[51] Wirnt, *Wigalois*, ll. 2315–23. Despite Elisabeth Lienert's claim that the narrator's comments about his time are more or less unrelated to the plot, the behaviour recommended in the comments is here exemplified and problematized by Wigalois, see Lienert, 'Zur Pragmatik höfischen Erzählens: Erzähler und Erzählerkommentare in Wirnts von Grafenberg *Wigalois*', *Archiv für das Studium der neueren Sprachen und Literaturen*, 234 (1997), 263–75 (pp. 273–5).

52 Wirnt, *Wigalois*, ll. 2324–9.
53 Ibid., ll. 5233–40, 11204–9, 11352–6 and 8061–93.
54 Ibid., ll. 8262, *rein*; 8264, *kiusche*; 8273, *valschlôs*; 9221, *rein*; 9229, *reiner lîp*.
55 Ibid., ll. 11210–37.
56 Ibid., ll. 5314–5504.
57 Research has stressed that this narrative technique of trimming down the traditional heroic adventures of young Siegfried to a short embedded narration, after having introduced him at length as an ideal courtly knight in the second *aventiure*, is part of an attempt to make the story more courtly and reduce the heroic elements. For example, Ursula Schulze, *Das Nibelungenlied* (Stuttgart: Reclam, 1997), pp. 136–41; Jan-Dirk Müller, *Spielregeln des Untergangs: Die Welt des Nibelungenliedes* (Tübingen: Niemeyer, 1998), pp. 125–36.
58 *Nibelungenlied*, ed. Brackert, stanza 100.
59 *Eckenlied: Fassung L*, ed. Martin Wierschin, Altdeutsche Textbibliothek, 78 (Tübingen: Niemeyer, 1974), stanza 24, ll. 1–6.
60 Pfaffe Lamprecht, *Alexander*, ed. Karl Kinzel, Germanistische Handbibliothek, 6 (Halle: Verlag der Buchhandlung des Waisenhauses, 1884), ll. 934–7, *Gebeizet was sîn brunne in eines wurmes blûte . . . Hurnen was siu veste*.
61 Dietrich von der Glezze, 'Der Borte', in *Gesammtabenteuer. Hundert altdeutsche Erzählungen*, ed. Friedrich Heinrich von der Hagen, 3 vols (Stuttgart: Cotta, 1850), I, pp. 449–78 (ll. 639–43); Der Stricker, *Daniel von dem Blühenden Tal*, ed. Michael Resler, 2nd, rev. edn, Altdeutsche Textbibliothek, 92 (Tübingen: Niemeyer, 1995 [1983]), ll. 4035–48. Further references to hardened armour and skin in S. Singer, 'Die romanischen Elemente des *Nibelungenliedes*', in Singer, *Germanisch-romanisches Mittelalter* (Zurich: Niehaus, 1935), pp. 232–54 (pp. 244–7). On iron and weapons toughened in blood and in the ashes of basilisks (dragons) in medieval fiction and technical writing, see Emil Ploss, 'Wielands Schwert Mimung und die alte Stahlhärtung', *Beiträge zur Geschichte der deutschen Sprache und Literatur*, 79 (1957), 110–28. 'Dragon's blood', probably a resin, was also recommended in medical texts to staunch blood, for example, in Ortolf's *Arzneibuch*, in remedies for healing wounds by a rabid dog or other poisonous animals, p. 163 (ch. 140); other bleeding wounds, p. 165 (chs 144 and 145); against excess menstrual flow, pp. 156–7 (ch. 131); nosebleeds, p. 129 (ch. 94); spitting blood, pp. 137–8 (ch. 107); and blood in urine, pp. 154–5 (ch. 128); as well as intestinal prolapse, p. 149 (ch. 122).
62 *Nibelungenlied*, ed. Brackert, stanza 100, l. 4–stanza 101, l. 2.
63 Ibid., stanzas 458 and 675; on Siegfried's layers of 'skin' and their visibility, see also Müller, *Spielregeln*, pp. 243–8 and 257–61. I share Müller's general view of the actions as not psychologically motivated, although my estimation of the role of blood is higher.
64 *Nibelungenlied*, ed. Brackert, stanzas 902 and 938, *zwischen die herte*.

[65] Ibid., stanza 981, ll. 2–3, *er schôz in durch daz kriuze, daz von der wunden spranc daz bluot im von dem herzen vaste an die Hagenen wât*, 'spurt' is also used in 675 and 1986, 'break forth' in 458 and 1010.

[66] Uta Störmer-Caysa, however, has argued again that it could also serve to present Kriemhild as trying to murder her husband, see Störmer-Caysa, 'Kriemhild's erste Ehe: ein Vorschlag zum Verständnis von Siegfrieds Tod im *Nibelungenlied*', *Neophilologus*, 83 (1999), 93–113.

[67] *Nibelungenlied*, ed. Brackert, stanzas 981, 988, 998; similarly, 'Hagen was struck down by Siegfried's hands', not Siegfried himself, 986.

[68] Ibid., stanzas 188, 199 and 218.

[69] Ibid., stanzas 981, 982, 988, 981, 982, 983 and 986.

[70] Ibid., stanzas 203, 205 and 212.

[71] Ibid., stanzas 205, 214 and 217.

[72] See Katherine Rowe, '"God's handy worke"', in Hillmann and Mazzio, *Body in Parts*, pp. 285–309.

[73] *Nibelungenlied*, ed. Brackert, stanza 286, *Dô stuont sô minneclîche daz Sigmundes kint, sam er entworfen waere als ein permint*.

[74] Ibid., stanzas 1986, 2219, 2284 and 810; *jâ sihe ich durch die helme von swerten springen daz bluot; dô sluoc Gêrnôten Rüedeger der degen durch helm vlinsherten, daz nider vlôz daz bluot; Sigestap der küene den bluotegen bach hiu ûz herten ringen; mit drîen starken wunden die er dem künege sluoc durch eine wîze brünne diu was guot genuoc daz swert an sînen ecken brâhte ûz wunden bluot*; similarly 205, 2279, 2296 and 2360.

[75] Ibid., stanza 1775, ll. 1–3.

[76] Ibid., stanza 2248, l. 1, *blôzer*, stanza 2250, l. 1, *Dô garte sich die wîse durch des tumben rât*.

[77] Ibid., stanza 2253.

[78] Ibid., stanza 2299.

[79] See Müller, *Spielregeln*, pp. 430–4. On medieval blood-revenge see Rainer Zacharias, 'Die Blutrache im deutschen Mittelalter', *Zeitschrift für deutsches Altertum*, 91 (1961/62), 167–201. The idea of revenge, and especially Hagen's images of paying Etzel back for the wine by killing his son, stresses the concept of exchange and debt that is crucial to this text, see Irmgard Gephart, *Geben und Nehmen im* Nibelungenlied *und in Wolframs von Eschenbach* Parzival, Studien zur Germanistik, Anglistik und Komparatistik, 122 (Bonn: Bouvier, 1994), pp. 8–99.

[80] *Nibelungenlied*, ed. Brackert, stanzas 353 and 629, *er trug si ime herzen, si was im sô der lîp; si wart im sô sîn lîp*.

[81] Ibid., stanzas 1007–11 and 1069.

[82] In the light of my analysis of the lack of human agency in this chain, H. B. Willson's view that the characters in the *Nibelungenlied* react to blood with Christian compassion is unsustainable: Willson, 'Blood and wounds in the *Nibelungenlied*', *Modern Language Review*, 55 (1960), 40–50.

[83] *Die Nibelungenklage: synoptische Ausgabe aller vier Fassungen*, ed. Joachim Bumke (Berlin: de Gruyter, 1999).

84 Wirnt, *Wigalois*, ll. 156–8.

85 Ibid., ll. 3123–4, *der besten lop erwerben od mänlîch ersterben*.

86 Ibid., ll. 3407–11, 4699–4700, 4965, 4971, 4976–7, 6461–87, 3165–9, 6003–5, 6043–50, 6061, 2613–19, 2998–9, 2490–4, 3014–15, 3037–47, 3057–8 and 3078.

87 One giant (raping the maiden), two knights (the one offering beds and the one owning the dog), the dragon Pfetan, the dwarf Karrioz, King Garel of Mirmidone, the beast Marrien, Roaz and many in battle die at Wigalois's hands. Only the second giant, Hojir, Azzadac, Ruel and an old man survive their battles with him.

88 Stricker, *Daniel*, ll. 1284–9 and 1301–9.

89 Ibid., ll. 1326–31.

90 Ibid., ll. 1877–1941.

91 Ibid., ll. 1917–23.

92 Ibid., ll. 4329–4518.

93 Torsten Haferland, *Die Darstellung von Verletzungen und Krankheiten und ihrer Therapie in mittelalterlicher deutscher Literatur unter gattungsspezifischen Aspekten*, Beiträge zur älteren Literaturgeschichte (Heidelberg: Winter, 1991).

94 Stricker, *Daniel*, l. 4437, *zersnîden*.

95 Ibid., ll. 4783–91.

96 Ibid., ll. 5320–1 and 6473–4, *disen . . ., der mit ir bluote wolde baden; jener . . ., der in dem bluote badete*.

97 Ibid., for example, ll. 752–60.

98 McCracken, *Curse of Eve*, esp. pp. 1–20.

99 Stricker, *Daniel*, ll. 5290–5376.

100 Ibid., ll. 5623–81 (ll. 5657–9), 'this was a strong, manly attitude: however many fell into the blood, the others would not despair', *daz was ein starker mannes muot: swie vil ir viel in daz bluot, die andern wolden niht verzagen*.

101 Ibid., ll. 3600, 5109, 5156–7 and 5585, *das rôte saf*.

102 Ibid., ll. 3576–3601, 5109, 5156–7 and 5585, *der edel künic Artûs; der küene helt Parzivâl*.

103 Ibid., ll. 5897–6198.

104 Ibid., ll. 7106–13.

105 See Oliver F. Emerson, 'Legends of Cain, especially in Old and Middle English', *Publications of the Modern Language Association of America*, 21 (1906), 831–929.

106 Stricker, *Daniel*, ll. 4933–4, *ich bringe iuch schiere an ein stat dâ ich muoz lîden ein bat*.

107 Ibid., ll. 5680–1, *sô er in dem bluote muoste baden unz an die stunde daz er ertranc*.

108 See Friedrich Bode, *Die Kampfesschilderungen in den mittelhochdeutschen Epen* (Greifswald: Adler, 1909), for example, pp. 227 and 237; Ulrike Sprenger, 'Zum Schwimmen im Blut (Sg. 24, 7/8)', *Zeitschrift für deutsche Philologie*, 101/3 (1982), 321–33.

109 Stricker, *Daniel*, ll. 5108–10, 'he became so poor that he lost his blood as

well as life and goods', *er muoste werden alsô arm daz er verlôs sîn bluot, darzuo lîp unde guot*; see Ingrid Hahn, 'Das Ethos der *kraft*: zur Bedeutung des Massenschlachten in Strickers *Daniel von dem Blühenden Tal*, *Deutsche Vierteljahrsschrift für Literaturwissenschaft und Geistesgeschichte*, 59 (1985), 173–92.

110 Stricker, *Daniel*, ll. 125–33. Without linking it to the issues of bodies and permeability, Hedda Ragotzky has shown that the frequent crises befalling Arthur's court are not coincidental, but rather a result of its own rules, see Ragotzky, *Gattungserneuerung und Laienunterweisung in den Texten des Strickers*, Studien und Texte zur Sozialgeschichte der Literatur, 1 (Tübingen: Niemeyer, 1981), pp. 57–62. Werner Schröder follows her, but sees Stricker's attempt to explore and expose this intrinsic problem of Arthurian ideals as a parody, assuming his intention was to undermine the genre, see Schröder, 'Der synkretistische Roman des Wirnt von Gravenberg: Unerledigte Fragen an den *Wigalois*', *Euphorion*, 80 (1986), 235–77. Stephen L. Wailes and Günter Zimmermann have both convincingly argued that the much-discussed parodistic and comic elements do not undermine *Daniel's* functioning as a romance, see Wailes, 'Wolfram's *Parzivâl* and Der Stricker's *Daniel von dem Blühenden Tal*, *Colloquia Germanica*, 26 (1993), 299–315 (p. 312); and Zimmermann, 'Der gefangene Parzival: Gedanken zur Komik in Strickers *Daniel*', in Danielle Buschinger and Wolfram Spiewok (eds), *Perceval-Parzival hier et aujourd'hui et autres essais sur la littérature allemande du Moyen Age et de la Renaissance pour fêter les 95 ans de Jean Fourquet*, Wodan: Greifswälder Beiträge zum Mittelalter, 48, Series 3, Tagungsbände und Sammelschriften, 28 (Greifswald: Reineke, 1994), pp. 303–15.

111 Stricker, *Daniel*, ll. 4035–48.

112 Ibid., for example, ll. 432–3.

113 Ibid., ll. 3598–3601, 5155 and 5669.

Chapter 3

1 *Secreta mulierum*, ed. Schleissner, ll. 1947–8, *der man wirdiger ist dan dy fraw*.

2 Laqueur, *Making Sex*, pp. 1–154 (p. 8).

3 Ibid., p. viii.

4 Jean-Paul Sartre, *Being and Nothingness: An Essay on Phenomenological Ontology*, tr. Hazel E. Barnes (London: Routledge, 1969 [1943]), esp. pp. 600–15 (p. 601).

5 See Michèle Le Doeuff, *Hipparchia's Choice: An Essay Concerning Women, Philosophy, etc.*, tr. Trista Selous (Oxford: Blackwell, 1991 [1989]), pp. 58–97; Grosz, *Volatile Bodies*, pp. 194–5; Margery Collins and Christine Pierce, 'Holes and slime: sexism in Sartre's psychoanalysis', in Carol C. Gould and Marx W. Wartofsky, *Women and Philosophy: Toward a Theory of Liberation* (New York: G. P. Putnam's Sons, 1976), pp. 112–27.

6   Butler, *Bodies that Matter*, p. 16.
7   Ibid., p. 53.
8   'To matter' in the sense of 'to be significant' is not easily applicable to the gender distinction. Although men are clearly more valued than women, both genders are equally significant in the sense that one cannot be constructed without the other. So when Peggy McCracken argues throughout *Curse of Eve* that women's blood does not signify beyond their bodies, this distracts from the fact that women's bodies are highly significant in themselves.
9   Butler, *Bodies that Matter*, p. 32.
10 Aristotle, *Generation of Animals*, ed. and tr. A. L. Peck (London: Heinemann, 1963 [1942]), pp. 184–5 (2. 738b).
11 Ibid., pp. 384–7 (2. 765b).
12 *Secreta mulierum*, ed. Schleissner, ll. 105–21.
13 Ibid., ll. 108–10.
14 *Matery*, ibid., ll. 183, 185, 186, 187, 212, 222, 234, 236, 237, 239, etc.; *die matery die menstrum haist*, ibid., ll. 171–2, 216–17 and 220; *U on dem Selben fluß ist zw wissen, Das das lateinisch wort menstrum Jn den Frauen nichtz anders ist, wan ein wbrige matery die do kompt von essen vnd von drincken das die Selb fraw newst*, ibid., ll. 152–4. Clm 22297 uses *materia* much less, but still considers *menstruum* to be the name of the female seed.
15 Aristotle, *Generation of Animals*, pp. 389–91 (2. 766a).
16 Ibid., pp. 400–1 and 460–1 (2. 767b and 775a).
17 *Secreta mulierum*, ed. Schleissner, ll. 2695–8.
18 'Rheinfränkische Himmelfahrt Mariae', ed. Karl L. Weigand, *Zeitschrift für deutsches Alterthum*, 5 (1845), 515–64, ll. 1481–2, 1492 and 149–50, *die mensheit ich von ir genam; ich bin ir fleihz vn ir blvt; ein fleihz vn ein blvt; von mvterlicher spvnne fleizh vn blvt gewunne*. For further references, see Ellington, pp. 47 and 70–2; and Vincent, *Holy Blood*, pp. 128–9.
19 Mechthild, *Fließendes Licht*, pp. 266–8 (4. 14).
20 Ibid., pp. 166–8 (3. 4).
21 See Charles T. Wood, 'The doctors' dilemma: sin, salvation and the menstrual cycle in medieval thought', *Speculum*, 56 (1981), 710–27; and Dyan Elliott, *Fallen Bodies: Pollution, Sexuality and Demonology in the Middle Ages*, The Middle Ages Series (Philadelphia: University of Pennsylvania Press, 1999), pp. 109–16.
22 Song of Songs 8: 6, 'put me as a seal upon thy heart', *pone me ut signaculum super cor tuum*.
23 *'Die heilige Regel für ein vollkommenes Leben': Eine Cisterzienserarbeit des XIII. Jahrhunderts aus der Handschrift Additional 9048 des British Museum*, ed. Robert Priebsch, Deutsche Texte des Mittelalters, 16 (Berlin: Weidmann, 1909), p. 75.
24 *Secreta mulierum*, ed. Schleissner, ll. 151–4 and 2724–2808.
25 Ibid., ll. 2899–2903.
26 But the bloody nature of menstruum does shine through: the *Secreta* stresses the 'blood-colouredness' (*varb alls blut*) of menstruum, which is elaborated

upon in a question dedicated to just this issue (ibid., ll. 171–4). That it is 'similar in shape to raw blood' (*recht yn gestalt als roh blut*) is mentioned again in the following question concerning which hole the fluid exits from, anus or vulva (ibid., ll. 185–7). Further hints at the bloody nature of menstruum are that, like a fake virgin, the menstruating woman is betrayed by her blood-coloured urine (ibid., ll. 2297–2311); that the mirror a menstruating woman looks into also gets bloody (ibid., ll. 626–32); and that nosebleeds are an equivalent to menstrual flow as an alternative outlet for blood (ibid., ll. 2645–51 and 2658–70).

[27]   Ibid., ll. 187–214.

[28]   Ibid., ll. 2173–6. While it is normally the German text that uses wordy lists of synonyms, not the Latin, Clm 22297 repeats verbs stressing this cohesion: '*Et* lac eius de ma*m*illis ei*u*s spissu*m* et be*n*e digestu*m* ita q*u*od sep*er* (*recte* super) *ali*q*u*od politu*m* et tersu*m* cor*p*us pona*tur* no*n* di*vi*detur (*recte* dividatur) *sed p*artes *con*stabu*nt* et no*n* fluent . . . H*aec* om*n*ia su*nt* signa ad masc*u*linu*m*' (fol. 41v, 9–12).

[29]   *Secreta mulierum*, ed. Schleissner, ll. 2176–9, *zutailt sich nicht*.

[30]   Ibid., ll. 2186–9, *vngedait vnd dun, zurfleust*.

[31]   Ibid., ll. 2179–81, *zergan*.

[32]   Ibid., ll. 2201–6 and 2683–94, *dick, wol gdaitt, zurfleust, zu schmeltz*.

[33]   Ibid., ll. 2944–69, *dunne fruht*.

[34]   Ibid., ll. 187–213.

[35]   Ibid., ll. 187–93.

[36]   See, for example, Elliott, *Fallen Bodies*, esp. pp. 14–34.

[37]   Wood, 'Doctors' dilemma', pp. 713–17.

[38]   See Peggy McCracken, 'The curse of Eve: female bodies and Christian bodies in Heloise's Third Letter', in Bonnie Wheeler (ed.), *Listening to Heloise: The Voice of a Twelfth-Century Woman* (New York: St Martin's Press, 2000), pp. 217–31; Joan Cadden, *Meanings of Sex Difference in the Middle Ages: Medicine, Science and Culture*, Cambridge History of Medicine (Cambridge: Cambridge University Press, 1993), pp. 70–9 and 174; *The Trotula: An English Translation of the Medieval Compendium of Women's Medicine*, ed. and tr. Monica Green (Philadelphia: University of Pennsylvania Press, 2001), pp. 19–22. For a corrective to the assumption that menstruation is universally seen as polluting in all cultures, see Thomas Buckley and Alma Gottlieb (eds), *Blood Magic: The Anthropology of Menstruation* (Berkeley: University of California Press, 1988).

[39]   Mechthild, *Fließendes Licht*, p. 340 (5. 9); see also pp. 176–8 (3. 9).

[40]   The *Fließendes Licht* again associates all blood, not just menstrual fluid, with sin, when the sinners' souls in purgatory are marked by blood, ibid., p. 96 (2. 8), and when the narrator's own blood is referred to as 'my sinful life-blood', p. 122 (2. 24), *min sundiges herzebluot*. Similarly linking blood with evil, a devil tempting the soul is bloody, 'a big devil, fiery, bloody, black, with claws and horn and eyes of glass', ibid., p. 274 (4. 17), *ein grosse tufel, furig, bluotig, swartze, mit takken und mit hornen und mit glasougen*. On a

Jungian basis, James C. Franklin, however, interprets liquidity in the *Fließendes Licht* as entirely positive and neglects all associations of blood with sin, Franklin, *Mystical Transformations: The Imagery of Liquids in the Work of Mechthild von Magdeburg* (Cranbury, NJ: Associated University Presses, 1978). On Mechthild reinterpretation of women as messy bodies see also Sara S. Poor, *Mechthild of Magdeburg and her Book: Gender and the Making of Textual Authority*, Middle Ages Series (Philadelphia: University of Pennsylvania Press, 2004); Poor, 'Mechthild von Magdeburg, gender, and the "unlearned tongue"', *Journal of Medieval and Early Modern Studies*, 31 (2001), 213–50; and Poor, 'Cloaking the body in text: the question of female authorship in the writings of Mechthild von Magdeburg', *Exemplaria*, 12/2 (2000), 417–53.

41 Hartlieb, *Secreta mulierum*, pp. 135–7.

42 See Irven M. Resnick, 'Medieval roots of the myth of Jewish male menses', *Harvard Theological Review*, 93/3 (2000), 241–63; Irven M. Resnick, 'Roots of the myth of Jewish male menses in Jacques de Vitry's *History of Jerusalem*', *International Guest Lecture Series*, Ingeborg Rennert Center for Jerusalem Studies, Bar-Ilan University (Israel), 3 (1998), 1–27; Peter Biller, 'A scientific view of Jews from Paris around 1300', *Micrologus*, 9 (2001), 137–68; Peter Biller, 'Views of Jews from Paris around 1300: Christian or "scientific"?', in Diana Wood (ed.), *Christianity and Judaism: Papers Read at the 1991 Summer Meeting and the 1992 Winter Meeting of the Ecclesiastical History Society*, Studies in Church History, 29 (Oxford: Blackwell, 1992), pp. 187–207; Willis Johnson, 'The myth of Jewish male menses', *Journal of Medieval History*, 24 (1998), 273–95; David S. Katz, 'Shylock's gender: Jewish male menstruation in early modern England', *Review of English Studies*, NS 50, no. 200 (1999), 440–62. While Biller in 2001 and Resnick in 2000 make references to some of the *Secreta mulierum* versions, they have not cited Hartlieb's translation; this is why I here quote it at length.

43 On such medieval notions of ethnicity, see Robert Bartlett, *The Making of Europe: Conquest, Colonization, and Cultural Change, 950–1350* (Harmondsworth: Penguin, 1993), esp. pp. 197–242. On the bloodshedder Cain as a forefather to Jews and monsters, see John Block Friedman, *The Monstrous Races in Medieval Art and Thought* (Cambridge, MA: Harvard University Press, 1981), pp. 87–107 (p. 103); Ruth Mellinkoff, 'Cain and the Jews', *Journal of Jewish Art*, 6 (1979), 16–38.

44 *Secreta mulierum*, ed. Schleissner, ll. 1715–26.

45 Ibid., ll. 268–71, 247–9 and 2724–58.

46 Ibid., ll. 599–612.

47 Pliny, *Natural History*, ed. and tr. Harris Rackham, 10 vols, Loeb Classical Library (London: Heinemann, 1938–63), II (1961 [1942]), pp. 548–9 (7. 64), tr. Rackham.

48 Ortolf, *Arzneibuch*, p. 161 (ch. 137), *alz eyn kynt geborn vnde enphenget wert von boseme blode*; *Secreta mulierum*, ed. Schleissner, l. 2383. Women

çan affect embryos not only through blood, but even by their thoughts, turning them into whatever they think about during the conception, ibid., ll. 1922–30.

49 *Secreta mulierum*, ed. Schleissner, ll. 1458–1596 (l. 1532, *starck vnd krefftig*; and l. 1525, *plode vnd nit starck*). The uterus itself is also referred to as a 'fleshy skin' or 'fleshy hide' surrounding the embryo and foetus, ibid., for example, ll. 2532–3, 2579–80, 1646, *flaischen fell* or *flaischen haudt*). Clm 22297 simply has *matrix*.

50 Ibid., ll. 668–73 and 899–900.

51 Ibid., ll. 1569–73 and 1593–6.

52 Ibid., ll. 30–85. The initial advice to shield the *Secreta* from children is the only instance where masculinity and childhood are contrasted with one another, while the author at the same time claims to have a 'young and simple mind' himself, ibid., ll. 13–20, *mein klainer vnd Junger sun*.

53 Ibid., for example, ll. 2140–4 and 2649–51. The commentary claims that nosebleeds can also indicate a miscarriage, ibid., ll. 2658–70.

54 Ibid., ll. 1405–12.

55 McCracken, *Curse of Eve*, esp. pp. 61–91.

56 Ibid., ll. 1621–47.

57 Ortolf, *Arzneibuch*, p. 89 (ch. 21). That women's milk is also used in various remedies only highlights its potency, ibid., p. 121 (ch. 83); p. 127 (ch. 91); and p. 133 (ch. 100). On the risks breastfeeding was believed to present to the infant, see William F. MacLehose, 'Nurturing danger: high medieval medicine and the problem(s) of the child', in John Carmi Parsons and Bonnie Wheeler (eds), *Medieval Mothering*, New Middle Ages, 3 (New York: Garland, 1996), pp. 3–24.

58 *Secreta mulierum*, ed. Schleissner, ll. 584–94.

59 Ibid., ll. 612–26.

60 Ibid., ll. 2312–15 and 632–6. Ortolf also believes that men can become leprous during sex with a healthy woman, who passes on a previous partner's leprosy, without linking that to menstruation, Ortolf, *Arzneibuch*, p. 161 (ch. 137), 'when a woman has a leprous man, whoever comes to her after that, becomes leprous', *daz eyn wyb eynen vsseczigen man hat, wer dar nach to er kumt, der wert vssetisch*.

61 *Secreta mulierum*, ed. Schleissner, ll. 2480–5.

62 Ibid., for example, l. 2363, *krebs*; *Bartholomäus*, ed. Pfeiffer, pp. 24 and 48, *siechtuom*.

63 *Secreta mulierum*, ed. Schleissner, ll. 2390–2405.

64 Ibid., ll. 2416–19.

65 See also ibid., ll. 2335–6.

66 Ibid., ll. 2377–82.

67 Ibid., ll. 1671–2.

68 Ibid., ll. 626–32.

69 Aristotle, 'On Dreams', in Aristotle, *On the Soul, Parva Naturalia, On Breath*, ed. and tr. W. S. Hett, rev. edn, Loeb Classical Library, 288 (London: Heinemann and Cambridge, MA: Harvard University Press, 1957

[1936]), pp. 348–71 (pp. 356–7, part II, para. 459b); Pliny, *Natural History*, II (1961 [1942]), p. 548 (7. 64).

70 The narrator tells us she eventually 'returned his senses to him', but 'kept his heart'; and Parzival's waking question is: 'Ah, my lady and wife, who has taken your body away?', Wolfram, *Parzival*, 302, ll. 3–5; 302, ll. 7–8; see also 283, l. 22; *im gap her wider witze sîn von Pelrapeir diu künegîn diu behielt iedoch sîn herze dort; ôwê vrouwe unde wîp, wer hât benomen mit dînen lîp?* Most scholars agree that a union takes place; Herbert Ernst Wiegand speaks of Parzival and Condwiramurs 'becoming one internally' (*innerliches Einswerden*), in Wiegand, *Studien zur Minne und Ehe in Wolframs Parzival und Hartmanns Artusepik*, Quellen und Forschungen zur Sprach- und Kulturgeschichte der germanischen Völker, NS 49 (Berlin: de Gruyter, 1972), p. 154; Walter Delabar emphasizes that this unit of the couple is poised against the outside world of the Arthurian court, see Delabar, '*Ûfgerihtiu sper: zur Interaktion in der Blutstropfenepisode in Wolframs Parzival*', in Helmut Brall, Barbara Haupt and Urban Küsters (eds), *Personenbeziehungen in der mittelalterlichen Literatur*, Studia humaniora, 25 (Düsseldorf: Droste, 1994), pp. 321–46 (pp. 339–46).

71 Wolfram, *Parzival*, 302, l. 11, *bin ichz?* 'is it me?'

72 Ibid., 283, l. 17, *unversunnen*; 287, l. 9; 288, l. 9; 283, l. 22, Condwiramurs *zuct im wizzenlîchen sin*; and 289, l. 2, *wan er schiet von den witzen dô*; similarly 300, l. 17; 302, l. 3; and 802, ll. 1–5. This is against Eberhard Nellmann, who believes that a negative evaluation in the excursus contrasts with the presentation of the plot, Nellmann, *Wolframs Erzähltechnik: Untersuchungen zur Funktion des Erzählers* (Wiesbaden: Steiner, 1973), pp. 142–4.

73 Wolfram, *Parzival*, 293, l. 5, *gewalt tuon*. Negative effects on the narrator, ibid., 287, ll. 10–18; on Solomon, ibid., 289, ll. 16–17; and on all men in two excursuses on love, ibid., 291, l. 1–293, l. 18; and 586, ll. 14–18.

74 Joachim Bumke, *Die Blutstropfen im Schnee*, Hermaea Germanistische Forschungen, NS 94 (Tübingen: Niemeyer, 2001), esp. pp. 111–16; Hans Dewald, *Minne und sgrâles âventiur: Äußerungen der Subjektivität und ihre sprachliche Vergegenwärtigung in Wolframs 'Parzival'*, Göppinger Arbeiten zur Germanistik, 158 (Göppingen: Kümmerle, 1975), pp. 73–5. Wiegand also assumes that Parzival perceives his ecstasy as blissful, but believes that this stands in contrast to its negative effects in the plot, where he is left defenceless against the attacks, see Wiegand, *Studien*, pp. 157–8. For a bibliography and the most detailed discussion on this episode, see Bumke, *Blutstropfen*, pp. 1–2 and 59–62.

75 Wirnt, *Wigalois*, l. 1484, *lûter als ein spiegelglas*.

76 Ibid., ll. 1511–13.

77 *Wigamur*, ed. Danielle Buschinger, Göppinger Arbeiten zur Germanistik, 320 (Göppingen: Kümmerle, 1987), ll. 1100–21.

78 Wirnt, *Wigalois*, ll. 2363–6.

79 Ibid., ll. 948–9, 4270, 4133–5, 9725–30, 7521, 7466–7, 8316, 9781, 4594–5, 4606, 10361–88, 4616–18 and 4836–46.

80 Ibid., ll. 4113–6, 4137–8, 4166–8, 4216–17, 4244 and 11375; *sînes herzen ṡuòt; er ir was alsam der lîp; rehte konschaft; ein lîp; gevangen.*
81 Ibid., ll. 906–12. For a more positive reading of this unity of lovers in *Wigalois* see Ingrid Hahn, 'Gott und Minne, Tod und *triuwe*: Zur Konzeption des *Wigalois* des Wirnt von Grafenberg', in Brall et al. (eds), *Personenbeziehungen*, pp. 37–60 (pp. 51–60).
82 Wirnt, *Wigalois*, ll. 2764 (*schôz*); 2578, 2591, 2755, 2936, 2997 and 2841–55. For the importance of Hojir in *Wigalois* see Andreas Klare, 'Überlegungen zur Literarisierung von historischen Figuren am Beispiel des Hoyer von Mansfeld in Wirnts *Wigalois*', *Leuvense Bijdragen*, 83 (1994), 485–521, and Volker Honemann, '*Wigalois*' Kampf mit dem roten Ritter: Zum Verständnis der Hojir-Aventiure in Wirnts *Wigalois*', in Honemann et al. (eds), *German Narrative Literature of the Twelfth and Thirteenth Centuries: Studies Presented to Roy Wisbey on his Sixty-Fifth Birthday* (Tübingen: Niemeyer, 1994), pp. 347–62.
83 Jacquart and Thomasset, *Sexuality and Medicine*, p. 74 (without references).
84 Wirnt, *Wigalois*, ll. 6406–6515, 7921–8006 and 5314–92. Critics discussing these passages have remained curiously silent about the unusual constellation of a female opponent for an Arthurian knight, for instance, Stephan Fuchs, *Hybride Helden: Gwigalois und Willehalm: Beiträge zum Heldenbild und zur Poetik des Romans im frühen 13. Jahrhundert*, Frankfurter Beiträge zur Germanistik (Heidelberg: Winter, 1997), pp. 159–63; Peter Kern, 'Die Auseinandersetzung mit der Gattungstradition im *Wigalois* Wirnts von Grafenberg', in Friedrich Wolfzettel (ed.) *Artusroman und Intertextualität*, Beiträge zur deutschen Philologie (Giessen: Schmitz, 1990), pp. 73–83 (pp. 77–8); and Schröder, 'Der synkretistische Roman', pp. 252–5.
85 See Battersby, *Phenomenal Woman*; Grosz, *Volatile Bodies*, esp. pp. 160–210; and Margrit Shildrick, *Leaky Bodies and Boundaries: Feminism, Postmodernism and (Bio-) Ethics* (London: Routledge, 1997).
86 Kathleen Coyne Kelly, *Performing Virginity and Testing Chastity in the Middle Ages*, Routledge Research in Medieval Studies, 2 (London: Routledge, 2000), esp. pp. 12 and 28; Jocelyn Wogan-Browne, 'Chaste bodies: frames and experiences', in Kay and Rubin (eds), *Framing Medieval Bodies*, pp. 24–42 (p. 24); Anke Bernau, Ruth Evans and Sarah Salih (eds), *Medieval Virginities*, Religion and Culture in the Middle Ages (Cardiff: University of Wales Press, 2003), in particular, Jane Cartwright, 'Virginity and chastity tests in medieval Welsh prose', pp. 56–79; Sarah Salih, *Versions of Virginity in Late Medieval England* (Woodbridge: Brewer, 2001), esp. pp. 107–65; McCracken, *Curse of Eve*, pp. 2–6.
87 *Secreta mulierum*, ed. Schleissner, ll. 2576–7, *so ist auch ein ytliche tochter zu helssenn wan Jr menstruum zum ersten kompt.*
88 Ibid., ll. 140–5.
89 *Bartholomäus*, ed. Pfeiffer, p. 42, *ist si niht ein dirne, so beseichet si sich.*
90 'Kaiser Lucius' Tochter', in *Deutsche Märendichtung*, ed. Fischer, ll. 272–7.
91 On 'evil women' in a German version of the *Dolopathos* narrative, see

Katya Skow Obenaus, 'The whole is the sum of its parts: misogyny as a unifying factor in *Die sieben weisen Meister*', *Fifteenth-Century Studies*, 26 (2001), 169–82.

92 'Kaiser Lucius' Tochter', in *Deutsche Märendichtung*, ed. Fischer, ll. 4 and 8, *wol geboren, von hocher art* and *diener*.

93 The view of the family as held together by *sippebluot*, and as violated by a woman trading sexual favours on her own, is spelled out in Dietrich, 'Borte', in *Gesammtabenteuer*, l. 195; see also chapter 4. On Portia's similar resistance, see Karen Newman, 'Reprise: gender, sexuality and theories of exchange in *The Merchant of Venice*', in Nigel Wood (ed.), *The Merchant of Venice*, Theory in Practice (Buckingham: Open University Press, 1996), pp. 102–23.

94 'Kaiser Lucius' Tochter', in *Deutsche Märendichtung*, ed. Fischer, ll. 611–13.

95 Ibid., ll. 548–50 and 572.

96 *Nibelungenlied*, ed. Brackert, stanzas 325–8, *ein küneginne gesezzen über sê*.

97 Ibid., stanza 673.

98 Ibid., stanza 675, see also chapter 2.

99 Jerold C. Frakes also convincingly reads the fight as a rape, Frakes, *Brides and Doom: Gender, Property, and Power in Medieval German Women's Epic*, The Middle Ages Series (Philadelphia: University of Pennsylvania Press, 1994), esp. pp. 96–136.

100 'Beringer', in *Die historien von dem ritter beringer* (Strasbourg: Matthias Brant, 1495); modern German translation in *Schwankerzählungen des deutschen Mittelalters*, tr. Hanns Fischer (Munich: Beck, 1967), pp. 47–54.

101 Dietrich, 'Borte', in *Gesammtabenteuer*, ll. 639–43.

102 *Secreta mulierum*, ed. Schleissner, ll. 1502–4.

103 Ibid., ll. 2315–36 (ll. 2315–19). The thirteenth-century Latin version formulates likewise: '*Est etiam notandum et diligenter memorie imprimendum quod mulieres antique quibus menstrua fluunt uel quedam ut in pluribus quibus menstrua retenta sunt sepe (recte semper?) si inspiciant (recte inspiciunt) pueros in cunis iacentes toxicant eos uisu ut ait albertus contractatu suo de menstruis mulierum*' (Clm 22297, fol. 43r, 8–13). Much work has been done on related beliefs in the evil eye, in particular by folklorists, see, for example, Alan Dundes (ed.), *The Evil Eye: A Folklore Casebook*, Garland Folklore Casebooks, 2 (New York: Garland, 1981). On further similar beliefs about menstrual pollution in natural philosophical and medical texts see Claude Thomasset, 'Le corps féminin ou le regard empêché', *Micrologus*, 1 (1993), 99–114.

104 See Jacquart and Thomasset, *Sexuality and Medicine*, pp. 188–93; Lochrie, *Covert Operations*, pp. 98–118; Claude Thomasset, 'La femme au Moyen Age: les composantes fondamentales de sa représentation, immunité – impunité', *Ornicar*, 22–3 (1981), 223–38.

105 *Secreta mulierum*, ed. Schleissner, ll. 2319–25 and 2363–9. The eyes of the baby are vulnerable also in Ortolf, *Arzneibuch*, p. 88 (ch. 20). On the material effects of gazes, see also Suzannah Biernoff, *Sight and Embodiment in the Middle Ages*, The New Middle Ages (Basingstoke: Palgrave, 2002).

106 *Secreta mulierum*, ed. Schleissner, ll. 2331–5.

107 Fernando Salmon and Montserrat Cabré i Pairet, 'Fascinating women: the evil eye in medical scholasticism', in Roger French et al. (ed.), *Medicine from the Black Death to the French Disease* (Aldershot: Ashgate, 1998), pp. 53–84. They have found such beliefs in much early sixteenth-century Spanish natural philosophy, amongst others, in Diego Alvarez Chanca's *Tractatus de fascinatione* (*c.* 1499); Antonio de Cartagena's *Libellus de fascinatione* (1499); Martin de Andosilla's *De Superstitionibus* (1510); Martin de Castañega's *Tratado de las superticiones y hechicerías* (1527); and López de Corella's *Treszientas preguntas de cosas naturals* (1546). See also Shulamith Shahar, *Growing Old in the Middle Ages: 'Winter Clothes Us in Shadow and Pain'*, tr. Yael Lotan (New York: Routledge, 1997 [1995]), esp. pp. 43–4 and 151–2.

108 Facsimile of 1st edn and commentary: Heinrich Institoris and Jakob Sprenger, *Malleus maleficarum*, ed. André Schnyder, 2 vols (Göppingen: Kümmerle, 1991–3), fol. 9r (part I, question 2); German tr.: Heinrich Kramer (Institoris), *Der Hexenhammer. Malleus maleficarum*, tr. Günter Jerouschek and Wolfgang Behringer (Munich: dtv, 2000), p. 168; no critical edn is available. See *Women's Secrets*, tr. Lemay, pp. 49–58. For the link between the images of the menstrual woman and the witch (as well as of the vampire), see Shuttle and Redgrove, *Wise Wound*, esp. pp. 197–259.

109 Norman Cohn, *Europe's Inner Demons: The Demonization of Christians in Medieval Christendom*, 2nd edn (London: Pimlico, 1993), esp. pp. 35–41 and 162–6; and Jeffrey Burton Russell, *Witchcraft in the Middle Ages* (Ithaca, NY: Cornell University Press, 1972). Historical records of cannibalism by Christian crusaders are discussed, for example, in Geraldine Heng, 'Cannibalism, the first crusade and the genesis of medieval romance', *Differences*, 10 (1998), 98–173. Mongols were also accused of cannibalism by various writers, see Michael Uebel, 'Unthinking the monster: twelfth-century responses to Saracen alterity', in Jeffrey Jerome Cohen (ed.), *Monster Theory: Reading Culture* (Minneapolis: University of Minnesota Press, 1996), pp. 264–91 (pp. 282 and 290–1).

110 Institoris and Sprenger, *Malleus maleficarum*, fol. 9v (part I, question 2), tr. Kramer, *Hexenhammer*, p. 171; Pliny, *Natural History*, III (1967 [1940]), pp. 57–8 (8. 33), and VIII (1963), ed. and tr. W. H. S. Jones, pp. 225–6 (29. 19); and Isidore of Seville, *Etymologiarum sive originvm*, ed. W. M. Lindsay, 2 vols (Oxford: Clarendon, 1911), II (12. 4, definitions 6 and 7). For a first introduction to medieval beliefs about the basilisk, see Marianne Sammer, 'Basilisk – regulus: eine bedeutungsgeschichtliche Skizze', in Ulrich Müller and Werner Wunderlich (eds), *Dämonen – Monster – Fabelwesen*, Mittelaltermythen, 2 (St Gallen: Fachverlag für Wissenschaft und Studium, 1999), pp. 135–60.

111 *Libellus de formatione hominis in vtero, vel ut notiori Titulo, Secreta mulierum* (Antwerp: Mart. Caesar, 1538), pages not numbered (ch. 10).

112 *De Secretis mulierum* (Lyons: Quadratus, 1580), quoted in *Women's Secrets*, tr. Lemay, p. 130.

[113] Wirnt, *Wigalois*, ll. 4697–8; see also ll. 5063–5, 5058, 1025–6 and 5055–6. *The Prose Salernitan Questions*, ed. Brian Lawn, Auctores Britannici Medii Aevi, 5 (London: Oxford University Press, for the British Academy, 1979), p. 49 (question B 105); pp. 68–9 (question B 138); pp. 129–30 (question B 268) and p. 298 (question N 30).

[114] Wirnt, *Wigalois*, ll. 7363–6 and 7399–7401. Ingeborg Henderson sees all the monsters that Wigalois fights as Cain's kin (sharing the features traditionally believed to be characteristic of his descendants), which could create another link between these creatures and the blood which their ancestor famously shed, Henderson, 'Dark figures and eschatological imagery in Wirnt von Gravenberg's *Wigalois*', in Edward R. Haymes and Stephanie Cain van D'Elden (eds), *The Dark Figure in Medieval German and Germanic Literature*, Göppinger Arbeiten zur Germanistik, 448 (Göppingen: Kümmerle, 1986), pp. 99–113 (pp. 108–10).

[115] Salmon and Cabré, 'Fascinating women', p. 68; see also Joan Copjec, 'Vampires, breast-feeding and anxiety', *October*, 58 (1998), 24–43 (p. 27). Approaching someone from behind, in the way that Daniel approaches not only the bloodsuckers, but also the blood-bather, is a related idea; Stricker, *Daniel*, ll. 4792–5; see Claude Gaignebet, 'Véronique ou l'image vraie', *Anagrom*, 7–8 (1976), 45–70 (esp. pp. 51–5). Besides, if it is indeed leprosy that the blood-bather suffers from, it could be caused by him having been conceived during a menstrual period, and would make him into another opponent with 'menstrous' overtones.

[116] On the singular status of the three ladies' autobiographical narratives in the romance see Volker Honemann, 'Daniel monologisiert, der Riese berichtet, drei Damen erzählen: Aspekte der Figurenrede im *Daniel von dem Blühenden Tal* des Strickers', in Harald Haferland and Norbert Mecklenburg (eds), *Erzählungen in Erzählungen: Phänomene der Narration in Mittelalter und früher Neuzeit*, Forschungen zur Geschichte der älteren deutschen Literatur, 19 (Munich: Fink, 1996), pp. 221–32 (pp. 230–1).

[117] See his long hesistant musings, Stricker, *Daniel*, for example, ll. 1739–1876.

[118] Ibid., ll. 1579–80, 1581–91 and 1266–71.

[119] Konrad von Würzburg, 'Silvester', ll. 661–713.

[120] Ibid., ll. 771–835.

[121] Samantha Riches, *St George: Hero, Martyr and Myth* (Stroud: Sutton, 2000), pp. 156–78.

[122] Alexander Barclay, *The Life of St George*, ed. William Nelson, Early English Text Society, os 230 (London: Oxford University Press, 1955), ll. 521–5.

[123] Ibid., l. 528, *hyr wombe insaciate no hunger coude indure.*

[124] Ibid., ll. 542–6. The dragons in the George and Sylvester legends in the *Passional* (c.1280–1300), a widespread German collection of saints' lives derived mostly from the famous *Legenda aurea* by Jacobus de Voragine (d. 1298), also have a poisonous stench and gaze and an insatiable appetite, but no other links to menstruation, *Das Passional*, 3 vols, I and II, ed. Karl A. Hahn (Frankfurt/Main: Broenner, 1845), III, ed. Karl Köpke (Quedlinburg:

Basse, 1857), 'Sylvester', III, pp. 62–93; 'Georg', III, pp. 253–65. *Mandeville's Travels* (c.1357) tells of a virgin who was turned into a dragon herself, *Mandeville's Travels*, ed. P. Hamelius, Early English Text Society, os 153 (London: Kegan Paul, Trench & Trübner, 1919), pp. 14–16.

125 Jean d'Arras, *Mélusine: Roman du XIVe siècle*, ed. Louis Stouff (Djion: Publications de l'Université, 1932); Thüring von Ringoltingen, 'Melusine', in *Romane des 15. und 16. Jahrhunderts*, ed. Jan-Dirk Müller, Bibliothek der frühen Neuzeit, 1 (Frankfurt/Main: Deutscher Klassiker-Verlag, 1990), pp. 9–176; examples for the woman-serpent in paradise are discussed in Riches, *St George*, pp. 156–8; see also McCracken, *Curse of Eve*, pp. 79–91. As a starting point into the abundant research on Melusine, see Jeanne-Marie Boivin and Proinsias MacCana (eds), *Mélusines continentales et insulaires* (Paris: Champion, 1999) and Donald Maddox and Sara Sturm-Maddox (eds), *Melusine of Lusignan: Founding Fiction in Late Medieval France* (Athens, GA: University of Georgia Press, 1996).

126 Claude Gaignebet, 'Véronique ou l'image vraie', esp. pp. 60–2; repeated in Claude Gaignebet and Jean-Dominique Lajoux, *Art profane et religion populaire au Moyen Age* (Paris: Presses Universitaires de France, 1985), p. 137; Jacquart and Thomasset, *Sexuality and Medicine*, p. 74; François Clier-Colombani, *La fée Mélusine au Moyen Age: Images, mythes et symboles* (Paris: Léopard d'or, 1991), pp. 155–7; in relation to the siren also in Gilbert Durand, *Les structures anthropologiques de l'imaginaire: Introduction à l'archétypologie générale* (Paris: Bordas, Collection Etudes Supérieures, 1969), pp. 114–15; quoted again in David Williams, *Deformed Discourse: The Function of the Monster in Mediaeval Thought and Literature* (Exeter: University of Exeter Press, 1996), p. 188.

127 Thüring, 'Melusine', p. 97.

128 A wide range of reproductions are accessible in Clier-Colombani, *La fée Mélusine*, appendix, and Gaignebet and Lajoux, *Art profane*, esp. pp. 141–51.

129 Stephen G. Nichols mentions 'the feminine body forsaken by Melusine in assuming, in the place of the female sex, the serpent's tail, itself a form of usurpation of male authority' (p. 154), and goes on to discuss what he sees as this usurpation, Nichols, 'Melusine between myth and history: profile of a female demon' in Maddox and Sturm-Maddox (eds), *Melusine of Lusignan*, pp. 137–64 (pp. 154–8). For a similar reading of Melusine as both maternal and phallic, and for her lineage as monstrous, see Gabrielle M. Spiegel, 'Maternity and monstrosity: reproductive biology in the *Roman de Mélusine*', in Maddox and Sturm-Maddox (eds), *Melusine of Lusignan*, pp. 100–24.

130 On Melusine's body guaranteeing the integrity of the lineage, see Sylvia Huot, 'Dangerous embodiments: Froissart's Harton and Jean d'Arras's Melusine', *Speculum*, 78/2 (April 2003), 400–20 (esp. p. 420); and for a reading of Melusine passing on her lineage through blood (which is simplistically set against semen), see Douglas Kelly, 'The domestication of the marvelous in the Melusine romances', in Maddox and Sturm-Maddox (eds), *Melusine of Lusignan*, pp. 32–47; see also McCracken, *Curse of Eve*, pp. 77–91.

[131] Thomas Schürmann finds no proof of a persistent belief in vampires as revenants during the Middle Ages, in Schürmann, *Nachzehrerglauben in Mitteleuropa*, Schriftenreihe der Kommission für ostdeutsche Volkskunde in der Gesellschaft für Volkskunde, 51 (Marburg: Elwert, 1990), esp. pp. 32–42. For a psychoanalytic introduction to vampires, see Alan Dundes, 'The vampire as bloodthirsty revenant: a psychoanalytic post mortem', in Dundes (ed.), *The Vampire: A Casebook* (Madison: University of Wisconsin Press, 1998), pp. 150–75. On bloodsucking women and monsters see previous chapters and Bettina Bildhauer, 'Bloodsuckers: the construction of female sexuality in medieval science and fiction', in Liz Herbert McAvoy and Teresa Walters (eds), *Consuming Narratives: Gender and Monstrous Appetites in the Middle Ages and the Renaissance* (Cardiff: University of Wales Press, 2002), pp. 104–15.

[132] *Eckenlied*, ed. Wierschin, stanza 21, ll. 9–13. For references to other versions of this episode in the Dietrich legends, see Wolfgang Dinkelacher, 'Ortnit', in Ruh (ed.), *Die deutsche Literatur des Mittelalters: Verfasserlexikon*, VII (Berlin: de Gruyter, 1989), cols 58–67 (col. 65).

[133] 'Wolfdietrich B', ed. Oscar Jänicke, in Arthur Amelung and Jänicke (eds), *Ortnit und die Wolfdietriche*, 2 vols, Deutsches Heldenbuch, 3 and 4 (Berlin: Weidmann, 1871–3), II (1873), pp. 165–301 (p. 268, *aventiure* IV, stanza 684).

[134] See Claude Lecouteux, who highlights the overlaps between this dragon with sleep-inducing powers and the basilisk, Lecouteux, 'Des Königs Ortnit Schlaf', *Euphorion*, 73 (1979), 347–55; but Heino Gehrts makes the not incompatible point that this sleep is simply a standard fairytale motif when a hero is about to die, Gehrts, 'Der Schlaf des Drachenkämpfers Ortnit', *Euphorion*, 77 (1983), 342–4. Uta Störmer-Caysa offers a simple reading of the sucking as pulling Ortnit into the evil children's realm in Störmer-Caysa, 'Ortnits Mutter, die Drachen und der Zwerg', *Zeitschrift für deutsches Altertum und deutsche Literatur*, 128 (1998), 282–308. Joyce Tally Lionarons uses Girard to argue that this and other episodes in which the dragon wins are always already embedded in wider narratives in which the dragon is overcome after all, see Joyce Tally Lionarons, ' "Sometimes the dragon wins": unsuccessful dragon fighters in medieval literature', in Loren C. Gruber (ed.), *Essays in Old, Middle, Modern English and Old Icelandic in Honour of Raymond J. Tripp, Jr* (Lewiston, NY: Edwin Mullen, 2000), pp. 301–16; on dragons as Cain's kin and thereby related to the original bloodshed, see Emerson, 'Legends of Cain'; and Zacharias P. Thundy, 'The dragon in *Beowulf*: Cain's seed, heresy and Islam', ibid., pp. 201–300.

[135] *Secreta mulierum*, ed. Schleissner, ll. 2093–7. The Latin text does not have the comparison to breastfeeding, but does speaks of sucking, too: 'Signum conceptionis est si vir existens in coitu sentiat virgam suam sugi et attrahi quadam clausura et pressura factam ex parte vulvue mulieris' (Clm 22297, fol. 41r, 12–15).

[136] *Secreta mulierum*, ed. Schleissner, ll. 2940–3.

[137] Ibid., ll. 2909–14 and 2922–5; similarly: 'Igitur etiam sperma amplius emissum a uiro nimis desiccat quia uirtutem humectandi et calefaciendi habet(.)

corpsi pöre (*recte* corpore) au*t* exsiccato si*ne* hu*m*ido extracto sit debilitat*io* uite *et* per *consequen*s mors(.) *et* hoc *est* cau*s*a qu*are* illi q*ui* mu*ltum et* frequ*enter* coiu*nt* (*recte* coeunt) n*on* su*nt* longe uite q*uia* corpo*r*a eo*rum* a *natur*ali hu*m*ido desiccantur q*ue* desiccat*io est causa* mortis . . . *est* e*nim* generali*ter* vnu*m* (*recte* verum) q*uod* masculi femellis lo*n*gioris uite su*nt* si fuerint coit*iui*' (Clm 22297, fols 49r, 6–49v, 1 and 8–10). In the resolution of abbreviations, I have used the common medieval spelling 'que' for 'quae' throughout.

138 *Secreta mulierum*, ed. Schleissner, ll. 2441–3.

139 Ibid., ll. 232–9, similarly ll. 2144–50, where the retained menstrual blood is referred to as women's seed, *Same der Frauen*.

140 Ibid., ll. 2153–9 (ll. 2155–8).

141 Ibid., ll. 2311–12 and 2373–5.

142 Ibid., ll. 2160–6.

143 Ibid., ll. 2885–2903. For a discussion of various theories on the origin of semen, see Reynolds, *Food and the Body*, pp. 9–10, 250–3 and passim; Cadden, *Meanings of Sex Difference*, pp. 32 and 180; Jacquart and Thomasset, *Sexuality and Medicine*, pp. 52–60. Other cravings mentioned are those for earth or coal, prototypically dry substances that could balance women's moisture (ibid., ll. 2106–7); apples, the prototypical object of a woman's sinful desire since Adam and Eve (Clm 22297, fol. 41v, 1–3; and *Secreta mulierum*, ed. Schleissner, ll. 2632–47); and meat, fresh flesh (Clm 22297, fol. 41v, 1–3).

144 See Bynum, *Holy Feast and Holy Fast*, passim; and Peter Dinzelbacher, 'Das Blut Christi in der Religiösität des Mittelalters', in Kruse and Rudolf (eds), *900 Jahre Heilig-Blut-Verehrung*, pp. 415–34.

145 Mechthild, *Fließendes Licht*, p. 42 (1. 22).

146 Ibid., p. 42 (1. 22).

147 See also ibid., p. 94 (2. 7); and p. 120 (2. 24).

148 For example, ibid., pp. 36–8 (1. 17–20); and p. 176 (3. 9).

149 Ibid., p. 90 (2. 4).

150 Ibid., p. 512 (6. 39); see also in combination with mirrors, p. 514 (6. 41). For images of mirrors in the *Fließendes Licht* see Burkhard Hasebrink, 'Spiegel und Spiegelung im *Fließenden Licht der Gottheit*', in Walter Haug and Wolfram Schneider-Lastin (eds), *Deutsche Mystik im abendländischen Zusammenhang: Neu erschlossene Texte, neue methodische Ansätze, neue theoretische Konzepte* (Tübingen: Niemeyer, 2000), pp. 157–74.

151 *Heilige Regel*, ed. Priebsch, p. 27.

152 Hans Folz, 'Jüdischer Wucher', in Folz, *Reimpaarsprüche*, pp. 310–18, ll. 265–6, *wy dy pluthunt saugen und melcken Der armen cristen plut und schweiß*; Folz, 'Hausratbüchlein', in Folz, *Reimpaarsprüche*, pp. 358–68, ll. 259–61, *Süg yn an yder hant ein per, Das yms plut auß den negeln drüng, Er meint, das im vil pas gelüng*.

153 Mechthild, *Fließendes Licht*, p. 42 (1. 22) and p. 82 (2. 3). Mary desires the soul or the union between Christ and the soul in return when Christ enters the soul with the words: 'Mother, I will gladly lay myself into the site of your

desire', ibid. p. 90 (2. 4), *Muoter, ich wil mich gerne legen in die stat diner girde.*

[154] Ibid., pp. 40–2 (1. 22).

[155] Ibid., p. 42 (1. 22).

[156] Ibid., p. 82 (2. 3); *mit offenen wunden, bluotig, unverbunden*; ibid., p. 482 (6. 24); *ze glicher wis alse die milch, die ich von miner megetlichen muoter soug*; Mary's milk from grace also p. 366 (5. 23).

[157] Songs of Songs, 4: 12; Ezekiel 44: 1–3; see also Ellington, pp. 61–2 and 70.

[158] *Heilige Regel*, ed. Priebsch, p. 2.

[159] Penetration is an important and usually threatening experience throughout the text. For example, the Devil shoots arrows at the hermit to tempt him (ibid., p. 11); being penetrated by fiery snakes entering the throat and heart and sucking her breasts is a punishment in hell for a sinful woman (ibid., p. 38); and penetration by Devils pushing two red-hot knives through his head and feet is a punishment for an unrepentant man (ibid., pp. 39–40). On the other hand, divinity, in the form of a dove, enters the body through the natural opening of the mouth (ibid., p. 47).

[160] Ibid., for example, pp. 1 and 2.

[161] See also Beckwith, *Christ's Body*, on the hierarchized, but coherent body of Christ.

[162] *Heilige Regel*, ed. Priebsch, p. 69, *Ysaias: 'Alle unzer gerechtekeit werden wuor Gotez gerichte unreiner dan ie dekein duch wurde daz zu wibez suchede gehoret.'*

[163] Ibid., pp. 42–3.

[164] Brun, *Hohes Lied*, ll. 2292–2303.

[165] Ibid., ll. 4130–4367.

[166] Ibid., ll. 2954–77.

[167] Ibid., ll. 3882–93, 3927–77 (as opposed to the open garden of the paradise) and 3790–7; also ll. 4773–89.

[168] Ibid., ll. 2947–50 and 2761–4. There are also other courtly motives in Mary's description, for example, her feet are 'set in a knightly fashion' (ibid., l. 4606, *rittirlich gestellet*); she is balm, drink and food for men wounded in fights in her service (ibid., ll. 6107–46).

[169] Ibid., ll. 3831–67 and 2636–46.

[170] Bernardino of Siena, '*Sermo 61: Feria quarta post resurrectionem: De superadmirabili gratia et gloria Matris Dei*', in *Opera Omnia*, ed. Pacifici M. Perantoni and P. Augustini Sépinski, 9 vols (Quaracchi: Collegium S. Bonaventurae, 1950–65), II (1950), pp. 371–97 (p. 376, article I, chapter IV), corrected tr. after Diane Spivey Ellington, *From Sacred Body to Angelic Soul: Understanding Mary in Late Medieval and Early Modern Europe* (Washington, DC: Catholic University of America Press, 2001), p. 63.

[171] Song of Songs 4: 2, *dentes tui sicut greges*; Brun, *Hohes Lied*, ll. 2978–3145 (ll. 3120–5). That these sheep that are her teeth are at the same time read as Christ creates its own problems for the boundaries of Mary's body, who now somehow contains her son in her teeth.

[172] Brun, *Hohes Lied*, ll. 4084–4100.

[173] Song of Songs 7: 4, in Brun's *Hohes Lied* quoted as *nasus tuus sicut turris Salomonis quae respicit contra Damascum*; the Vulgate and Douay-Rheims versions have 'tower of Libanus' (*turris libani*) instead.

[174] Brun, *Hohes Lied*, ll. 2375–84.

[175] Ibid., ll. 2385–90.

[176] Konrad, 'Silvester', ll. 3431–3562; further references are collected in Köhler, 'Die Erde als jungfräuliche Mutter Adams'.

[177] Brun, *Hohes Lied*, for example, ll. 2625–9 and 3427–3636; see also 2895–2945.

[178] Ibid., ll. 3521–32.

[179] Ibid., ll. 2625–9.

[180] Pliny, *Natural History*, II, p. 548 (7. 64); see above in this chapter, pp. 97–8.

[181] *Secreta mulierum*, ed. Schleissner, ll. 1894–7 (l. 1895), *uberflussigkait der matery*.

[182] Williams, *Deformed Discourse*, pp. 174–5.

[183] *Secreta mulierum*, ed. Schleissner, p. 152; Erlangen, Universitätsbibliothek, MS B 33 (Irm. 1492).

Chapter 4

[1] Douglas, *Purity and Danger*, p. 116, see my introduction, p. 9.

[2] Ernst H. Kantorowicz, *The King's Two Bodies: A Study in Mediaeval Political Theology* (Princeton: Princeton University Press, 1957), pp. 194–206; John of Salisbury, *Policraticus*, ed. Clement Charles Julian Webb, 2 vols (Oxford: Clarendon, 1909), 5. 2. Pouchelle draws attention to the fact that not only was society metaphorically represented as a body, but the body was also imagined in medical writing as a society, a kingdom, with rulers, a workforce and cooperating members, Pouchelle, *Body and Surgery*, pp. 109–24.

[3] *Schwabenspiegel*, ed. Eckhardt, I (1972), pp. 48–50; II, pp. 64–5; and *Sachsenspiegel: Landrecht und Lehnrecht*, ed. Friedrich Ebel, 3rd, rev. edn (Stuttgart: Reclam, 1999 [1953]), 1. 3. 3 (p. 31). A diagram in a thirteenth-century manuscript shows a similar family line extending backwards and forwards through the generations and sideways to the siblings and cousins in the shape of an arrow superimposed on and at the same time held by a body; Grenoble, Bibliothèque Municipale, MS 34, fol. 185r, reproduced and briefly described in Jacques Le Goff, *Medieval Civilisation, 400–1500*, tr. Julia Barrow (Oxford: Blackwell, 1988 [1964]), pl. 16. Conversely, relationships between organs are also imagined as those of a mother, father and daughter in Henri de Mondeville's *Chirurgie* (c.1306–20), see Pouchelle, *Body and Surgery*, p. 124.

[4] *Decrees of the Ecumenical Councils*, ed. Tanner, I, p. 201 (Canon 16), *honores ecclesiastici sanguinis non sunt sed meriti*, tr. Tanner; Dietrich, 'Der Borte', in *Gesammtabenteuer*, l. 195; Wolfram, *Parzival*, 470, l. 23, and 740, l. 3; 'Rheinfränkische Himmelfahrt Mariae', ed. Weigand, l. 1492, see also

ll. 1481–2 and 150–2. Further references to blood as 'kinship', see '*Bluot*', in Matthias Lexer, *Mittelhochdeutsches Handwörterbuch*, 3 vols (Leipzig: Hirzel, 1872–8), I (1872), col. 316, and '*Sippebluot*', in Benecke et al., *Mittelhochdeutsches Wörterbuch*, I (1854), p. 219. Uli Linke argues that in Proto-Indo-European, the term for blood uniting a family group (**es-r*) was the same as for blood inside the body, while there was a different term for blood outside the body (**kreu*), Linke, 'Blood as metaphor in Proto-Indo-European', *Journal of Indoeuropean Studies*, 13 (1985), 333–76. Adrian Parvulescu, 'Blood and IE. kinship terminology', *Indogermanische Forschungen*, 94 (1989), 67–88, argues that many Indo-European kinship terms also mean 'of one's own blood'.

5 Isidore of Seville, *Etymologiarum*, I (9. 6, definition 4).

6 Hans Folz, 'Adam und Eva' in Folz, *Reimpaarsprüche*, pp. 150–63, l. 296, *unser fleisch und plut*.

7 Walter Delabar, *Erkantiu sippe und hoch geselleschaft: Studien zur Funktion des Verwandtschaftsverbandes in Wolfram von Eschenbachs Parzival*, Göppinger Arbeiten zur Germanistik, 518 (Göppingen: Kümmerle, 1990), esp. pp. 237–47.

8 Wolfram, *Parzival*, 475, ll. 22–5.

9 Ibid., 740, l. 3.

10 Ibid., 464, ll. 16–22.

11 Ibid., 465, ll. 1–6.

12 Without much reference to blood, the problematic concept of kinship and its relation to sin in *Parzival* and in this episode in particular has been discussed by numerous scholars, for example, Elisabeth Schmid, *Familiengeschichten und Heilsmythologie: Die Verwandtschaftsstrukturen in den französischen und deutschen Gralromanen des 12. und 13. Jahrhunderts*, Beihefte zur Zeitschrift für romanische Philologie (Tübingen: Niemeyer, 1986), pp. 171–204; Karl Bertau, *Über Literaturgeschichte: Literarischer Kunstcharakter und Geschichte in der höfischen Epik um 1200* (Munich: Beck, 1983), pp. 47–66; Bertau, 'Versuch über Verhaltenssemantik von Verwandten im *Parzival*', in Bertau, *Neun Versuche über Subjektivität und Ursprünglichkeit in der Geschichte* (Munich: Beck, 1983), pp. 190–240; Ursula Storp, *Väter und Söhne: Tradition und Traditionsbruch in der volkssprachlichen Literatur des Mittelalters*, Item mediävistische Studien, 2 (Essen: Item, 1994), pp. 61–81; Delabar, *Erkantiu sippe*, pp. 293–308; Peter Czerwinski, *Der Glanz der Abstraktion: Frühe Formen von Reflexivität im Mittelalter: Exempel einer Geschichte der Wahrnehmung* (Frankfurt/Main: Campus, 1989), pp. 160–77; Wilhelm Busse, 'Verwandtschaftsstrukturen im *Parzival*', *Wolfram-Studien*, 5 (1979), 116–34; and Julius Schwietering, 'Natur und *art*', *Zeitschrift für deutsches Altertum und deutsche Literatur*, 91 (1961/62), 108–37.

13 Mechthild, *Fließendes Licht*, p. 340 (5. 9).

14 John 19: 34; Augustine of Hippo, *In Joannis Evangelium*, ed. Migne, *Patrologia Latina*, 35 (1841), cols 1579–1976 (col. 1953, tractate 120, para. 2);

translation: Augustine, *Tractates on the Gospel of John 112–24/Tractates on the First Epistle of John*, tr. John W. Rettig, The Fathers of the Church, 92 (Washington, DC: Catholic University of America Press, 1995), pp. 50–5 (p. 51); Thomas Aquinas agreed with him: Aquinas, *Super Evangelium S. Ioannis*, p. 455 (para. 2458); see also Berg, 'Traktat des Gerhard von Köln', p. 440; and chapter 1, pp. 29–31.

15 *Decrees of the Ecumenical Councils*, ed. Tanner, I, p. 360 (canon 1), tr. and emphasis Tanner. The context is yet again an invocation of blood as proof to defend against Franciscan doubts the belief that Christ took a true human body from the virgin.

16 Brun, *Hohes Lied*, ll. 10139–54 (ll. 10444–51).

17 *Heilige Regel*, ed. Priebsch, p. 74; Genesis 2: 11–12.

18 Esp. Caroline Walker Bynum, *Holy Feast and Holy Fast*; and Bynum, 'The body of Christ in the later Middle Ages: a reply to Leo Steinberg', in Bynum, *Fragmentation and Redemption: Essays on Gender and the Human Body in Medieval Religion* (New York: Zone, 1992), pp. 79–117.

19 McCracken, *Curse of Eve*, esp. pp. 6–20 and 41–60.

20 Mechthild, *Fließendes Licht*, p. 176 (3. 9) and p. 40 (1. 22).

21 Ibid., pp. 338–40 (5. 9), see also p. 178 (3. 9).

22 Ibid., p. 178 (3. 9), see also pp. 404–6 (5. 34) and p. 482 (6. 24).

23 Ibid., p. 482 (6. 24).

24 Ibid., p. 83 (2. 3), p. 42 (1. 22) and p. 406 (5. 34).

25 Ibid., pp. 404–6 (5. 34) and pp. 462–4 (6. 15).

26 Ibid., p. 324 (5. 3).

27 Ibid., p. 44 (1. 22), p. 82 (2. 3), p. 148 (3. 1) and p. 340 (5. 9).

28 Ibid., p. 96 (2. 8) and p. 210 (3. 21).

29 On this understanding of sin and redemption, see Arnold Angenendt, 'Sühne durch Blut', *Frühmittelalterliche Studien*, 18 (1984), 437–67; and John Bossy, *Christianity in the West 1400–1700* (Oxford: Oxford University Press, 1985), pp. 3–6. On the logic of sacrifice, see also Allen J. Frantzen, *Bloody Good: Chivalry, Sacrifice and the Great War* (Chicago: University of Chicago Press, 2004); René Girard, *The Scapegoat*, tr. Yvonne Freccero (London: Athlone, 1986 [1982]); Girard, *Violence and the Sacred*, tr. Patrick Gregory (Baltimore: Johns Hopkins University Press, 1977 [1972]); and Joyce E. Salisbury, *The Blood of Martyrs: Unintended Consequences of Ancient Violence* (New York: Routledge, 2004), pp. 131–49.

30 See, for example, the *Hohes Lied*, which frequently presents blood as the central tool of redemption, in passages like: 'with the blood that flowed from his body when he died for us, he glorified us'; 'those who I redeemed with the blast of my blood'; 'those whom God freed with his blood'; 'those whom I have redeemed from the Devil's comforts with my blood'; 'water and blood, which he has freed the doves from the Devil's blast'; Brun, *Hohes Lied*, ll. 7670–3, 8236, 8882, 9236–7 and 9305–7; *daz blut daz uz sime libe gink, do her den tot durch uns empfing . . . do mite her uns machte schone; di ich irlosete mit mines blutes doz; di got losete mit sinem blute; di*

ich von des tubels spute han irlost mit minem blute; wazzer und blut . . . do mite her von des tubels doz di turteltuben hat geloset.

31 See, for example, Waszink, 'Blut'; Wißmann, 'Blut, 1: Religionsgeschichtlich'; Böcher, 'Blut II: Biblische und frühjüdische Auffassungen'.

32 Angenendt, 'Sühne durch Blut', pp. 457–66.

33 Mechthild, *Fließendes Licht*, p. 404 (5. 34), see also p. 526 (7. 1), p. 290 (4. 22) and p. 110 (2. 20).

34 Ibid., pp. 120–4 (2. 24).

35 Ibid., p. 184 (3. 10) and p. 240 (4. 2).

36 Ibid., pp. 334–8 (p. 336; 5. 8), *mit bluotigem herzen, herzebluot, muoterliche pine.*

37 Ibid., p. 96 (2. 8), pp. 120–4 (2. 24) and p. 484 (6. 26).

38 Ibid., p. 60 (1. 44).

39 Ibid., p. 134 (2. 25), *herre, din bluot und min ist ein, unbewollen.*

40 Ibid., p. 120 (2. 24), p. 20 (1. 1), p. 102 (2. 18), see also God carving the soul into his wounds, p. 160 (3. 2).

41 Ibid., p. 132 (2. 25), *Wenne min fleisch mir entvallet, min bluot vertrukent, min gebein kellet, min adern krimpfent und min herze smilzet nach diner minne.*

42 Ibid., p. 96 (2. 8). Underlying Theophilus' pact in the *Hohes Lied* is also the idea that blood is a spiritual commodity that can be traded, like Christ buys us with his blood, and Magdalene buys herself with her tears, Brun, *Hohes Lied*, ll. 11894 and 5235.

43 *Heilige Regel*, ed. Priebsch, p. 75.

44 Ibid., p. 15, *daz gelt sins heiligen blutes.*

45 Ibid., p. 45, *Diz ander laster: daz der mensche versturzet und ime selben unnuze machet daz heilige bluot daz unser herre durch alle di sundere gizen wolde.*

46 Ibid., p. 78; see, for example, Caroline Walker Bynum, ' ". . . And woman his humanity": female imagery in the religious writing of the later Middle Ages', in Bynum, *Fragmentation and Redemption*, pp. 151–79.

47 *Heilige Regel*, ed. Priebsch, p. 75.

48 Ibid., p. 89.

49 Ibid., pp. 47–8. Similarly, without reference to blood, a devil admits that if all the water on earth and in the sea were ink, it would not be enough to describe even the smallest of the joys he experienced in heaven, ibid., p. 25.

50 The lady in the *Dolopathos* threatens that the creditor will be 'torn into a thousand pieces'; Helena in *Cursor mundi* rules that the Jew shall have his tongue cut out for swearing in court (if not for the bond of flesh itself); in *Zelauto*, the punishment is indeed an eye for an eye; in the *Pecorone*, decapitation awaits.

51 *Cursor mundi*, ed. Morris, ll. 21729–21730, *of cros god boȝt our saule liuis, þer-on he gaf him-self ransoun.*

52 Gundacker von Judenburg, *Christi Hort*, Deutsche Texte des Mittelalters, 18, ed. J. Jaschke (Berlin: Weidmann 1910), ll. 1127–30; see also, for example, 'Buch der Rügen', ed. Theodor von Karajan, *Zeitschrift für*

deutsches Alterthum, 2 (1842), 6–92 (ll. 1359–62); *Der Saelden Hort*, ed. Heinrich Adrian, Deutsche Texte des Mittelalters, 26 (Berlin: Weidmann, 1927), ll. 9382–99.

53 Brun, *Hohes Lied*, ll. 3120–5.

54 On *mors* as derived from *morsus*, see, for example, Alois M. Haas, *Todesbilder im Mittelalter: Fakten und Hinweise in der deutschen Literatur* (Darmstadt: Wissenschaftliche Buchgesellschaft, 1989), pp. 42–3.

55 Brun, *Hohes Lied*, ll. 3908–20 (ll. 3919–20), *er shol rechen mein plût an den juden, das wirt im gût*.

56 James Shapiro, *Shakespeare and the Jews* (New York: Columbia University Press, 1996); see also Stephen F. Kruger, 'Conversion and medieval sexual, religious, and racial categories', in Karma Lochrie, Peggy McCracken and James A. Schultz (eds), *Constructing Medieval Sexuality*, Medieval Cultures, 11 (Minneapolis: University of Minnesota Press, 1997), pp. 158–79.

57 *Nibelungenlied*, ed. Brackert, stanza 88.

58 Ibid., stanzas 53–9 and 78.

59 Jan-Dirk Müller, 'Motivationsstrukturen und personale Identität im *Nibelungenlied*: Zur Gattungsdiskussion um "Epos" oder "Roman" ', in Fritz Peter Knapp (ed.), Nibelungenlied *und* Klage, *Sage und Geschichte, Struktur und Gattung: Passauer Nibelungenliedgespräche 1985* (Heidelberg: Winter, 1987), pp. 221–56; similarly Müller, *Spielregeln*, pp. 153–9.

60 *Nibelungenlied*, ed. Brackert, stanza 110. On this clash, see also Schulze, *Nibelungenlied*, pp. 178–83; and Müller, *Spielregeln*, pp. 170–7 and 399–409.

61 *Nibelungenlied*, ed. Brackert, stanza 112, ll. 1–3.

62 Ibid., stanza 127, ll. 1–3.

63 On spaces in the *Nibelungenlied*, see also Müller, *Spielregeln*, pp. 297–343.

64 *Nibelungenlied*, ed. Brackert, stanzas 325–8.

65 Ibid., stanzas 1290–4.

66 Ibid., stanza 1558, ll. 2–3, *ez habent fîande die lieben herren mîn, dar umbe ich niemen vremden füere in ditze lant*.

67 Ibid., stanzas 1617 and 1619.

68 Ibid., stanza 1591, ll. 3–4, *sît daz ich vîende hân verdienet ûf der straze, wir werden sicherlîch bestân*.

69 Ibid., stanzas 1744–7, 1761–3, 1775, 1852–4 and 1861–4.

70 Ibid., stanzas 1957 and 1973–80.

71 Ibid., stanzas 1983–2003.

72 Ibid., stanza 2088.

73 Stricker, *Daniel*, ll. 34 and 89–93. In political discourse, the physical presence and performance of a ruler's body were similarly important as a guarantee of social coherence; the monarch had one human, mortal, body, but also embodied the commonwealth; Kantorowicz, *King's Two Bodies*; Jacques Le Goff, 'Head or heart? The political use of body metaphors in the Middle Ages', in Feher (ed.), *Fragments for a History of the Human Body*, III, pp. 13–26; Hedda Ragotzky and Horst Wenzel (eds), *Höfische Repräsentation: Das Zeremoniell und die Zeichen* (Tübingen: Niemeyer, 1990).

[74] Stricker, *Daniel*, ll. 72–4 and 136–42.

[75] Ibid., l. 86, *sich dâ niht verlaegen*.

[76] Ibid., ll. 87–8, *er fuogte ir êre in alle wîs, dâvon bejagte er den prîs*.

[77] Ibid., ll. 83–6.

[78] Ibid., ll. 66–7.

[79] Ibid., ll. 64–6.

[80] Ibid., ll. 381–5, *sô man vil lieben friunt sol*.

[81] Ibid., ll. 8931–3.

[82] Ibid., for example, ll. 508–27 and 740–60.

[83] Ibid., ll. 646–711 and 734–7.

[84] Ibid., ll. 2481–2551 and 3921.

[85] Ibid., for example, ll. 4817–19 and 4465–9.

[86] Ibid., ll. 4342, 2499–2551, 3921 and 744.

[87] Ibid., ll. 1913 and 276; Claude Lecouteux claims that Der Stricker introduced these monsters simply in order to describe something new and strange, Lecouteux, 'Das bauchlose Ungeheuer: Des Strickers *Daniel von dem Blühenden Tal*, 1879ff.', *Euphorion*, 71 (1977), 272–6.

[88] Stricker, *Daniel*, for example, ll. 6371–3.

[89] *Decrees of the Ecumenical Councils*, ed. Tanner, I, pp. 229–30 (canon 1), tr. Tanner. On the increased emphasis on Christ's body in the eucharistic sense and the concept of *societas christiana*, see Rubin, *Corpus Christi*, pp. 12–14.

[90] *Decrees of the Ecumenical Councils*, ed. Tanner, I, p. 266 (canon 68); Jeremy Cohen, *The Friars and the Jews: The Evolution of Medieval Anti-Judaism* (Ithaca, NY: Cornell University Press, 1982), pp. 248–64. Attempts to regulate what counts as inside and outside this Christian union also meant that the status of monstrous demons had to be made unambiguous: they had intentionally left the community of the good, it was decided, *Decrees of the Ecumenical Councils*, ed. Tanner, I, p. 230 (canon 1).

[91] Ibid., I, p. 239 (canon 9), tr. Tanner, *tanquam unum corpus diversa capita, quasi monstrum*.

[92] Konrad, 'Silvester', l. 1902, *houbet*; see Kantorowicz, *King's Two Bodies*, pp. 194–206.

[93] See also Robert Mills, 'Jesus as monster', in Bettina Bildhauer and Mills (eds), *The Monstrous Middle Ages* (Cardiff: University of Wales Press, 2003), pp. 28–54.

[94] *Decrees of the Ecumenical Councils*, ed. Tanner, I, p. 244 (canon 18), quoted above, chapter 2 (p. 64).

[95] Der Stricker, 'Die Pfaffendirne', in Der Stricker, *Kleindichtung*, ed. Wolfgang Wilfried Moelleken, 5 vols, Göppinger Arbeiten zur Germanistik, 107, I–V (Göppingen: Kümmerle, 1973–8), IV (1977), pp. 41–3 (ll. 17–21), *zechelche, sin hailiger leichnam und sin blut*.

[96] Brun, *Hohes Lied*, ll. 3077–8, *sin hut wart an dem cruze gedenet, daz ir breite alle di werlde begreift*.

[97] Ibid., ll. 9859–65.

[98] *Heilige Regel*, ed. Priebsch, p. 1.

[99] Ibid., p. 2. In the *Hohes Lied*, too, Mary appears both as an object of adoration and as a believer herself. Perhaps this intermediate position is described when she is said to unite 'us' with Christ like the neck unites head and body, Brun, *Hohes Lied*, ll. 3419–25.

[100] For edns see Ernst Sommerbrodt, *Die Ebstorfer Weltkarte* (Hanover: Hahn, 1891); Konrad Miller (ed.), *Monialium Ebstorfensium Mappamundi/Die Ebstorfkarte*, Mappaemundi: Die ältesten Weltkarten, 5 (Stuttgart: Roth, 1896); 'Ebskart' under kulturinformatik.uni-lueneburg.de. 'Corners' here denote the intersections of the diagonals of the square map with the circumference of the earth. The spatial layout is analysed in Hartmut Kugler, 'Die Ebstorfer Weltkarte: ein europäisches Weltbild im deutschen Mittelalter', *Zeitschrift für deutsches Altertum und deutsche Literatur*, 116 (1987), 1–29 (pp. 20–2); Hartmut Kugler, 'Hochmittelalterliche Weltkarten als Geschichtsbilder', in Hans-Werner Goetz (ed.), *Hochmittelalterliches Geschichtsbewusstsein im Spiegel nichthistorischer Quellen* (Berlin: Akademie Verlag, 1998), pp. 179–98 (pp. 187–94). On the representational system of the Ebstorf map see also Hartmut Kugler (ed.), *Ein Weltbild vor Columbus: Die Ebstorfer Weltkarte: Interdisziplinäres Kolloquium 1988*, Acta humaniora (Weinheim: VCH, 1991); Birgit Hahn-Woernle, *Die Ebstorfer Weltkarte* (Ebstorf: Kloster Ebstorf, 1987); Uwe Ruberg, 'Mappae mundi des Mittelalters im Zusammenwirken von Text und Bild', in Christel Meier und Uwe Ruberg (eds), *Text und Bild: Aspekte des Zusammenwirkens zweier Künste in Mittelalter und früher Neuzeit* (Wiesbaden: Reichert, 1980), pp. 550–92; Jerzy Strzelczyk, 'Die Legende von den Ebstorfer Märtyrern als Zeugnis über die politischen und ethnischen Verhältnisse in Nordostdeutschland im Mittelalter', *Lĕtopis*, B 18 (1971), 54–79; and Jürgen Wilke, *Die Ebstorfer Weltkarte*, 2 vols, Veröffentlichungen des Institut für historische Landesforschung der Universität Göttingen, 39 (Bielefeld: Verlag für Regionalgeschichte, 2004). On Gog and Magog as forging rather than disrupting a group identity, see Victor I. Scherb, 'Assimilating giants: the appropriation of Gog and Magog in medieval and early modern England', *Journal of Medieval and Early Modern Studies*, 3/1 (2002), 59–84. From a different perspective, I discuss this map and some of the following material in 'Blood, Jews and monsters in medieval culture', in Bildhauer and Mills (eds), *Monstrous Middle Ages*, pp. 75–96.

[101] *Hic inclusit Alexander duas gentes immundas Gog et Magog, quas comites habebit Antichristus. Hii humanis carnibus vescuntur et sanguinem bibunt.*

[102] In the use of a crumb of earth as a substitute for a host, for example, in an emergency last communion, the idea of Christ's body as the earth is literalized. For references to this practice in medieval fiction, see Wilhelm Wackernagel, 'Erde der Leib Christi', *Zeitschrift für deutsches Altertum und deutsche Literatur*, 6 (1848), pp. 288–9. On Christ's body as the Church in the thirteenth century, see also Walter H. Principe, '*Quaestiones* concerning Christ from the first half of the thirteenth century, IV: *quaestiones* from Douai MS. 434, Christ as head of the Church; the unity of the mystical body',

Mediaeval Studies, 44 (1982), 1–82; and Beckwith, *Christ's Body*, esp. pp. 30–3.

103 Gog and Magog are here similarly multiplied, as if to show they can attack many individual and collective bodies. The caption of the northern ocean island Taracontum also informs us that it is inhabited by the cannibalistic Gog and Magog. Several other cannibals are present on the map; one image depicts the Massagetes in Scythia as similarly slaughtering and eating the right foot of a bleeding victim.

104 Jeffrey Jerome Cohen, 'Monster culture (seven theses)', in Cohen (ed.), *Monster Theory*, pp. 3–25 (p. 7).

105 Ute Schwab, 'Blut trinken und im Bier ertrinken: zur Trinkmetaphorik bei Saxo Grammaticus im Vergleich zu einigen Zeugnissen der germanischen Heldendichtung, besonders des *Nibelungenlieds*', in *Saxo Grammaticus tra storiografia e letteratura*, ed. Carlo Santini (Rome: Calamo, 1992), pp. 367–415 (pp. 367–8), *Antibankett*.

106 *Nibelungenlied*, ed. Brackert, stanzas 1960–1 (stanza 1960, l. 3), *nu trinken wir die minne und gelten des küneges wîn*.

107 Ibid., stanza 1981.

108 Ibid., stanzas 2114–17.

109 See Müller, *Spielregeln*, pp. 424–34; and extended discussion of the drinking metaphors in epics in Schwab, 'Blut trinken'; and Ute Schwab, 'Weinverschütten und Minnetrinken: Verwendung und Umwandlung metaphorischer Hallentopik im *Nibelungenlied*', in Klaus Zatloukal (ed.), *Pöchlarner Heldenliedgespräch: Das Nibelungenlied und der mittlere Donauraum*, Philologica Germanica, 12 (Vienna: Fassbaender, 1990), pp. 59–101.

110 Berthold, *Predigten*, I, pp. 357–72. A largely unmodified edn of this sermon with commentary and modern German translation appears again in Berthold von Regensburg, *Vier Predigten Mittelhochdeutsch/Neuhochdeutsch*, ed. Werner Röcke (Stuttgart: Reclam, 1983), pp. 142–83 and 222–34.

111 Berthold, *Predigten*, I, p. 367. Judas is also associated with blood since he famously sold Christ's blood for 'blood money' with which a 'field of blood' was bought (for example, ibid., I, p. 160). Berthold calls blood in general a sign of sin in the Bible, see Frank G. Banta, *Predigten und Stücke aus dem Kreise Bertholds von Regensburg (Teilsammlung Y^{III})*, Göppinger Arbeiten zur Germanistik, 621 (Göppingen: Kümmerle, 1995), p. 92. Jezebel is described as wearing yellow, which Berthold condemns throughout his sermons, and elsewhere sees fit for demarcating Jewesses, Berthold, *Predigten*, I, p. 415.

112 Matthew 13: 4.

113 Berthold, *Predigten*, I, p. 258, *Wan er hât in getunget mit sînem edeln minneclîchen herzbluote, wan dâ mite wart diu erde begozzen*.

114 See above, chapter 2, pp. 65–6, chapter 3, p. 130; Berthold elsewhere also uses this image (Banta, *Predigten*, p. 89). Christ here assumes Cain's role of a field farmer, his crucifix being likened to a plough and his blood to fertilizer, as opposed to the shepherd Abel. In the shorter version of this sermon, Christ problematically both buys and at the same time fertilizes the field

with his blood, perhaps indicating the double role of his blood as having bought salvation for us and still being required as a reminder of his passion, to ensure piety and thus salvation, see Berthold, *Predigten*, II (1880), p. 239. Another field of blood that can be uncomfortably linked to this one is the field that was bought with Judas' thirty coins of 'blood money' (Matthew 27: 6–9; Acts 1: 18–19).

[115] Cohen, *Friars and Jews*, p. 235.

[116] Berthold, *Predigten*, I, p. 362, *diu îsenîniu mûre dannoch dâ vor sî unde den acker schirme vor jüden unde vor heiden unde vor ketzern.*

[117] Ibid., I, p. 363, *Wan jüden suln sie alsô schirmen alse die kristen an ir lîbe und an ir guote, wan sie sint in den fride genomen.* If they became too numerous, however, one would have to defend oneself against them as against heathens, see ibid., I (1862), p. 363.

[118] The relationship of the three walls to each other is also unclear. If someone who broke the first wall (presumably from the outside) would still face the second one, and if the third wall is the narrow individual one, it seems likely that the walls are concentric and treated from the outside to the inside; this in turn implies that the papal Christian community is regarded as more inclusive than worldly society. In another, shorter version of this sermon, however, worldly and papal walls have changed place, ibid., II, pp. 238–41.

[119] Andrew Colin Gow, *The Red Jews: Antisemitism in an Apocalyptic Age 1200–1600*, Studies in Medieval and Reformation Thought, 55 (Leiden: Brill, 1995), pp. 3–4; see 2 Kings 17, Ezekiel 38–9 and Revelation 20: 7–10.

[120] Ruth Mellinkoff, *Outcasts: Signs of Otherness in Northern European Art of the Late Middle Ages*, 2 vols (Berkeley: University of California Press, 1993), I, pp. 229–30; for example, II, fig. 3.4; Ruth Mellinkoff, *Antisemitic Hate Signs in Hebrew Illuminated Manuscripts from Medieval Germany* (Jerusalem: Center for Jewish Art, Hebrew University of Jerusalem, 1999), pp. 23–7. Mellinkoff also mentions other elements frequently found in anti-Semitic images, such as Hebrew letters, or mouths drawn as a long horizontal line or with heavy lips, that are not present here.

[121] Gavin I. Langmuir, *Toward a Definition of Antisemitism* (Berkeley: University of California Press, 1990), pp. 262–81. In 1247, Innocent IV had received complaints from German Jews that they were accused of cannibalism, of eating Christian children's hearts at Passover: Julius Aronius, *Regesten zur Geschichte der Juden im fränkischen und deutschen Reiche bis zum Jahre 1273* (Berlin: Nathansen & Lamm, 1902), p. 242. On later variations of the blood libel legend and ritual murder accusations, see, for instance, Ronnie Po-chia Hsia, *The Myth of Ritual Murder: Jews and Magic in Reformation Germany* (New Haven: Yale University Press, 1988).

[122] Gow, *Red Jews*, pp. 49–53.

[123] See, for instance, Miri Rubin, *Gentile Tales*; Langmuir, *Toward a Definition*; Denise L. Despres, 'Cultic anti-Judaism and Chaucer's Little Clergeon', *Modern Philology*, 91 (1994), 413–27; Christoph Cluse, 'Blut ist im Schuh: Ein Exempel zur Judenverfolgung des "Rex Armleder"', in Friedhelm

Burgard, Christoph Cluse and Alfred Haverkamp (eds), *Liber amicorum necnon et amicarum für Alfred Heit: Beiträge zur Geschichte und geschichtlichen Landeskunde*, Trierer historische Forschungen, 28 (Trier: Verlag Trierer Historische Forschungen, 1996), pp. 371–92; Israel Jacob Yuval, 'Christliche Symbolik und jüdische Martyrologie zur Zeit der Kreuzzüge', in Alfred Haverkamp (ed.), *Juden und Christen zur Zeit der Kreuzzüge*, Vorträge und Forschungen, 47 (Sigmaringen: Thorbecke, 1999), pp. 87–106. Although he rests his assumption that the social body is imagined as held together by blood on loose associations, Jeffrey Jerome Cohen shows that the multi-ethnic community of Norwich came together by accusing Jews of shedding the blood of William of Norwich in 1144, Cohen, 'The flow of blood in medieval Norwich', *Speculum*, 79 (2004), 26–65.

Bibliography

Manuscripts

Basle, University Library, MS 0.I.18
Cologne, Stadtarchiv, W 4° 24*
Erlangen, Universitätsbibliothek, MS B33 (Irm. 1492)
Grenoble, Bibliothèque Municipale, MS 34
London, British Library, Harley MS 3719
London, Wellcome Library, MS 49
Munich, Bayerische Staatsbibliothek, Cgm 121
Munich, Bayerische Staatsbibliothek, Cgm 458
Munich, Bayerische Staatsbibliothek, Clm 22297 (Windberg 97)
Munich, Bayerische Staatsbibliothek, Clm 22300 (Windberg 100)
Oxford, Bodleian Library, Fairfax MS 14
Strasbourg, Bibliothèque Nationale, MS 2929

Printed sources

Angenendt, Arnold, 'Sühne durch Blut', *Frühmittelalterliche Studien*, 18 (1984), 437–67.

Anzieu, Didier, *The Skin Ego*, tr. Chris Turner (New Haven: Yale University Press, 1989 [1985]).

Aristotle, 'On Dreams', in Aristotle, *On the Soul, Parva Naturalia, On Breath*, ed. and tr. W. S. Hett, rev. edn, Loeb Classical Library, 288 (London: Heinemann, and Cambridge, MA: Harvard University Press, 1957 [1936]), pp. 348–71.

—— *Generation of Animals*, ed. and tr. A. L. Peck (London: Heinemann, 1963 [1942]).

Aronius, Julius, *Regesten zur Geschichte der Juden im fränkischen und deutschen Reiche bis zum Jahre 1273* (Berlin: Nathansen & Lamm, 1902).

Ashe, Laura, 'The Short Charter of Christ: an unpublished longer version, from Cambridge University Library, MS Add. 6686', *Medium Aevum*, 72/1 (2003), 32–48.

Augustine of Hippo, *In Joannis Evangelium*, ed. Jacques-Paul Migne, Patrilogiae Cursus Completus: Series Latina (Paris: Migne), 35 (1841), cols 1579–1976.

—— *Confessions*, tr. Henry Chadwick, Oxford World's Classics (Oxford: Oxford University Press, 1991).

—— *Tractates on the Gospel of John 112–24/Tractates on the First Epistle of John*, tr. John W. Rettig, The Fathers of the Church, 92 (Washington, DC: Catholic University of America Press, 1995).

Bacon, Roger, *Opus majus*, ed. John Henry Bridges, 3 vols (Oxford: Clarendon, 1897).

—— *Secreta secretorum cum glossis et notulis*, in *Opera hactenus inedita Roger Baconi*, ed. Robert Steele, 16 vols (Oxford: Clarendon, 1909–40), V (1909).

—— *Opus Majus*, tr. Robert Belle Burke, 2 vols (Philadelphia: University of Pennsylvania Press, 1928).

Bakhtin, Mikhail, *Rabelais and his World*, tr. Helene Iswolsky (Bloomington: Indiana University Press, 1984 [1965]).

Banta, Frank G., *Predigten und Stücke aus dem Kreise Bertholds von Regensburg (Teilsammlung Y^{III})*, Göppinger Arbeiten zur Germanistik, 621 (Göppingen: Kümmerle, 1995).

Barclay, Alexander, *The Life of St George*, ed. William Nelson, Early English Text Society, os 230 (London: Oxford University Press, 1955).

'Bartholomäus', in *Zwei deutsche Arzneibücher aus dem XII. und XIII. Jahrhundert*, ed. Franz Pfeiffer, Sitzungsberichte der österreichischen Akademie der Wissenschaften Wien, Philosophisch-historische Klasse, 42 (Vienna: Gerold's Sohn, 1863), pp. 20–51.

Bartlett, Robert, *The Making of Europe: Conquest, Colonization, and Cultural Change, 950–1350* (Harmondsworth: Penguin, 1993).

Battersby, Christine, *The Phenomenal Woman: Feminist Metaphysics and the Patterns of Identity* (Oxford: Polity, 1998).

Beckwith, Sarah, *Christ's Body: Identity, Culture and Society in Late Medieval Writings* (London: Routledge, 1993).

Benecke, Georg Friedrich, Wilhelm Müller and Friedrich Zarncke (eds), *Mittelhochdeutsches Wörterbuch*, 3 vols (Leipzig: Hirzel, 1854–61).

Benthien, Claudia, *Skin: On the Cultural Border between Self and World*, tr. Thomas Dunlap (New York: Columbia University Press, 2002 [1999]).

Berg, Klaus, 'Der Traktat des Gerhard von Köln über das kostbarste Blut Christi aus dem Jahre 1280', in N. Kruse and H.-U. Rudolf (eds), *900 Jahre Heilig-Blut-Verehrung in Weingarten*, I, pp. 435–84.

'Beringer', in *Die historien von dem ritter beringer* (Straßburg: Matthias Brant, 1495).

'Beringer', in *Schwankerzählungen des deutschen Mittelalters*, tr. Hanns Fischer (Munich: Beck, 1967), pp. 47–54.

Bernardino of Siena, 'Sermo 61: Feria quarta post resurrectionem: De superadmirabili gratia et gloria Matris Dei', in *Opera Omnia*, ed. Pacifici M. Perantoni and P. Augustini Sépinski, 9 vols (Quaracchi: Collegium S. Bonaventurae, 1950–65), II (1950), pp. 371–97.

Bernau, Anke, Ruth Evans and Sarah Salih (eds), *Medieval Virginities, Religion and Culture in the Middle Ages* (Cardiff: University of Wales Press, 2003).

Bertau, Karl, *Über Literaturgeschichte: Literarischer Kunstcharakter und Geschichte in der höfischen Epik um 1200* (Munich: Beck, 1983).

—— 'Versuch über Verhaltenssemantik von Verwandten im *Parzival*', in Bertau, *Neun Versuche über Subjektivität und Ursprünglichkeit in der Geschichte* (Munich: Beck, 1983), pp. 190–240.

Berthold von Regensburg, 'Von drin mûren', in Berthold, *Predigten*, I (1862), pp. 357–72.

—— 'Von den zehen geboten unsers Herren', in Berthold, *Predigten*, I (1862), pp. 264–88.

—— *Vollständige Ausgabe seiner Predigten*, ed. Franz Pfeiffer, 2 vols (Vienna: Braumüller, 1862–80).

—— *Vier Predigten Mittelhochdeutsch/Neuhochdeutsch*, ed. Werner Röcke (Stuttgart: Reclam, 1983).

Biddick, Kathleen, 'Genders, bodies, borders: technologies of the visible', *Speculum*, 68 (1993), 389–418.

—— 'The cut of genealogy: pedagogy in the blood', *Journal of Medieval and Early Modern Studies*, 30/3 (Fall 2000), 449–62.

Biernoff, Suzannah, *Sight and Embodiment in the Middle Ages*, The New Middle Ages (Basingstoke: Palgrave, 2002).

Bildhauer, Bettina, 'Bloodsuckers: the construction of female sexuality in medieval science and fiction', in Liz Herbert McAvoy and Teresa Walters (eds), *Consuming Narratives: Gender and Monstrous Appetites in the Middle Ages and the Renaissance* (Cardiff: University of Wales Press, 2002), pp. 104–15.

—— 'Blood, Jews and monsters in medieval culture', in Bildhauer and R. Mills (eds), *The Monstrous Middle Ages* (Cardiff: University of Wales Press, 2003), pp. 75–96.

—— and Robert Mills (eds), *The Monstrous Middle Ages* (Cardiff: University of Wales Press, 2003).

Biller, Peter, 'Views of Jews from Paris around 1300: Christian or "scientific"?', in Diana Wood (ed.), *Christianity and Judaism: Papers Read at the 1991 Summer Meeting and the 1992 Winter Meeting of the Ecclesiastical History Society*, Studies in Church History, 29 (Oxford: Blackwell, 1992), pp. 187–207.

—— 'A scientific view of Jews from Paris around 1300', *Micrologus*, 9 (2001), 137–68.

Böcher, Otto, 'Blut II: Biblische und frühjüdische Auffassungen', in G. Krause and G. Müller (eds), *Theologische Realenzyklopädie*, VI (Berlin: de Gruyter, 1980), cols 729–36.

Bode, Friedrich, *Die Kampfesschilderungen in den mittelhochdeutschen Epen* (Greifswald: Adler, 1909).

Boivin, Jeanne-Marie, and Proinsias MacCana (eds), *Mélusines continentales et insulaires* (Paris: Champion, 1999).

Bossy, John, *Christianity in the West 1400–1700* (Oxford: Oxford University Press, 1985).

Boureau, Alain, 'The sacrality of one's own body in the Middle Ages', *Yale French Studies*, 86 (1994), 5–17.

Bradburne, James M. (ed.), *Blood: Art, Power, Politics, and Pathology* (Munich: Prestel, 2001).

Brain, Peter, *Galen on Bloodletting: A Study of the Origins, Developments and Validity of his Opinions* (Cambridge: Cambridge University Press, 1986).

Brall, Helmut, Barbara Haupt and Urban Küsters (eds), *Personenbeziehungen in der mittelalterlichen Literatur*, Studia humaniora, 25 (Düsseldorf: Droste, 1994).

Brun von Schönebeck, *Das Hohe Lied*, ed. Arwed Fischer, Bibliothek des litterarischen Vereins in Stuttgart, 198 (Tübingen: Litterarischer Verein Stuttgart, 1893).

'Buch der Rügen', ed. Theodor von Karajan, *Zeitschrift für deutsches Alterthum*, 2 (1842), 6–92.

Buckley, Thomas, and Alma Gottlieb (eds), *Blood Magic: The Anthropology of Menstruation* (Berkeley: University of California Press, 1988).

Bumke, Joachim, *Wolfram von Eschenbach*, Sammlung Metzler, 36 (Stuttgart: Metzler, 2004 [1991]).

—— *Die Blutstropfen im Schnee*, Hermaea Germanistische Forschungen, NS 94 (Tübingen: Niemeyer, 2001).

Busse, Wilhelm, 'Verwandtschaftsstrukturen im *Parzival*', *Wolfram-Studien*, 5 (1979), 116–34.

Butler, Judith, *Gender Trouble: Feminism and the Subversion of Identity* (New York: Routledge, 1999 [1990]).

—— *Bodies that Matter: On the Discursive Limits of 'Sex'* (New York: Routledge, 1993).

—— 'Revisiting bodies and pleasures', *Theory, Culture and Society*, 16/2 (1999), 11–20.

—— 'How can I deny that these hands and this body are mine?', in Tom Cohen, Barbara Cohen, J. Hillis Miller, and Andrzej Warminski (eds), *Material Events: Paul de Man and the Afterlife of Theory* (Minneapolis: University of Minnesota Press, 2001), pp. 254–73.

—— *Undoing Gender* (New York: Routledge, 2004).

Bynum, Caroline Walker, *Jesus as Mother: Studies in the Spirituality of the High Middle Ages* (Berkeley: University of California Press, 1982).

—— *Holy Feast and Holy Fast: The Religious Significance of Food to Medieval Women*, The New Historicism: Studies in Cultural Poetics (Berkeley: University of California Press, 1987).

—— *Fragmentation and Redemption: Essays on Gender and the Human Body in Medieval Religion* (New York: Zone, 1991).

—— '". . . And woman his humanity": female imagery in the religious writing of the later Middle Ages', in Bynum, *Fragmentation and Redemption*, pp. 151–79.

—— 'The body of Christ in the later Middle Ages: a reply to Leo Steinberg', in Bynum, *Fragmentation and Redemption*, pp. 79–117.

—— *The Resurrection of the Body in Western Christianity, 200–1336*, Lectures on the History of Religions, ns 15 (New York: Columbia University Press, 1995).

—— 'Why all the fuss about the body? A medievalist's perspective', *Critical Inquiry*, 22 (Autumn 1995), 1–33.

—— 'Blood of Christ', *Church History*, 71/4 (December 2002), 685–714.

Bynum, William F., and Roy Porter (eds), *Medicine and the Five Senses* (Cambridge: Cambridge University Press, 1993).

Cadden, Joan, *Meanings of Sex Difference in the Middle Ages: Medicine, Science and Culture*, Cambridge History of Medicine (Cambridge: Cambridge University Press, 1993).

Caesarius of Heisterbach, *Dialogus miraculorum*, ed. Joseph Strange, 2 vols (Cologne: Lempertz, 1851).

—— *The Dialogue on Miracles*, tr. Henry von Essen Scott and Charles Cooke Swinton Bland, 2 vols (London: Routledge, 1929).

Camporesi, Piero, *Juice of Life: The Symbolic and Magic Significance of Blood*, tr. Robert R. Barr (New York: Continuum, 1995 [1988]).

Cartwright, Jane, 'Virginity and chastity tests in medieval Welsh prose', in Anke Bernau, Ruth Evans and Sarah Salih (eds), *Medieval Virginities* (Cardiff: University of Wales Press, 2003), pp. 56–79.

Clark, Stuart, *Thinking with Demons: The Idea of Witchcraft in Early Modern Europe* (Oxford: Oxford University Press, 1997).

Clier-Colombani, Francois, *La fée Mélusine au Moyen Age: Images, mythes et symboles* (Paris: Léopard d'or, 1991).

Cluse, Christoph, 'Blut ist im Schuh: Ein Exempel zur Judenverfolgung des "Rex Armleder"', in Friedhelm Burgard, Christoph Cluse and Alfred Haverkamp (eds), *Liber amicorum necnon et amicarum für Alfred Heit: Beiträge zur Geschichte und geschichtlichen Landeskunde*, Trierer historische Forschungen, 28 (Trier: Verlag Trierer Historische Forschungen, 1996), pp. 371–92.

Cohen, Jeffrey Jerome (ed.) *Monster Theory: Reading Culture* (Minneapolis: University of Minnesota Press, 1996).

—— 'Monster culture (seven theses)', in Cohen (ed.), *Monster Theory*, pp. 3–25.

—— *Medieval Identity Machines*, Medieval Cultures, 35 (Minneapolis: University of Minnesota Press, 2003).

—— 'The flow of blood in medieval Norwich', *Speculum*, 79 (2004), 26–65.

Cohen, Jeremy, *The Friars and the Jews: The Evolution of Medieval Anti-Judaism* (Ithaca, NY: Cornell University Press, 1982).

Cohn, Norman, *Europe's Inner Demons: The Demonization of Christians in Medieval Christendom*, 2nd edn (London: Pimlico, 1993).

Collins, Margery, and Christine Pierce, 'Holes and slime: sexism in Sartre's psychoanalysis', in Carol C. Gould and Marx W. Wartofsky, *Women and Philosophy: Toward a Theory of Liberation* (New York: G. P. Putnam's Sons, 1976), pp. 112–27.

Copjec, Joan, 'Vampires, breast-feeding and anxiety', *October*, 58 (1998), 24–43.

Crossgrove, William, *Die deutsche Sachliteratur des Mittelalters* (Bern: Lang, 1994).

Cursor mundi (The Cursur o' the World): A Northumbrian Poem of the XIVth Century in Four Versions, ed. Richard Morris, 3 vols, Early English Text Society, os 57, 59, 62, 66, 68, 99, 101 (London: Kegan Paul, Trench, Trübner, 1874–93).

Czerwinski, Peter, *Der Glanz der Abstraktion: Frühe Formen von Reflexivität im Mittelalter: Exempel einer Geschichte der Wahrnehmung* (Frankfurt/Main: Campus, 1989).

Das Nibelungenlied: Mittelhochdeutscher Text und Übertragung, ed. and tr. Helmut Brackert (Frankfurt/Main: Fischer, 1970–1).

'Das Nonnenturnier', in *Die deutsche Märendichtung des 15. Jahrhunderts*, ed. H. Fischer (Munich: Beck, 1966), pp. 31–47.

Das Passional, 3 vols, I and II, ed. Karl A. Hahn (Frankfurt/Main: Broenner, 1845), III, ed. Karl Köpke (Quedlinburg: Basse, 1852).

De Secretis mulierum (Lyons: Quadratus, 1580).

Decrees of the Ecumenical Councils, ed. and tr. Norman P. Tanner, 2 vols (London: Sheed & Ward, 1990).

Delabar, Walter, *Erkantiu sippe und hoch geselleschaft: Studien zur Funktion des Verwandtschaftsverbandes in Wolfram von Eschenbachs*

Parzival, Göppinger Arbeiten zur Germanistik, 518 (Göppingen: Kümmerle, 1990).

—— 'Ûfgerihtiu sper: Zur Interaktion in der Blutstropfenepisode in Wolframs Parzival', in H. Brall et al. (eds), Personenbeziehungen in der mittelalterlichen Literatur (Düsseldorf: Droste, 1994), pp. 321–46.

Deleuze, Gilles, and Félix Guattari, Anti-Oedipus: Capitalism and Schizophrenia, tr. Robert Hurley, Mark Seem and Helen R. Lane (London: Athlone, 1984 [1972]).

Der Saelden Hort, ed. Heinrich Adrian, Deutsche Texte des Mittelalters, 26 (Berlin: Weidmann, 1927).

Dérrien, Eve, 'Le sang et la saignée dans le roman médiéval en vers', Lettres Romanes, 51/1–2 (February–May 1997), 3–18.

Despres, Denise L., 'Cultic anti-Judaism and Chaucer's Little Clergeon', Modern Philology, 91 (1994), 413–27.

Dewald, Hans, Minne und sgrâles âventiur: Äußerungen der Subjektivität und ihre sprachliche Vergegenwärtigung in Wolframs 'Parzival', Göppinger Arbeiten zur Germanistik, 158 (Göppingen: Kümmerle, 1975).

Die deutsche Märendichtung des 15. Jahrhunderts, ed. Hanns Fischer, Münchner Texte und Untersuchungen zur Literatur des Mittelalters, 12 (Munich: Beck, 1966).

Diederichsen, Uwe, 'Das Fleischpfand', in Ulrich Mölk (ed.), Literatur und Recht (Göttingen: Wallstern, 1996), pp. 138–49.

'Die gestohlene Monstranz', in Eine Schweizer Kleinepiksammlung des fünfzehnten Jahrhunderts, ed. Hanns Fischer, Altdeutsche Textbibliothek, 65 (Tübingen: Niemeyer, 1965), pp. 84–6.

'Die heilige Regel für ein vollkommenes Leben': Eine Cisterzienserarbeit des XIII. Jahrhunderts aus der Handschrift Additional 9048 des British Museum, ed. Robert Priebsch, Deutsche Texte des Mittelalters, 16 (Berlin: Weidmann, 1909).

Die Nibelungenklage: synoptische Ausgabe aller vier Fassungen, ed. Joachim Bumke (Berlin: de Gruyter, 1999).

Dietrich von der Glezze, 'Der Borte', in Gesammtabenteuer. Hundert altdeutsche Erzählungen, ed. Friedrich Heinrich von der Hagen, 3 vols (Stuttgart: Cotta, 1850), I, pp. 449–78.

Dinkelacher, Wolfgang, 'Ortnit', in K. Ruh (ed.), Die deutsche Literatur des Mittelalters: Verfasserlexikon, VII (Berlin: de Gruyter, 1989), cols 58–67.

Dinshaw, Carolyn, Chaucer's Sexual Poetics (Madison: University of Wisconsin Press, 1989).

—— Getting Medieval: Sexualities and Communities, Pre- and Postmodern (Durham, NC: Duke University Press, 1999).

Dinzelbacher, Peter, 'Das Blut Christi in der Religiösität des Mittelalters', in N. Kruse and H.-U. Rudolf (eds), *900 Jahre Heilig-Blut-Verehrung in Weingarten* (Sigmaringen: Thorbecke, 1994), pp. 415–34.

Douglas, Mary, *Purity and Danger: An Analysis of the Concepts of Pollution and Taboo* (London: Routledge, 1966).

—— *Leviticus as Literature* (Oxford: Oxford University Press, 1999).

Duden, Barbara, 'A repertory of body history' in M. Feher (ed.), *Fragments for a History of the Human Body* (New York: Zone, 1989), III, pp. 471–578.

Dundes, Alan (ed.), *The Evil Eye: A Folklore Casebook*, Garland Folklore Casebooks, 2 (New York: Garland, 1981).

—— 'The vampire as bloodthirsty revenant: a psychoanalytic post mortem', in Dundes (ed.), *The Vampire: A Casebook* (Madison: University of Wisconsin Press, 1998), pp. 150–75.

Durand, Gilbert, *Les structures anthropologiques de l'imaginaire: Introduction à l'archétypologie générale* (Paris: Bordas, Collection Études Supérieures, 1969).

Eamon, William, *Science and the Secrets of Nature: Books of Secrets in Medieval and Early Modern Culture* (Princeton: Princeton University Press, 1994).

Eckenlied: Fassung L, ed. Martin Wierschin, Altdeutsche Textbibliothek, 78 (Tübingen: Niemeyer, 1974).

Elias, Norbert, *The Civilizing Process: Sociogenetic and Psychogenetic Investigations*, ed. Eric Dunning, Johan Goudsblom and Stephen Mennell, tr. Edmund Jephcott, 2nd, rev. edn (Oxford: Blackwell, 2000 [1939]).

Ellington, Diane Spivey, *From Sacred Body to Angelic Soul: Understanding Mary in Late Medieval and Early Modern Europe* (Washington, DC: Catholic University of America Press, 2001).

Elliott, Dyan, *Fallen Bodies: Pollution, Sexuality and Demonology in the Middle Ages*, The Middle Ages Series (Philadelphia: University of Pennsylvania Press, 1999).

Emerson, Oliver F., 'Legends of Cain, Especially in Old and Middle English', *Publications of the Modern Language Association of America*, 21 (1906), 831–929.

Faure, Michel (ed.), *Le Sang au Moyen Age: Actes du quatrième colloque international de Montpellier Université Paul-Valéry 27–29 novembre 1997*, Les Cahiers du CRISIMA 4 (Montpellier: CRISIMA, Université Paul-Valéry, 1999).

Feher, Michel (ed.), *Fragments for a History of the Human Body*, 3 vols (New York: Zone, 1989).

Ferckel, Christoph, 'Die *Secreta mulierum* und ihr Verfasser', *Sudhoffs Archiv*, 38 (1954), 267–74.

Folz, Hans, *Die Reimpaarsprüche*, ed. Hanns Fischer, Münchner Texte und

Untersuchungen zur deutschen Literatur des Mittelalters, 1 (Munich: Beck, 1961).

—— 'Adam und Eva' in Folz, *Reimpaarsprüche*, pp. 150–63.

—— 'Beichtspiegel', in Folz, *Reimpaarsprüche*, pp. 188–210.

—— 'Hausratbüchlein', in Folz, *Reimpaarsprüche*, pp. 358–68.

—— 'Jüdischer Wucher', in Folz, *Reimpaarsprüche*, pp. 310–18.

Foucault, Michel, 'Nietzsche, genealogy, history', in Foucault, *Aesthetics, Method and Epistomology*, ed. James D. Faubion, *Essential Works of Foucault 1954–84*, II (New York: New Press, 1998 [1971]), pp. 369–91.

—— *The History of Sexuality, I, An Introduction*, tr. Robert Hurley (Harmondsworth: Penguin, 1981 [1976]).

—— 'Truth and power', in Foucault, *Power/Knowledge. Selected Interviews and Other Writings, 1972–1977*, ed. Colin Gordon (New York: Pantheon, 1980 [1977]), pp. 109–33.

Frakes, Jerold C., *Brides and Doom: Gender, Property, and Power in Medieval German Women's Epic*, The Middle Ages Series (Philadelphia: University of Pennsylvania Press, 1994).

Franklin, James C., *Mystical Transformations: The Imagery of Liquids in the Work of Mechthild von Magdeburg* (Cranbury, NJ: Associated University Presses, 1978).

Frantzen, Allen J., *Bloody Good: Chivalry, Sacrifice and the Great War* (Chicago: University of Chicago Press, 2004).

Friedman, John Block, *The Monstrous Races in Medieval Art and Thought* (Cambridge, MA: Harvard University Press, 1981).

Fuchs, Stephan, *Hybride Helden: Gwigalois und Willehalm: Beiträge zum Heldenbild und zur Poetik des Romans im frühen 13. Jahrhundert*, Frankfurter Beiträge zur Germanistik (Heidelberg: Winter, 1997).

Gaignebet, Claude, and Jean-Dominique Lajoux, *Art profane et religion populaire au Moyen Age* (Paris: Presses Universitaires de France, 1985).

Gaignebet, Claude, 'Véronique ou l'image vraie', *Anagrom*, 7–8 (1976), 45–70.

Garrett, Brian, 'Personal identity', in *Routledge Encyclopedia of Philosophy*, ed. Edward Craig, 10 vols (London: Routledge, 1998), VII, pp. 305–14.

Gaunt, Simon, *Gender and Genre in Medieval French Literature*, Cambridge Studies in French, 53 (Cambridge: Cambridge University Press, 1995).

Gehrts, Heino, 'Der Schlaf des Drachenkämpfers Ortnit', *Euphorion*, 77 (1983), 342–4.

'Georg', in *Das Passional*, III, ed. K. Köpke (Quedlinburg: Basse, 1852), pp. 253–65.

Gephart, Irmgard, *Geben und Nehmen im* Nibelungenlied *und in Wolframs von Eschenbach* Parzival, Studien zur Germanistik, Anglistik und Komparatistik, 122 (Bonn: Bouvier, 1994).

Gesta romanorum, ed. Hermann Oesterley (Berlin: Weidmann, 1872).

Gil-Sotres, Pedro, 'Derivation and revulsion: the theory and practice of medieval phlebotomy', in Luis Garcia Ballester, Roger French, Jon Arrizabalaga and Andrew Cunningham (eds), *Practical Medicine from Salerno to the Black Death* (Cambridge: Cambridge University Press, 1993), pp. 110–56.

Giovanni Fiorentino, *Il Pecorone*, ed. Enzo Esposito, Classici italiani minori, 1 (Ravenna: Longo, 1974).

Girard, René, *Violence and the Sacred*, tr. Patrick Gregory (Baltimore: Johns Hopkins University Press, 1977 [1972]).

—— *The Scapegoat*, tr. Yvonne Freccero (London: Athlone, 1986 [1982]).

'Gold und Zers', in *Die deutsche Märendichtung des 15. Jahrhunderts*, ed. H. Fischer (Munich: Beck, 1966), pp. 431–43.

Gottfried von Straßburg, *Tristan*, ed. and tr. Rüdiger Krohn, 3 vols (Stuttgart: Reclam, 1996 [1980]).

Gow, Andrew Colin, *The Red Jews: Antisemitism in an Apocalyptic Age 1200–1600*, Studies in Medieval and Reformation Thought, 55 (Leiden: Brill, 1995).

Grantley, Darryll, and Nina Taunton (eds), *The Body in Late Medieval and Early Modern Culture* (Aldershot: Ashgate, 2000).

Green, Monica H., ' "Traittié tout de mençonges": the *Secrés des dames*, "Trotula," and attitudes toward women's medicine in fourteenth- and early-fifteenth-century France', in Marilynn Desmond (ed.), *Christine de Pizan and the Categories of Difference* (Minneapolis: University of Minnesota Press, 1998), pp. 146–78.

—— 'From "Diseases of Women" to "Secrets of Women": the transformation of gynecological literature in the later Middle Ages', *Journal of Medieval and Early Modern Studies*, 30/1 (Winter 2000), 5–39.

Greenblatt, Stephen, *Marvelous Possessions: The Wonder of the New World* (Oxford: Clarendon Press, 1991).

—— and Catherine Gallagher, 'The wound in the wall', in Greenblatt and Gallagher, *Practicing New Historicism* (Chicago: University of Chicago Press, 2000), pp. 75–109.

Groebner, Valentin, *Defaced: The Visual Culture of Violence in the Late Middle Ages*, tr. Pamela Selwyn (New York: Zone, 2004 [2003]).

Grosz, Elizabeth, *Volatile Bodies: Toward a Corporeal Feminism*, Theories of Representation and Difference (Bloomington: Indiana University Press, 1994).

Gruber, Loren C. (ed.), *Essays in Old, Middle, Modern English and Old Icelandic in Honour of Raymond J. Tripp, Jr* (Lewiston, NY: Edwin Mullen, 2000).

Grubmüller, Klaus, 'Kaiser Lucius' Tochter: Zur Vorgeschichte von Shakespeares *Kaufmann von Venedig*', in U. Mölk (ed.), *Literatur und Recht* (Göttingen: Wallstein, 1996), pp. 94–137.

Guerriri, Anna Maria, 'Il sangue nella tradizione poetica germanica', in F. Vattioni (ed.), *Sangue e antropologia nella biblica nella patristica*, II, Sangue e antropologia, 4 (Rome: Pia Unione Prezissimo Sangue, 1982), pp. 907–34.

Gumbrecht, Hans Ulrich, *In 1926: Living at the Edge of Time* (Cambridge, MA: Harvard University Press, 1997).

Gundacker von Judenburg, *Christi Hort*, Deutsche Texte des Mittelalters, 18, ed. J. Jaschke (Berlin: Weidmann 1910).

Haas, Alois M., 'Mechthilds von Magdeburg dichterische *heimlichkeit*', in Rüdiger Schnell (ed.), *Gotes und der werlde hulde: Literatur in Mittelalter und Neuzeit: Festschrift für Heinz Rupp zum 70. Geburtstag* (Berne: Francke, 1989), pp. 206–23.

—— *Todesbilder im Mittelalter: Fakten und Hinweise in der deutschen Literatur* (Darmstadt: Wissenschaftliche Buchgesellschaft, 1989).

Haferland, Torsten, *Die Darstellung von Verletzungen und Krankheiten und ihrer Therapie in mittelalterlicher deutscher Literatur unter gattungsspezifischen Aspekten*, Beiträge zur älteren Literaturgeschichte (Heidelberg: Winter, 1991).

Hahn, Ingrid, 'Das Ethos der *kraft*: Zur Bedeutung des Massenschlachten in Strickers *Daniel von dem Blühenden Tal*', *Deutsche Vierteljahrsschrift für Literaturwissenschaft und Geistesgeschichte*, 59 (1985), 173–92.

—— 'Gott und Minne, Tod und *triuwe*: Zur Konzeption des *Wigalois* des Wirnt von Grafenberg', in H. Brall et al. (eds), *Personenbeziehungen in der mittelalterlichen Literatur* (Düsseldorf: Droste, 1994), pp. 37–60.

Hahn-Woernle, Birgit, *Die Ebstorfer Weltkarte* (Ebstorf: Kloster Ebstorf, 1987).

Halberstam, Judith, *Skin Shows: Gothic Horror and the Technology of Monsters* (Durham NC: Duke University Press, 1995).

Hamburger, Jeffrey F., *Nuns as Artists: The Visual Culture of a Medieval Convent*, California Studies in the History of Art, 37 (Berkeley: University of California Press, 1997).

Haraway, Donna J., 'A cyborg manifesto: science, technology, and socialist-feminism in the late twentieth century', in Haraway, *Simians, Cyborgs and Women: The Reinvention of Nature* (New York: Routledge, 1991), pp. 149–81.

Hartlieb, Johann, *Übersetzung des* Dialogus Miraculorum *von Caesarius von Heisterbach*, ed. Karl Drescher, Deutsche Texte des Mittelalters, 33 (Berlin: Weidmann, 1929).

—— *Secreta mulierum mit Glosse in der deutschen Bearbeitung von Johann Hartlieb*, ed. Kristian Bosselmann-Cyran, Würzburger medizin-historische Forschungen, 36 (Pattensen/Hanover: Wellm, 1985).

Hartmann von Aue, *Iwein*, ed. Georg Friedrich Benecke and Karl

Lachmann, tr. Thomas Cramer (Berlin: de Gruyter, 1981 [1966]).

—— *Der arme Heinrich*, ed. Hermann Paul and Kurt Gärtner, Altdeutsche Textbibliothek, 3 (Tübingen: Niemeyer, 2001).

Hasebrink, Burkhard, 'Spiegel und Spiegelung im *Fließenden Licht der Gottheit*', in Walter Haug and Wolfram Schneider-Lastin (eds), *Deutsche Mystik im abendländischen Zusammenhang: Neu erschlossene Texte, neue methodische Ansätze, neue theoretische Konzepte* (Tübingen: Niemeyer, 2000), pp. 157–74.

'Heilige Regel für ein vollkommenes Leben': Eine Cisterzienserarbeit des XIII. Jahrhunderts aus der Handschrift Additional 9048 des British Museum, ed. Robert Priebsch, Deutsche Texte des Mittelalters, 16 (Berlin: Weidmann, 1909).

Heimbach-Steins, Marianne, 'Gottes und des Menschen "heimlichkeit": zu einem Zentralbegriff der mystischen Theologie Mechthilds von Magdeburg', in Claudia Brinker, Urs Herzog, Niklaus Largier and Paul Michel (eds), *Contemplata aliis tradere: Studien zum Verhältnis von Literatur und Spiritualität* (Berne: Lang, 1995), pp. 71–86.

Henderson, Ingeborg, 'Dark figures and eschatological imagery in Wirnt von Gravenberg's *Wigalois*', in Edward R. Haymes and Stephanie Cain van D'Elden (eds), *The Dark Figure in Medieval German and Germanic Literature*, Göppinger Arbeiten zur Germanistik, 448 (Göppingen: Kümmerle, 1986), pp. 99–113.

Heng, Geraldine, 'Cannibalism, the first crusade and the genesis of medieval romance', *Differences*, 10 (1998), 98–173.

Hill, Boyd H., 'A medieval German wound man: Wellcome MS 49', *Journal of the History of Medicine and Allied Sciences*, 20 (1965), 334–57.

Hillmann, David, and Carla Mazzio (eds), *The Body in Parts: Fantasies of Corporeality in Early Modern Europe* (London: Routledge, 1997).

—— and —— 'Introduction: individual parts', in Hillmann and Mazzio (eds), *The Body in Parts*, pp. xi–xxix.

Honemann, Volker, 'Wigalois' Kampf mit dem roten Ritter: zum Verständnis der Hojir-Aventiure in Wirnts *Wigalois*', in Honemann et al. (eds), *German Narrative Literature of the Twelfth and Thirteenth Centuries: Studies Presented to Roy Wisbey on his Sixty-Fifth Birthday* (Tübingen: Niemeyer, 1994), pp. 347–62.

—— 'Daniel monologisiert, der Riese berichtet, drei Damen erzählen: Aspekte der Figurenrede im *Daniel von dem Blühenden Tal* des Strickers', in Harald Haferland and Norbert Mecklenburg (eds), *Erzählungen in Erzählungen: Phänomene der Narration in Mittelalter und früher Neuzeit*, Forschungen zur Geschichte der älteren deutschen Literatur, 19 (Munich: Fink, 1996), pp. 221–32.

Hsia, Ronnie Po-chia, *The Myth of Ritual Murder: Jews and Magic in Reformation Germany* (New Haven: Yale University Press, 1988).

Huot, Sylvia, 'Dangerous embodiments: Froissart's Harton and Jean d'Arras's Melusine', *Speculum*, 78/2 (April 2003), 400–20.

Innocent III, 'De sacro altaris mysterio', in Innocent III, *Opera Omnia*, ed. Jacques-Paul Migne, 4 vols, Patrologia Cursus Completus: Series Latina (Paris: Migne, 1855), CCXVII, cols 773–916.

Institoris, Heinrich, and Jakob Sprenger, *Malleus maleficarum*, ed. André Schnyder, 2 vols (Göppingen: Kümmerle, 1991–3).

Isidore of Seville, *Etymologiarum sive originvm*, ed. W. M. Lindsay, 2 vols (Oxford: Clarendon, 1911).

Jean d'Arras, *Mélusine: Roman du XIVe siècle*, ed. Louis Stouff (Djion: Publications de l'Université, 1932).

Johannes de Alta Silva, *Dolopathos, sive, De rege et septem sapientibus*, ed. Hermann Oesterley (Strasbourg: Trübner, 1873).

—— *Dolopathos or the King and the Seven Wise Men*, tr. Brady B. Gilleland, Medieval and Renaissance Texts and Studies, 2 (Binghampton, NY: Center for Medieval and Early and Renaissance Studies, 1981).

John of Salisbury, *Policraticus*, ed. Clement Charles Julian Webb, 2 vols (Oxford: Clarendon, 1909).

Johnson, Willis, 'The myth of Jewish male menses', *Journal of Medieval History*, 24 (1998), 273–95.

Jones, Peter Murray, *Medieval Medical Miniatures* (London: British Library, 1984).

Jordan, William Chester, 'Approaches to the court scene in the bond story: equity and mercy or reason and nature', *Shakespeare Quarterly*, 33 (1982), 49–59.

'Kaiser Lucius' Tochter', in *Die deutsche Märendichtung des 15. Jahrhunderts*, ed. H. Fischer (Munich: Beck, 1966), pp. 71–88.

Kantorowicz, Ernst H., *The King's Two Bodies: A Study in Mediaeval Political Theology* (Princeton: Princeton University Press, 1957).

Kasper, Walter, 'Der bleibende Gehalt der Heilig-Blut-Verehrung aus theologischer Sicht', in N. Kruse and H.-U. Rudolf (eds), *900 Jahre Heilig-Blut-Verehrung in Weingarten* (Sigmaringen: Thorbecke, 1994), pp. 377–86.

Katz, David S., 'Shylock's gender: Jewish male menstruation in early modern England', *Review of English Studies*, NS 50, no. 200 (1999), 440–62.

Kaufmann, Ekkehard, 'Körperverletzung', in Adalbert Erler and Kaufmann (eds), *Handwörterbuch zur deutschen Rechtsgeschichte*, 5 vols (Berlin: Schmidt, 1971–98), II (1978), cols 1159–63.

Kay, Sarah, 'Flayed skin as *objet a*: representation and materiality in Guillaume de Deguileville's *Pèlerinage de vie humaine*', in Jane E. Burns (ed.), *Medieval Fabrications: Dress, Textiles, Cloth Work, and Other Cultural Imaginings*, New Middle Ages Series (New York: Palgrave Macmillan, 2004), pp. 193–205 and 249–51.

—— and Miri Rubin (eds), *Framing Medieval Bodies* (Manchester: Manchester University Press, 1994).

Keil, Gundolf, '*Bartholomäus*', in K. Ruh (ed.), *Die deutsche Literatur des Mittelalters: Verfasserlexikon*, I (Berlin: de Gruyter, 1978), col. 609–15.

—— 'Ortolf von Baierland (von Würzburg)', in K. Ruh (ed.), *Die deutsche Literatur des Mittelalters: Verfasserlexikon*, VII (Berlin: de Gruyter, 1989), cols 67–82.

Keller, Evelyn Fox, 'Secrets of God, nature, and life', in Keller, *Secrets of Life, Secrets of Death: Essays on Language, Gender, and Science* (New York: Routledge, 1992 [1990]), pp. 56–72.

Kelly, Douglas, 'The domestication of the marvelous in the Melusine romances', in D. Maddox and S. Sturm-Maddox (eds), *Melusine of Lusignan* (Athens, GA: University of Georgia Press, 1996), pp. 32–47.

Kelly, Kathleen Coyne, *Performing Virginity and Testing Chastity in the Middle Ages*, Routledge Research in Medieval Studies, 2 (London: Routledge, 2000).

Kern, Peter, 'Die Auseinandersetzung mit der Gattungstradition im *Wigalois* Wirnts von Grafenberg', in Friedrich Wolfzettel (ed.) *Artusroman und Intertextualität*, Beiträge zur deutschen Philologie (Giessen: Schmitz, 1990), pp. 73–83.

Klare, Andreas, 'Überlegungen zur Literarisierung von historischen Figuren am Beispiel des Hoyer von Mansfeld in Wirnts *Wigalois*', *Leuvense Bijdragen*, 83 (1994), 485–521.

Kohler, Joseph, *Shakespeare vor dem Forum der Jurisprudenz*, 2nd edn (Berlin: Rothschild, 1919 [1883]).

Köhler, Reinhold, 'Die Erde als jungfräuliche Mutter Adams', *Germania*, 7 (1862), 476–80.

Konrad von Würzburg, 'Silvester', *Die Legenden*, ed. Paul Gereke, 3 vols (Halle/Saale: Niemeyer, 1925–7), I (1925).

Kramer, Heinrich (Institoris), *Der Hexenhammer. Malleus maleficarum*, tr. Günter Jerouschek and Wolfgang Behringer (Munich: dtv, 2000).

Kristeva, Julia, *Powers of Horror: An Essay on Abjection*, tr. Leon S. Roudiez (New York: Columbia University Press, 1982 [1980]).

Kruger, Stephen F., 'Conversion and medieval sexual, religious, and racial categories', in Karma Lochrie, Peggy McCracken and James A. Schultz (eds), *Constructing Medieval Sexuality*, Medieval Cultures, 11 (Minneapolis: University of Minnesota Press, 1997), pp. 158–79.

Kruse, Norbert, and Hans-Ulrich Rudolf (eds), *900 Jahre Heilig-Blut-Verehrung in Weingarten, 1094–1994*, 2 vols (Sigmaringen: Thorbecke, 1994).

Kugler, Hartmut, 'Die Ebstorfer Weltkarte: ein europäisches Weltbild im deutschen Mittelalter', *Zeitschrift für deutsches Altertum und deutsche Literatur*, 116 (1987), 1–29.

226   BIBLIOGRAPHY

—— (ed.), *Ein Weltbild vor Columbus: Die Ebstorfer Weltkarte: Inter-disziplinäres Kolloquium 1988*, Acta Humaniora (Weinheim: VCH, 1991).

—— 'Hochmittelalterliche Weltkarten als Geschichtsbilder', in Hans-Werner Goetz (ed.), *Hochmittelalterliches Geschichtsbewusstsein im Spiegel nichthistorischer Quellen* (Berlin: Akademie Verlag, 1998), pp. 179–98.

Kunze, Konrad, and Hansjürgen Linke, 'Theophilus', in K. Ruh (ed.), *Die deutsche Literatur des Mittelalters: Verfasserlexikon*, IX (Berlin: de Gruyter, 1995), cols 775–82.

Kuriyama, Shigesa, *The Expressiveness of the Body and the Divergence of Greek and Chinese Medicine* (New York: Zone, 1999).

Kusche, Brigitte, 'Zur *Secreta mulierum*-Forschung', *Janus*, 62 (1975), 103–23.

Küsters, Urban, 'Narbenschriften: zur religiösen Literatur des Spätmittelalters', in J.-D. Müller and H. Wenzel (eds), *Mittelalter* (Stuttgart: Hirzel, 1999), pp. 81–110.

Langmuir, Gavin I., *Toward a Definition of Antisemitism* (Berkeley: University of California Press, 1990).

Laqueur, Thomas, *Making Sex: Body and Gender from the Greeks to Freud* (Cambridge, MA: Harvard University Press, 1990).

Largier, Niklaus, 'Der Körper der Schrift: Text und Bild am Beispiel einer Seuse-Handschrift des 15. Jahrhunderts', in J.-D. Müller and H. Wenzel (eds), *Mittelalter* (Stuttgart: Hirzel, 1999), pp. 241–71.

Lavin, Marilyn Aronberg, 'The altar of Corpus Domini in Urbino: Paolo Uccello, Joos van Ghent, Piero della Francesca', *Art Bulletin*, 19/1 (March 1967), 1–24.

Le Doeuff, Michèle, *Hipparchia's Choice: An Essay Concerning Women, Philosophy, etc.*, tr. Trista Selous (Oxford: Blackwell, 1991 [1989]).

Le Goff, Jacques, *Medieval Civilisation, 400–1500*, tr. Julia Barrow (Oxford: Blackwell, 1988 [1964]).

—— 'Head or heart? The political use of body metaphors in the Middle Ages', in M. Feher (ed.), *Fragments for a History of the Human Body* (New York: Zone, 1989), III, pp. 13–26.

Lecouteux, Claude, 'Das bauchlose Ungeheuer: Des Strickers *Daniel von dem Blühenden Tal*, 1879ff.', *Euphorion*, 71 (1977), 272–6.

—— 'Des Königs Ortnit Schlaf', *Euphorion*, 73 (1979), 347–55.

Lexer, Matthias, *Mittelhochdeutsches Handwörterbuch*, 3 vols (Leipzig: Hirzel, 1872–8).

Lex Salica: 100 Titel-Text, ed. Karl August Eckhardt, Germanenrechte Neue Folge, Abteilung Westgermanisches Recht (Weimar: Böhlau, 1953).

Libellus de formatione hominis in vtero, vel ut notiori Titulo, Secreta mulierum (Antwerp: Mart. Caesar, 1538).

Lienert, Elisabeth, 'Zur Pragmatik höfischen Erzählens: Erzähler und Erzählerkommentare in Wirnts von Grafenberg *Wigalois*', *Archiv für das Studium der neueren Sprachen und Literaturen*, 234 (1997), 263–75.

Linke, Uli, 'Blood as metaphor in Proto-Indo-European', *Journal of Indoeuropean Studies*, 13 (1985), 333–76.

——— *Blood and Nation: The European Aesthetics of Race*, Contemporary Ethnography (Philadelphia: University of Pennsylvania Press, 1999).

Lionarons, Joyce Tally, ' "Sometimes the dragon wins": unsuccessful dragon fighters in medieval literature', in L. C. Gruber (ed.), *Essays in Old, Middle, Modern English and Old Icelandic in Honour of Raymond J. Tripp, Jr* (Lewiston, NY: Edwin Muller, 2000), pp. 301–16.

Lixfeld, Hannsjost, 'Fleischpfand', in *Enzyklopädie des Märchens. Handwörterbuch zur historischen und vergleichenden Erzählforschung*, ed. Kurt Ranke, 11 vols (Berlin: de Gruyter, 1975–), IV (1984), cols 1256–62.

Lloyd, Genevieve, *The Man of Reason: 'Male' and 'Female' in Western Philosophy* (Minneapolis: University of Minnesota Press, 1984).

Lochrie, Karma, 'Don't ask, don't tell: murderous plots and medieval secrets', in Louise Aranye Fradenburg and Carla Freccero (eds), *Premodern Sexualities* (New York: Routledge, 1996), pp. 137–52.

——— 'Desiring Foucault', *Journal of Medieval and Early Modern Studies*, 27/1 (Winter 1997), 3–16.

——— *Covert Operations: The Medieval Uses of Secrecy*, The Middle Ages Series (Philadelphia: University of Pennsylvania Press, 1999).

Lomperis, Linda, and Sarah Stanbury (eds), *Feminist Approaches to the Body in Medieval Literature* (Philadelphia: University of Pennsylvania Press, 1993).

McCracken, Peggy, 'The curse of Eve: female bodies and Christian bodies in Heloise's Third Letter', in Bonnie Wheeler (ed.), *Listening to Heloise: The Voice of a Twelfth-Century Woman* (New York: St Martin's Press, 2000), pp. 217–31.

——— *The Curse of Eve, the Wound of the Hero: Blood, Gender, and Medieval Literature* (Philadelphia: University of Pennsylvania Press, 2003).

MacLehose, William F., 'Nurturing danger: high medieval medicine and the problem(s) of the child', in John Carmi Parsons and Bonnie Wheeler (eds), *Medieval Mothering*, New Middle Ages, 3 (New York: Garland, 1996), pp. 3–24.

Maddox, Donald, and Sara Sturm-Maddox (eds), *Melusine of Lusignan: Founding Fiction in Late Medieval France* (Athens, GA: University of Georgia Press, 1996).

Mandeville's Travels, ed. P. Hamelius, Early English Text Society, os 153 (London: Kegan Paul, Trench & Trübner, 1919).

Mechthild von Magdeburg, *Das fließende Licht der Gottheit*, ed. Gisela

Vollmann-Profe, Bibliothek des Mittelalters, 19 (Frankfurt/Main: Deutscher Klassiker-Verlag, 2003).

Mellinkoff, Ruth, 'Cain and the Jews', *Journal of Jewish Art*, 6 (1979), 16–38.

—— *Outcasts: Signs of Otherness in Northern European Art of the Late Middle Ages*, 2 vols (Berkeley: University of California Press, 1993).

—— *Antisemitic Hate Signs in Hebrew Illuminated Manuscripts from Medieval Germany* (Jerusalem: Center for Jewish Art, Hebrew University of Jerusalem, 1999).

Milde, Vera, '*Si entrunnen alle scentlîchen dannen*: Christlich-jüdischer Disput in der Silvesterlegende der *Kaiserchronik*', in Ursula Schulze (ed.), *Juden in der deutschen Literatur des Mittelalters: Religiöse Konzepte – Feindbilder – Rechtfertigungen* (Tübingen: Niemeyer, 2002), pp. 13–34.

Miller, Konrad (ed.), *Monialium Ebstorfensium Mappamundi/Die Ebstorfkarte*, Mappaemundi: Die ältesten Weltkarten, 5 (Stuttgart: Roth, 1896).

Mills, Robert, 'Jesus as monster', in Bettina Bildhauer and Mills (eds), *The Monstrous Middle Ages* (Cardiff: University of Wales Press, 2003), pp. 28–54.

Mölk, Ulrich (ed.), *Literatur und Recht: Literarische Rechtsfälle von der Antike bis in die Gegenwart* (Göttingen: Wallstein, 1996).

Moormann van Kappen, Olav, 'Over de geschiednis van de baarproef in de Nederlanden', in Moormann van Kappen, *Lex Loci*, ed. E. C. Coppens et al., Rechtshistorische Reeks van het Gerard Noodt Instituut, 45 (Nijmegen: Gerard Noodt Instituut, 2000 [1985]), pp. 65–82.

Moriz von Craûn, ed. and tr. Stephanie Cain van d'Elden (New York: Garland, 1990).

Müller, Jan-Dirk, 'Motivationsstrukturen und personale Identität im *Nibelungenlied*: Zur Gattungsdiskussion um "Epos" oder "Roman" ', in Fritz Peter Knapp (ed.), Nibelungenlied *und* Klage, *Sage und Geschichte, Struktur und Gattung: Passauer Nibelungenliedgespräche 1985* (Heidelberg: Winter, 1987), pp. 221–56.

—— *Spielregeln des Untergangs: Die Welt des Nibelungenliedes* (Tübingen: Niemeyer, 1998).

—— and Horst Wenzel (eds), *Mittelalter: Neue Wege durch einen alten Kontinent* (Stuttgart: Hirzel, 1999).

Munday, Anthony, *Zelauto: The Fountaine of Fame*, ed. Jack Stillinger (Carbondale: Southern Illinois University Press, 1963 [1580]).

Nellmann, Eberhard, *Wolframs Erzähltechnik: Untersuchungen zur Funktion des Erzählers* (Wiesbaden: Steiner, 1973).

Newman, Karen, 'Reprise: gender, sexuality and theories of exchange in *The Merchant of Venice*', in Nigel Wood (ed.), *The Merchant of Venice*, Theory in Practice (Buckingham: Open University Press, 1996), pp. 102–23.

Nibelungenlied: Mittelhochdeutscher Text und Übertragung, ed. and tr. Helmut Brackert (Frankfurt/Main: Fischer, 1970–1).

Nichols, Stephen G., 'Melusine between myth and history: profile of a female demon', in D. Maddox and S. Sturm-Maddox (eds), *Melusine of Lusignan* (Athens, GA: University of Georgia Press, 1996), pp. 137–64.

Nutton, Vivian, 'Galen at the bedside: the methods of a medical detective', in William F. Bynum and Roy Porter (eds), *Medicine and the Five Senses* (Cambridge: Cambridge University Press, 1993), pp. 7–16.

—— 'Medicine in medieval western Europe, 1000–1500', in Lawrence I. Conrad et al. (eds), *The Western Medical Tradition, 800 BC to AD 1800* (Cambridge: Cambridge University Press, 1995), pp. 139–205.

Obenaus, Katya Skow, 'The whole is the sum of its parts: misogyny as a unifying factor in *Die sieben weisen Meister*', *Fifteenth-Century Studies*, 26 (2001), 169–82.

Ogris, W., 'Bahrprobe', in Adalbert Erler and Ekkehard Kaufmann (eds), *Handwörterbuch zur deutschen Rechtsgeschichte* (Berlin: Schmidt, 1971–98), I (1971), cols 283–5.

Ortolf von Baierland, *Das Arzneibuch Ortolfs von Baierland nach der ältesten Handschrift (14. Jahrhundert)*, ed. James Follan, Veröffentlichungen der Internationalen Gesellschaft für Geschichte der Pharmazie, NS 23 (Stuttgart: Wissenschaftliche Verlagsgesellschaft, 1963).

Parvulescu, Adrian, 'Blood and IE: kinship terminology', *Indogermanische Forschungen*, 94 (1989), 67–88.

Passional, 3 vols, I and II, ed. Karl A. Hahn (Frankfurt/Main: Broenner, 1845), III, ed. Karl Köpke (Quedlinburg: Basse, 1852).

Penna, Angelo, 'Il sangue nell' Antico Testamento', in F. Vattioni (ed.), *Sangue e antropologia biblica*, II, Sangue e antropologia, 2 (1981), pp. 379–402.

Pfaffe Lamprecht, *Alexander*, ed. Karl Kinzel, Germanistische Handbibliothek, 6 (Halle: Verlag der Buchhandlung des Waisenhauses, 1884).

Platelle, Henri, 'La voix du sang: le cadavre qui saigne en présence de son meutrier', in *Actes du 99e Congrès national des Sociétés savants, Besançon, 1974, Section de philologie et d'histoire jusqu'à 1610*, I, La Piété Populaire au Moyen Age (Paris: Bibliothèque Nationale, 1977), pp. 161–79.

Pliny, *Natural History*, ed. and tr. Harris Rackham, 10 vols, Loeb Classical Library (London: Heinemann, 1938–63).

Ploss, Emil, 'Wielands Schwert Mimung und die alte Stahlhärtung', *Beiträge zur Geschichte der deutschen Sprache und Literatur*, 79 (1957), 110–28.

Poor, Sara S., 'Cloaking the body in text: the question of female authorship in the writings of Mechthild von Magdeburg', *Exemplaria*, 12/2 (2000), 417–53.

—— 'Mechthild von Magdeburg, gender, and the "unlearned tongue"', *Journal of Medieval and Early Modern Studies*, 31 (2001), 213–50.

—— *Mechthild of Magdeburg and her Book: Gender and the Making of Textual Authority*, Middle Ages Series (Philadelphia: University of Pennsylvania Press, 2004).

Pouchelle, Marie-Christine, *The Body and Surgery in the Middle Ages*, tr. Rosemary Morris (Cambridge: Polity, 1990 [1983]).

—— 'Le sang et ses pouvoirs au Moyen Age', in *Affaires de Sang: Festschrift Arlette Farge*, Mentalités, 1 (Paris: Imago, 1988), pp. 17–41.

Principe, Walter H., '*Quaestiones* concerning Christ from the first half of the thirteenth century, IV: *quaestiones* from Douai MS. 434, Christ as head of the Church; the unity of the mystical body', *Mediaeval Studies*, 44 (1982), 1–82.

Pseudo-Albertus Magnus, 'Secreta Mulierum Cum Commento, Deutsch: Critical Text and Commentary', ed. Margaret Rose Schleissner (doctoral dissertation, University of Princeton, 1987).

Punday, Daniel, 'Foucault's body tropes', *New Literary History*, 31 (2000), 509–28.

Ragotzky, Hedda, *Gattungserneuerung und Laienunterweisung in den Texten des Strickers*, Studien und Texte zur Sozialgeschichte der Literatur, 1 (Tübingen: Niemeyer, 1981).

—— and Horst Wenzel (eds), *Höfische Repräsentation: Das Zeremoniell und die Zeichen* (Tübingen: Niemeyer, 1990).

Resnick, Irven M., 'Roots of the myth of Jewish male menses in Jacques de Vitry's *History of Jerusalem*', *International Guest Lecture Series, Ingeborg Rennert Center for Jerusalem Studies, Bar-Ilan University (Israel)*, 3 (1998), 1–27.

—— 'Medieval roots of the myth of Jewish male menses', *Harvard Theological Review*, 93/3 (2000), 241–63.

Reynolds, Philip Lyndon, *Food and the Body: Some Peculiar Questions in High Medieval Theology*, Studien und Texte zur Geistesgeschichte des Mittelalters, 69 (Leiden: Brill, 1999).

'Rheinfränkische Himmelfahrt Mariae', ed. Karl L. Weigand, *Zeitschrift für deutsches Alterthum*, 5 (1845), 515–64.

Riches, Samantha, *St George: Hero, Martyr and Myth* (Stroud: Sutton, 2000).

Richter, Dieter, 'Die Allegorie der Pergamentbearbeitung: Beziehungen zwischen handwerklichen Vorgängen und der geistlichen Bildersprache des Mittelalters', in Gundolf Keil, Rainer Rudolf, Wolfram Schmitt and Hans J. Vermeer (eds), *Fachliteratur des Mittelalters: Festschrift für Gerhard Eis* (Stuttgart: Metzler, 1968), pp. 83–92.

Riha, Ortrun, *Ortolf von Baierland und seine lateinischen Quellen: Hochschulmedizin in der Volkssprache*, Wissensliteratur im Mittelalter, 10 (Wiesbaden: Reichert, 1992).

Roper, Lyndal, *Oedipus and the Devil: Witchcraft, Sexuality and Religion in Early Modern Europe* (London: Routledge, 1994).

Rowe, Katherine, ' "God's handy worke" ', in D. Hillmann and C. Mazzio, *The Body in Parts* (London: Routledge, 1997), pp. 285–309.

Ruberg, Uwe, 'Mappae mundi des Mittelalters im Zusammenwirken von Text und Bild', in Christel Meier und Uwe Ruberg (eds), *Text und Bild: Aspekte des Zusammenwirkens zweier Künste in Mittelalter und früher Neuzeit* (Wiesbaden: Reichert, 1980), pp. 550–92.

Rubin, Miri, *Corpus Christi: The Eucharist in Late Medieval Culture* (Cambridge: Cambridge University Press, 1991).

—— 'The body whole and vulnerable in fifteenth-century England', in Barbara Hanawalt and David Wallace (eds), *Bodies and Disciplines: Intersections of Literature and History in Fifteenth-Century England*, Medieval Cultures, 9 (Minneapolis: University of Minnesota Press, 1996), pp. 19–28.

—— *Gentile Tales: The Narrative Assault on Late Medieval Jews* (New Haven: Yale University Press, 1999).

Ruh, Kurt (ed.), *Die deutsche Literatur des Mittelalters: Verfasserlexikon*, 2nd, rev. edn, 11 vols (Berlin: de Gruyter, 1978–).

Russell, Jeffrey Burton, *Witchcraft in the Middle Ages* (Ithaca, NY: Cornell University Press, 1972).

Sachsenspiegel: Landrecht und Lehnrecht, ed. Friedrich Ebel, 3rd, rev. edn (Stuttgart: Reclam, 1999 [1953]).

Salih, Sarah, *Versions of Virginity in Late Medieval England* (Woodbridge: Brewer, 2001).

Salisbury, Joyce E., *The Blood of Martyrs: Unintended Consequences of Ancient Violence* (New York: Routledge, 2004).

Salmon, Fernando, and Montserrat Cabré i Pairet, 'Fascinating women: the evil eye in medical scholasticism', in Roger French et al. (ed.), *Medicine from the Black Death to the French Disease* (Aldershot: Ashgate, 1998), pp. 53–84.

Sammer, Marianne, 'Basilisk – regulus: eine bedeutungsgeschichtliche Skizze', in Ulrich Müller and Werner Wunderlich (eds), *Dämonen – Monster – Fabelwesen*, Mittelaltermythen, 2 (St Gallen: Fachverlag für Wissenschaft und Studium, 1999), pp. 135–60.

Sartre, Jean-Paul, *Being and Nothingness: An Essay on Phenomenological Ontology*, tr. Hazel E. Barnes (London: Routledge, 1969 [1943]).

Scherb, Victor I., 'Assimilating giants: the appropriation of Gog and Magog in medieval and early modern England', *Journal of Medieval and Early Modern Studies*, 3/1 (2002), 59–84.

Schmid, Elisabeth, *Familiengeschichten und Heilsmythologie: Die Verwandtschaftsstrukturen in den französischen und deutschen Gralromanen des 12. und 13. Jahrhunderts*, Beihefte zur Zeitschrift für romanische Philologie (Tübingen: Niemeyer, 1986).

Schnell, Bernhard, 'Die deutsche Medizinliteratur im 13. Jahrhundert: ein erster Überblick', in Christa Bertelsmeier-Kirst and Christopher Young (eds), *Eine Epoche im Umbruch: Volkssprachliche Literalität 1200–1300* (Tübingen: Niemeyer, 2003), pp. 249–65.

Schnell, Rüdiger, 'Rechtsgeschichte, Mentalitäten und Gattungsgeschichte: zur literarischen Autonomie im Mittelalter', in Joachim Heinzle (ed.), *Literarische Interessenbildung im Mittelalter: DFG Symposion 1991*, Germanistische Symposien Berichtbände, 14 (Stuttgart: Metzler, 1993), pp. 401–30.

Schröder, Werner, 'Der synkretistische Roman des Wirnt von Gravenberg: Unerledigte Fragen an den *Wigalois*', *Euphorion*, 80 (1986), 235–77.

Schulze, Ursula, *Das Nibelungenlied* (Stuttgart: Reclam, 1997).

Schürmann, Thomas, *Nachzehrerglauben in Mitteleuropa*, Schriftenreihe der Kommission für ostdeutsche Volkskunde in der Gesellschaft für Volkskunde, 51 (Marburg: Elwert, 1990).

Schwab, Ute, 'Weinverschütten und Minnetrinken: Verwendung und Umwandlung metaphorischer Hallentopik im *Nibelungenlied*', in Klaus Zatloukal (ed.), *Pöchlarner Heldenliedgespräch: Das Nibelungenlied und der mittlere Donauraum*, Philologica Germanica, 12 (Vienna: Fassbaender, 1990), pp. 59–101.

—— 'Blut trinken und im Bier ertrinken: Zur Trinkmetaphorik bei Saxo Grammaticus im Vergleich zu einigen Zeugnissen der germanischen Heldendichtung, besonders des *Nibelungenlieds*', in *Saxo Grammaticus tra storiografia e letteratura*, ed. Carlo Santini (Rome: Calamo, 1992), pp. 367–415.

Schwabenspiegel: Kurzform, ed. Karl August Eckhardt, 2 vols, Monumenta Germaniae historica, Fontes iuris Germanici antiqui, NS 4–5, 2nd edn (Hanover: Hahn, 1972–4), I (1972).

Schwietering, Julius, 'Natur und *art*', *Zeitschrift für deutsches Altertum und deutsche Literatur*, 91 (1961/62), 108–37.

Secreta mulierum, ed. Margaret Rose Schleissner (unpublished doctoral dissertation, University of Princeton, 1987).

Seebohm, Almuth, *Apokalypse, ars moriendi, medizinische Traktate, Tugend- und Lasterlehren: Die erbaulich-didaktische Sammelhandschrift London, Wellcome Institute for the History of Medicine, Ms. 49* (Munich: Lengenfelder, 1995).

Seuse, Heinrich, 'Leben', in *Deutsche Schriften*, ed. Karl Bihlmeyer (Frankfurt/Main: Minerva, 1961 [1907]), pp. 7–195.

Shahar, Shulamith, *Growing Old in the Middle Ages: 'Winter Clothes Us in Shadow and Pain'*, tr. Yael Lotan (New York: Routledge, 1997 [1995]).

Shakespeare, William, *The Merchant of Venice: Arden Shakespeare*, ed. John Russell Brown (London: Methuen, 1955).

Shapiro, James, *Shakespeare and the Jews* (New York: Columbia University Press, 1996).

Shildrick, Margrit, *Leaky Bodies and Boundaries: Feminism, Postmodernism and (Bio-)Ethics* (London: Routledge, 1997).

Shuttle, Penelope, and Peter Redgrove, *The Wise Wound: Menstruation and Everywoman*, 2nd, rev. edn (London: Boyars, 1999 [1978]).

Singer, S., 'Die romanischen Elemente des *Nibelungenliedes*', in Singer, *Germanisch-romanisches Mittelalter* (Zurich: Niehaus, 1935), pp. 232–54.

Smith, D. Vance, 'Body doubles: producing the masculine *corpus*', in Jeffrey Jerome Cohen and Bonnie Wheeler (eds), *Becoming Male in the Middle Ages*, The New Middle Ages, 4 (New York: Garland, 1997), pp. 3–19.

Sommerbrodt, Ernst, *Die Ebstorfer Weltkarte* (Hanover: Hahn, 1891).

Spalding, Mary Caroline, *The Middle English Charters of Christ*, Bryn Mawr College Monograph Series, 15 (Bryn Mawr, PA: Bryn Mawr College, 1914).

Spiegel, Gabrielle M., 'Maternity and monstrosity: reproductive biology in the *Roman de Mélusine*', in D. Maddox and S. Sturm-Maddox (eds), *Melusine of Lusignan* (Athens, GA: University of Georgia Press, 1996), pp. 100–24.

Sprenger, Ulrike, 'Zum Schwimmen im Blut (Sg. 24, 7/8)', *Zeitschrift für deutsche Philologie*, 101/3 (1982), 321–33.

Störmer-Caysa, Uta, 'Ortnits Mutter, die Drachen und der Zwerg', *Zeitschrift für deutsches Altertum und deutsche Literatur*, 128 (1998), 282–308.

—— 'Kriemhild's erste Ehe: ein Vorschlag zum Verständnis von Siegfrieds Tod im *Nibelungenlied*', *Neophilologus*, 83 (1999), 93–113.

Storp, Ursula, *Väter und Söhne: Tradition und Traditionsbruch in der volkssprachlichen Literatur des Mittelalters*, Item mediävistische Studien, 2 (Essen: Item, 1994).

Stricker, Der, 'Die Pfaffendirne', in Der Stricker, *Kleindichtung*, ed. Wolfgang Wilfried Moelleken, 5 vols, Göppinger Arbeiten zur Germanistik, 107, I–V (Göppingen: Kümmerle, 1973–8), IV (1977), pp. 41–3.

—— *Daniel von dem Blühenden Tal*, ed. Michael Resler, 2nd, rev. edn, Altdeutsche Textbibliothek, 92 (Tübingen: Niemeyer, 1995 [1983]).

—— *Der Pfaffe Amis: Mittelhochdeutsch/Neuhochdeutsch*, ed. Michael Schilling (Stuttgart: Reclam, 1994).

Strzelczyk, Jerzy, 'Die Legende von den Ebstorfer Märtyrern als Zeugnis über die politischen und ethnischen Verhältnisse in Nordostdeutschland im Mittelalter', *Lětopis*, B 18 (1971), 54–79.

Sullivan, Shannon, *Living across and through Skins: Transactional Bodies, Pragmatism and Feminism* (Bloomington: Indiana University Press, 2001).

'Sylvester', in *Das Passional*, III, ed. K. Köpke (Quedlinburg: Basse, 1852), pp. 62–93.

The Prose Salernitan Questions, ed. Brian Lawn, Auctores Britannici Medii Aevi, 5 (London: Oxford University Press, for the British Academy, 1979).

The Trotula: An English Translation of the Medieval Compendium of Women's Medicine, ed. and tr. Monica Green (Philadelphia: University of Pennsylvania Press, 2001).

Theweleit, Klaus, *Männerphantasien*, 2 vols, 2nd edn (Munich: Piper, 2000 [1977]).

Thomas Aquinas, *Super Evangelium S. Ioannis*, ed. P. Raphaelis Cai (Rome: Marietti, 1952).

Thomasset, Claude, 'La femme au Moyen Age: les composantes fondamentales de sa représentation, immunité – impunité', *Ornicar*, 22–3 (1981), 223–38.

—— 'Le corps féminin ou le regard empêché', *Micrologus*, 1 (1993), 99–114.

Thorndike, Lynn, 'Further considerations of the *Experimenta, Speculum Astronomia*, and *De Secretis mulierum* ascribed to Albertus Magnus', *Speculum*, 30 (1955), 413–43.

Thundy, Zacharias P., 'The dragon in *Beowulf*: Cain's seed, heresy and Islam', in L. C. Gruber (ed.), *Essays in Old, Middle, Modern English and Old Icelandic in Honour of Raymond J. Tripp. Jr* (Lewiston, NY: Edwin Muller, 2000), pp. 201–300.

Thüring von Ringoltingen, 'Melusine', in *Romane des 15. und 16. Jahrhunderts*, ed. Jan-Dirk Müller, Bibliothek der frühen Neuzeit, 1 (Frankfurt/Main: Deutscher Klassiker-Verlag, 1990), pp. 9–176.

Tobin, Frank, *Mechthild von Magdeburg: A Medieval Mystic in Modern Eyes*, Studies in German Literature, Linguistics and Culture: Literary Criticism in Perspective (Columbia, SC: Camden House, 1995).

Uebel, Michael, 'Unthinking the monster: twelfth-century responses to Saracen alterity', in J. J. Cohen (ed.), *Monster Theory* (Minneapolis: University of Minnesota Press, 1996), pp. 264–91.

Vattioni, Francesco (ed.), *Sangue e antropologia*, 16 vols (Rome: Pia Unione Prezissimo Sangue, 1981–9).

—— 'Sangue: vita o morte nella Bibbia?', in Vattioni (ed.), *Sangue e antropologia biblica*, II, Sangue e antropologia, 2 (1981), pp. 367–78.

Villani, Giovanni, *Nuova Cronica*, ed. Giuseppe Porta, Bibliotheca di scrittori italiani, 3 vols (Parma: Bembo, 1990–1).

Vincent, Nicholas, *Holy Blood: King Henry III and the Westminster Blood Relic* (Cambridge: Cambridge University Press, 2001).

Wackernagel, Wilhelm, 'Erde der Leib Christi', *Zeitschrift für deutsches Altertum und deutsche Literatur*, 6 (1848), pp. 288–9.

Wailes, Stephen L, 'Wolfram's *Parzivâl* and Der Stricker's *Daniel von dem Blühenden Tal*', *Colloquia Germanica*, 26 (1993), 299–315.

Wardale, Walter L., *The High German 'Bartholomaeus': Text, with Critical Commentary, of a Mediaeval Medical Book* ([Dundee:] Follan, 1993).

Waszink, Jan Hendrik, 'Blut', in *Reallexikon für Antike und Christentum: Sachwörterbuch zur Auseinandersetzung des Christentums mit der antiken Welt*, ed. Theodor Klauser, 18 vols (Stuttgart: Hiersemann, 1950–), II (1954), cols 459–73.

Weber, Hans Heinrich, *Studien zur deutschen Marienlegende des Mittelalters am Beispiel des Theophilus* (doctoral dissertation, University of Hamburg, 1966).

Weichenrieder, Lukas, 'Das Heilige Blut von Mantua', in N. Kruse and H.-U. Rudolf (eds), *900 Jahre Heilig-Blut-Verehrung in Weingarten* (Sigmaringen: Thorbecke, 1994), pp. 331–6.

Weidenhiller, P. Egino, *Untersuchungen zur deutschsprachigen katechetischen Literatur des späten Mittelalters* (Munich: Beck, 1965).

Wenger, Britta, 'Shylocks Pfund Fleisch: eine stoffgeschichtliche Untersuchung', *Shakespeare-Jahrbuch*, 65 (1929), 92–174.

Wenzel, Horst, 'Szene und Gebärde: zur visuellen Imagination im *Nibelungenlied*', *Zeitschrift für deutsche Philologie*, 111 (1992), 321–43.

Wiegand, Herbert Ernst, *Studien zur Minne und Ehe in Wolframs Parzival und Hartmanns Artusepik*, Quellen und Forschungen zur Sprach- und Kulturgeschichte der germanischen Völker, NS 49 (Berlin: de Gruyter, 1972).

Wigamur, ed. Danielle Buschinger, Göppinger Arbeiten zur Germanistik, 320 (Göppingen: Kümmerle, 1987).

Wilke, Jürgen, *Die Ebstorfer Weltkarte*, 2 vols, Veröffentlichungen des Institut für historische Landesforschung der Universität Göttingen, 39 (Bielefeld: Verlag für Regionalgeschichte, 2004).

Williams, David, *Deformed Discourse: The Function of the Monster in Mediaeval Thought and Literature* (Exeter: University of Exeter Press, 1996).

Willson, H. B., 'Blood and wounds in the *Nibelungenlied*', *Modern Language Review*, 55 (1960), 40–50.

Wirnt von Grafenberg, *Wigalois der Ritter mit dem Rade*, ed. J. M. N. Kapteyn, Rheinische Beiträge zur germanischen Philologie und Volkskunde, 9 (Bonn: Klopp, 1926).

Wißmann, Hans, 'Blut I: Religionsgeschichtlich', in Gerhard Krause and Gerhard Müller (eds), *Theologische Realenzyklopädie* (Berlin: de Gruyter, 1977–), VI (1980), cols 727–9.

Wogan-Browne, Jocelyn, 'Chaste bodies: frames and experiences', in S. Kay and M. Rubin (eds), *Framing Medieval Bodies* (Manchester: Manchester University Press, 1994), pp. 24–42.

'Wolfdietrich B', ed. Oscar Jänicke, in Arthur Amelung and Jänicke (eds), *Ortnit und die Wolfdietriche*, 2 vols, Deutsches Heldenbuch, 3 and 4 (Berlin: Weidmann, 1871–3), II (1873), pp. 165–301.

Wolfram von Eschenbach, *Parzival*, ed. Eberhard Nellmann, 2 vols, Bibliothek des Mittelalters, 8 (Frankfurt/Main: Deutscher Klassiker-Verlag, 1994).

Women's Secrets: A Translation of Pseudo-Albertus Magnus's 'De Secretis Mulierum with Commentaries', tr. Helen Rodnite Lemay, SUNY Series in Medieval Studies (Albany: State University of New York Press, 1992).

Wood, Charles T., 'The doctors' dilemma: sin, salvation and the menstrual cycle in medieval thought', *Speculum*, 56 (1981), 710–27.

Yuval, Israel Jacob, 'Christliche Symbolik und jüdische Martyrologie zur Zeit der Kreuzzüge', in Alfred Haverkamp (ed.), *Juden und Christen zur Zeit der Kreuzzüge*, Vorträge und Forschungen, 47 (Sigmaringen: Thorbecke, 1999), pp. 87–106.

Zacharias, Rainer, 'Die Blutrache im deutschen Mittelalter', *Zeitschrift für deutsches Altertum*, 91 (1961/62), 167–201.

Zimmermann, Günter, 'Der gefangene Parzival: Gedanken zur Komik in Strickers *Daniel*', in Danielle Buschinger and Wolfram Spiewok (eds), *Perceval-Parzival hier et aujourd'hui et autres essais sur la littérature allemande du Moyen Age et de la Renaissance pour fêter les 95 ans de Jean Fourquet*, Wodan: Greifswälder Beiträge zum Mittelalter, 48, Series 3, Tagungsbände und Sammelschriften, 28 (Greifswald: Reineke, 1994), pp. 303–15.

Zotto Tozzolli, Carla del, 'Il "sangue" nella tradizione evangelica germanica', in F. Vattioni (ed.), *Sangue e antropologia nella letteratura cristiana*, II, Sangue e antropologia, 6 (1983), pp. 1375–1420.

—— 'Il sangue nei testi germanici medievali', in F. Vattioni (ed.), *Sangue e antropologia nella teologia*, II, Sangue e antropologia, 15 (1989), pp. 1455–1522.

Index

Numbers in bold type indicate illustrations